2nd Edition

TEACHER
INTERVIEWS

How to Get Them & How to Get Hired!

ADVANTA
PUBLISHING

Printed in the United States of America

Library of Congress
Cataloging in Publication Division
101 Independence Ave., S.E.
Washington, D.C. 20540-4320
Library of Congress Control Number: 2001118203

ISBN NUMBER: 978-0-9712570-1-6

TABLE OF CONTENTS

"To my children, Robert and Kimberly
and to the Memory of my wife, Debra."

ACKNOWLEDGEMENTS

In any undertaking of significance, there are so many people who offer advice, encouragement, and keen insight that it is impossible to recognize everyone. However, the well from which I drew continued inspiration to strive and improve the ideas for this book has been the memory of my wife, Debbie. As it is with everyone who has lost a special partner or loved one in their life, their physical presence may be gone, but their voice and encouragement remain with us always. As I wrote these pages, I reflected back to her support and love often.

I want to give a special thanks to my two children, Robert and Kimberly who have patiently stood by their dad and helped in so many small ways. To my uncle, Archie W. Pollock, who again served as one of my primary proofreaders and advisors; his keen judgment from over thirty years in the public schools helped make this edition more accurate and current. Ms. Joan Smith was also a very important contributor to this edition. She acted as a proofreader and never complained no matter how many versions of a chapter came her way....or at what time they might have arrived. Her encouragement and insights were invaluable.

Although to mention by name all of the administrators, teachers, and colleagues who contributed information and critical ideas would be too lengthy, my conversations with them were instrumental in providing the foundation for this new edition. And a special thanks to Marc Taylor and Dana Alston of Marc Taylor Creative. Dana has been the creative genius behind the book's interior design and was also an essential editor for the project. Her patience and insight were indispensable in making this book come to life. Marc Taylor also gets a special thank you for his work in designing our new cover. His firm was always attentive to the ideas and goals I laid out for the project, and I could not be happier with the result.

Certainly, I cannot forget the hundreds of students and applicants to whom I have spoken about their interview experiences. The challenges surrounding teacher applicants today can only be fully understood by listening to those involved in the process. The feedback I received regarding the original version of Teacher Interviews has allowed me to know exactly where sound advice was offered and more work needed to be done. To all of them, I am grateful for sharing their experiences, concerns, and advice.

Before concluding, I want to salute all of you who will be undergoing interviews for a professional position in the coming weeks and months. You are the reason for this second edition, and I wish you well. If you are just beginning your career, I welcome you to one of the finest of all professions – teaching!

ABOUT THE AUTHOR

Dr. Pollock came to write about teacher interviews quite by accident. As an education professor at Georgian Court University, many students sought his advice as they were attempting to enter the job market and begin their teaching career. Because a discussion about negotiating the landscape from a degree to a teaching position did not lend itself to a short, thirty minute conversation Bob agreed to hold a half-day seminar for interested students. To prepare for this, he began to assemble appropriate handouts and a Power Point presentation. In so doing, Dr. Pollock realized a few handouts and short presentation hardly did justice to either the subject or the students; a different approach was needed.

Over the next year, Bob went to conferences around the country interviewing principals and other hiring managers to gather a cross-section of practices, questions, and teacher characteristics commonly sought in schools. The result of this research, combined with over twenty five years of his own interviewing experience, led to the publication of his first book, <u>Teacher Interviews: How to Get Them and How to Get Hired!</u>

The first edition was extremely well received and eventually rose to become the number one selling book on the subject of teacher interviews. It has since helped thousands of teachers obtain their desired teaching position. Colleges, universities, and job seekers of every level used this book to gain the insight necessary to navigate the difficult waters between the job search and the job offer.

Since the release of the first edition, a number of significant changes have taken place in the field of education and the job market. The competition for good teaching positions has grown, and the interviewing process has become more sophisticated. The knowledge gained from Bob's continued experience leading interview teams and added national research has converged to respond to these changes and produce this expanded Second Edition of Teacher Interviews. In it, Dr. Pollock shares new insights and secrets you can use to forge a path towards that great teaching position and future professional life…so good luck and enjoy the journey!

INTRODUCTION

There was once a television commercial that portrayed Abraham Lincoln at an employment agency seeking a job. The crusty agent behind the desk asked Abe a few questions such as: his level of education, did he have a chauffer's license, and did he have any previous work experience. At the conclusion of the interview, the agent said, "Well look, you seem like a bright guy, but let me just tell you, you ain't goin' nowhere without that piece of paper." It was the perfect depiction of an American notion that suggests prospects for a successful career are assured once a college degree is possessed. That perception continues to some degree even today. If only that was so. The reality is that a college degree does not always assure much of anything. All of us know of someone who has a college degree yet is not working in their chosen field or perhaps cannot even find worthy employment. Worse, it is often someone with a teaching major and certification!

Employment in today's teaching field, like employment in almost all professional fields, is highly competitive and challenging. The pathway to a successful interview with a good school district is *not* simple or direct. The interview process is more sophisticated and demanding than ever in the past. Because there will be strong competition for the better positions, only those who are knowledgeable and skilled are likely to prevail and receive the coveted job offer. The road between a college degree and a good job offer is littered with open pitfalls and traps that will sink the unaware candidate before he or she even realizes a critical mistake has been made. Interviewers will be armed with a bevy of tough questions and unanticipated interview strategies that can cost the uninformed or unprepared candidate any hope of securing the position.

Whether you are a traditional or **alternate route candidate**, this book is specifically designed to help you avoid the many interview dangers. It will give you the insight necessary to anticipate the tough questions, recognize what strategies are in use, and have powerful, difference making answers ready to separate you from the other applicants. It will provide you with step-by-step advice on how to navigate the entire job-seeking process and maximize your chances of landing the teaching position you want!

"I touch the future......I teach!"

—Christa McAuliffe
Teacher-Astronaut

A PASSION TO TEACH

Allow me to open this book by congratulating you on your decision to become a teacher. For every person, the decision to pursue a teaching career comes at different times and for different reasons. Whatever your reasons, I can assure you of one thing: you *will* be a positive force in the lives of hundreds, perhaps thousands, of children. The ideas you convey, motivation you provide, confidence you instill, and model you set will carry well beyond the classes you teach.

Your work will affect the quality of life for literally thousands of people. I know this sounds lofty, but I assure you it is true. Often, events that seem of almost no consequence to you can be of extraordinary importance to others. You think this far-fetched? Consider for a moment your own story. Go back through your personal history and think about those teachers who may have made a profound difference in your life. Was there a teacher who, at some opportune time became your advocate in a difficult situation? Did someone exhibit confidence in you when you perhaps lacked that confidence in yourself? Was there a mentor-teacher who guided you through some difficult waters? Or was there just that one special teacher who you simply admired and enjoyed being a part of his or her class? Which teachers inspired you? If you think back to those teachers, you will likely find the reason you have such strong feelings regarding your relationship is not centered on just one special event. Often, it was a series of very small exchanges or experiences that made the difference; occurrences that were almost always completely ordinary to the teacher, yet so very meaningful to you.

Consider for a moment what happened to Tara who was in Corey Romanak's class at Bridgewater Raritan High School. Are the actions on the part of this teacher likely to have left a lasting memory on all those present that day?

In an English class, Mr. Romanak started his lesson by telling the students that in the past he had been on an MTV game show called "Singled Out." The premise of the show was to keep answering questions correctly until you were the last person standing. Mr. Romanak then told the class that their review lesson for the day was going to duplicate that game show. As can happen, at about the middle of the competition, one of the boys stood and exclaimed, "This is really lame, I'm going to the boy's room," and left the room. Tara as well as number of others had been thinking something similar but continued just the same. As they got to the end of the game Tara found herself the winner! Mr. Romanak asked Tara, "Would you like to know what you won?" She just shrugged and said, "I guess so." He explained, "Well, when you win on a game show, they will tell you to open 'Door One' and see what you won. So go ahead and open the classroom door to see what you won." She opened the door and there stood the boy who left and, with flowers in hand, he asks her to the prom! Indeed, the young man's and Mr. Romanak's little ruse had made Tara more than just a contest winner.

How far will the reach of a teacher extend? In Tara's case, her experience is likely to last a lifetime. In most cases, teachers never really know how deeply they may have touched their students. What we do know is that when students are in the company of that special teacher, many will never again be quite the same. It is this dimension of our profession that provides each of us the passion to teach. When we are there to see the struggling student finally reach success, we are uplifted. When a student learns something new and provides us a smile to light the room, we are filled with inner happiness.

For each of us, someone has made a special impact on our life and significantly influenced the person we have become. Listen to Jane Lee, a geologist in San Antonio, Texas talk about her art teacher Mrs. Bee.

I'll never forget my art teacher, Mrs. Bee. I met her thirty four years ago when entering fourth grade. Most kids love to go to art class, and I was no exception. Her projects were creative and practical at the same time. Though I didn't become a professional artist, I received from her a few of life's important lessons; lessons that went far beyond the colorful walls of her classroom. Mrs. Bee believed in me. She challenged me to try new things and explore my creative abilities. She complimented me but also gave constructive criticism when I needed it. She held high expectations for me, and because she believed in me, I always tried to do more than was expected. She also taught me to finish what I started. The life lessons Mrs. Bee taught me may not have made me a famous artist, but they helped me in so many other ways. (McGuire and Abitz, 2001)

What a great testament to a wonderful teacher. The power of this story is that it is so familiar. Mrs. Bee is not uncommon. In fact, there are thousands of Mrs. Bees. For almost every one of us, there is a Mrs. Bee who taught us more than just a subject. They taught us how to live and how to be a better person. For those of us in the teaching profession we must always keep in mind the amount of power we hold. It is a power that reaches across generations and beyond even our own existence. It is from this desire to be such a positive influence in the lives of children that many of us derive our enthusiasm for teaching. Yet, with this capacity to influence comes an awesome responsibility. We must remain conscious of the potential impact we can have on students who sit in our class each day. And to be sure, not all our students will be easy to inspire and love. But, our love of working with children will always underlie everything that we do and it all begins with a first step.

You are ready to take that important step right now. Perhaps you are just graduating from college and looking for that first teaching position. Or perhaps you are already in the teaching field, but considering a new school or job opportunity. You might also have been out of teaching for a while and now wish to re-enter the profession. And, in some cases you are a prospective educator who has been involved in a different career for a number of years and now has decided to teach through one of the alternate routes. Whatever your current situation, you have prepared and are ready to put your talents and desire to teach into a classroom. BUT, if you fail to get the necessary interview or fail to make a dynamic impression on the committee, that passion will have no opportunity to evidence itself.

We need great teachers. The profession needs men and women just like you to come into its classes and work with the many young people who will be tomorrow's leaders. We need those who embody a genuine passion to teach. It is said that without our profession, none of the other professions can exist. The truth of that statement is what makes your decision to teach so important. Equally important is your ability to obtain that teaching position in the district and discipline to which you aspire. A teacher's best work is often achieved when he or she is in a position where he or she can feel professionally fulfilled. The teaching job market has many vacancies and you will have to choose wisely. More than that, you must prepare for the interviews that can lead to that truly special position. This is not easy.

13

THE MYTH OF TEACHER SHORTAGES:

Recently, you might have read of a teacher shortage in specific areas and some articles have suggested schools are finding it difficult to staff all of their classes. This is true. Schools often encounter fewer applicants in areas such as Foreign Language, Technology, Science, Mathematics, ESL, and Special Education. This reality can lead teachers to believe they need only apply and principals will be vying for their services. Alas, this is just not the case. Yes, if you are not concerned about the type school in which you work and are willing to relocate, a shortage can work to your advantage. In all other cases, heed the following warning. **BEWARE:** *Do not confuse a teacher shortage to mean an absence of competition.* Good schools and positions always have multiple applications. Granted, there is more competition in some districts than others, but there is always competition. You need strategies that will place you in front of that competition. You need sharp answers that will be noticed by the committee. You need the skills provided by this book.

Over the years, prospective teachers have asked me what they could expect in an interview. What questions might they be asked and how could they prepare? I recall a student who had been trying desperately to enter the teaching field and, after sending out 71 resumes, had not received even one interview. I asked to see her resume and cover letter. Both were neatly written and prepared with care, but they were quite routine and uninspired. The cover letter also contained a fatal error that would almost surely put her application in the "no interview" pile. Together we reworked both documents and readied them for a second round of mailings. From this more strategic second mailing, she received two interview invitations, and we met again to prepare for those interviews. My phone soon rang and she exclaimed, "I got the job! I got the job! They hired me!!" I could not have been happier for her. She was an excellent candidate with great potential. She was truly passionate about wanting to teach, but until she secured an interview where her talents and skill could be properly displayed, she was just one application in a large pile of others.

ALTERNATE ROUTE TEACHER: There are so many myths that surround the prospects and relative strengths regarding Alternate Route Teachers that it is impossible to address them all. But here are a few facts that everyone who genuinely wants to become a teacher, regardless of the route, should understand. First, there is no such thing as too many good teachers. Second, there is no guarantee that an individual coming through a college program will be any better than someone from an alternate route when it comes to a particular teacher vacancy. If you are someone who first traveled a different career path but more recently decided you wanted to become a teacher, then know that you are as good as any other candidate. One of the most important criteria to consider in teacher candidates is just how badly they want to teach. If you have been in the professional world, you have arrived at the decision to teach after a great deal of thought and consideration. Be confident; you are someone who brings a great deal to the interview table and needs to take a back seat to no one!

There are many different **alternate route paths,** and it is impossible for any book to address each one individually. Some programs offer clinical experiences, others include a segment of student teaching, and still others require only a college degree and enrollment in a state preparation program. It differs from state to state, but whatever your situation, we will offer you excellent advice on how to proceed in your application and interview process. If you have not fully investigated the various options for your state, this should be your first step. Once you have met the specific criteria to teach in your state, you are ready for this book and the opportunity to compete for a teaching position.

The biggest concern of the **alternate route candidate** and the interview team is the relative strength of every candidate's preparedness. Does he or she have the right pedagogical preparation? Does the prospect have sufficient classroom experience and understanding? Is this person a good professional "fit" to our school? In your case, the simple truth is that classroom experience may be the singular area where more traditionally trained candidates have the edge. Do not despair.

THE REAL QUESTION FOR ALTERNATE ROUTE TEACHERS:
The real question a district needs to answer in selecting a new teacher is not simply whether the person has sufficient previous "experience," but rather whether the person has sufficient "<u>capacity</u>" to be a great fit for the vacant teaching post.

As you go through the application and interview process, your goal is to prove you have the *capacity* to not only meet the requirements for the posted position, but also where you *exceed* the requirements! That is precisely where this book will prove an invaluable resource. Throughout these pages, you will see dozens of ideas and suggestions as to how you can demonstrate your qualifications and readiness to teach. Your application materials will sparkle with great qualifications for the post. Your answers to the interview questions will be sharp, on target, and compelling. You will command that interview because you know the kinds of questions to expect and you are ready! With these advantages, you will be in a position to not only prove yourself the equal of other candidates, but also the better of those candidates.

THE REAL VALUE OF THIS BOOK:

A friend of mine once told me how lucky I was to have secured a post in a very prestigious school district. I remember thinking at the time that luck had very little to do with my success. I had gone to that interview with a clear understanding of just what points I wanted to make and had prepared for weeks. A few great men, including Darrell Royal, the famous football coach at the University of Texas, defined luck as, *".... that time when opportunity and preparedness meet"* (Royal, et. al., 2005). My preparation and the recognition of opportunities for well crafted responses within the interview questions paid dividends. In that respect, I was lucky. Once you have read this book, you will be ready to create your own luck as well.

This book will provide strategies that will help put your resume at the top of the "must interview" list. It will provide answers to the many questions you have about how interviews are conducted, what questions to expect, and how to make your answer more powerful than that of other, less prepared candidates.

Each chapter of this book will provide valuable inside information that is rarely taught in college. Specific information on teacher interviews is difficult to find. Libraries provide little help with regard to teacher interviews and the Internet, although improved in recent years, lists only a few sites with any value. Most books on the topic are directed toward the business world and hold only passing relevance to your needs. *Teacher Interviews*, on the other hand, is *only* for prospective teachers and focuses entirely on proven ways to secure a teaching position. Regardless of whether you followed a traditional teacher education program or you are changing careers and arrived through an alternate route, this book will give you the upper hand in securing a great teaching position. You will know how to create your own personal brand that stands out from the other applicants. You will also know what mistakes and traps to avoid as you negotiate the process. Finally, when you begin your next search, you will have a complete game plan to attack the job market.

You have made a wise decision to keep this book in your library for review and study. From its pages you will gather the knowledge and confidence necessary to go into the right schools with the right answers. This will maximize your potential for success and minimize your chances of committing a fatal error. Remember, most people competing for the position *will not* have read this book. *You* will be the person in the room with the knowledge and that will give *you* the advantage!

The passion to teach is already inside your heart, but you need to secure the position you truly want and work in a district that meets your needs. To reach that goal, you need to brand yourself and market your skills in a compelling way. Study this book and take the necessary steps to aggressively get that great teaching position – THEN GO TEACH WITH A PASSION!!

WRITING AN EFFECTIVE COVER LETTER

The first document any school administrator will see from you is likely to be your cover letter. It is the first impression made on a reader who may decide your fate. As you can only make one first impression, it is essential that your cover letter present you as a first rate candidate who is well qualified and worth the time of an interview. The cover letter also provides the first illustration of your ability to present ideas in writing. I cannot tell you how many times I received cover letters so poorly done I did not even want to read the individual's resume. At the end of this chapter, you will know exactly how to construct an eye-catching cover letter that maximizes your chances for interview consideration. In addition, there are cover letter samples you can use to create your own letter. We will talk more about that later.

WRITING AN EFFECTIVE COVER LETTER IN THREE EASY STEPS:

The cover letter can be divided into a few simple parts, each set off as a paragraph. One key to effective writing is the ability to be concise! Understand that the person screening applications for this position might have from 50 to 500 resumes under review. That is correct, 500! He or she may take as little as thirty seconds to examine your resume and cover letter. Do you now see the need for a high impact cover letter? A three or four page letter is rarely read and often makes a poor impression. You must decide what information is essential and focus your writing energy to create a strong impact in a short space.

Before going further, I must tell you there are entire books on just the subject of writing cover letters. You can find them in any bookstore or library, and they are excellent. Nonetheless, in the field of education, there seem to be a few styles that are consistently successful. In this chapter, I have singled out the essential elements of those letters to help you remain simple and generate impact. Let us begin by looking at the basic parts of a sound cover letter.

FIRST: *Establish your interest in the position.*

Briefly explain how you know about the position, why you are qualified, and state your interest in the advertised opening. You want the reader to see you are excited about the position and prospect of working in his or her district or school.

SECOND: *Establish a match between the advertisement's identified employment requirements and your credentials.*

This is vitally important. Over half the cover letters a district receives contain a fatal flaw that eliminates them from consideration. This flaw must be avoided at all cost.

> **FATAL FLAW OF COVER LETTERS:** *The cover letter fails to clearly show how the candidate meets the stated requirements for the position.*

That is correct. The most frequent reason applications do not survive the screening process is the applicant's failure to establish early on how his or her credentials fit the criteria established for the position. Your cover letter must clearly and boldly establish how your background and skills match what the district has identified as its requirements. Yate in his book, Knock 'Em Dead, offers an effective way to make this connection; and yet, I rarely see it in use. He calls this method an executive summary (Yate, 2010). By using this simple design, your cover letters will clearly identify you as a match for the advertised position. Here is how that goal is achieved.

Step 1: *Review the advertisement to identify each and every requirement listed.* A typical ad might stipulate such things as:

New Jersey Elementary School Certificate Required
Knowledge of Current Reading Pedagogy
Previous Experience Working with Elementary Students
Ability to Work with Diverse Groups

Step 2: *Establish a match between your background and every requirement listed in the advertisement.*

Unless you quickly show an employer how you meet each of the criteria, you run the risk of being screened out on the first review. When someone is evaluating a few hundred resumes, it is easy for a reader to conclude a candidate is missing one or more of the required criteria and place his or her resume in the "no interview" pile. Your cover letter can preclude this possibility by creating a two-column table that lists each requirement on one side and how you meet that condition on the opposite side. Here is an example:

POSITION REQUIREMENTS	CREDENTIALS
NJ Certified Elementary Teacher	• *Hold NJ Elementary Teaching Certificate*
Knowledge of current reading pedagogy	• *Taught in both whole-language and literature based reading programs.* • *Possess strong phonics and traditional training.*
Experience with elementary students	• *Taught 3rd grade at Trenton Elementary School*
Ability to work with diverse groups	• *Received strong background in urban education principles from The College of New Jersey.* • *Experience teaching Hispanic, African-American and other ethnic groups.* • *Student taught in multicultural classes in Ewing, NJ.*

This block form is effective because it is so visually convincing. In a glance, the reader can see all of the criteria and how your qualifications match.

If you do not like the appearance of a table, you can achieve a similar effect by omitting the grid lines and using two columns with bullets. The information is the same, but you create a different visual affect.

ALTERNATE ROUTE CANDIDATE – BUT, what if you lack one or more of the criteria listed by the ad? Are you already out of the mix? Not necessarily. In this case, however, you are better advised to state your qualifications in paragraph form. A paragraph will allow you to selectively highlight strengths and de-emphasize points where your background may be less than a good match to the stated requirement. You need only be sure to sufficiently highlight your positive attributes so as to prevent any chance the reader will miss them as he or she rapidly scans your letter. For example, suppose your teaching experience was in a school where diversity was not a characteristic of your classes. A paragraph format will allow you to minimize that area of your background and focus on other strengths. Look at this illustration.

> *In reviewing your advertisement, I noted how my background and credentials match your needs. I currently hold a **New Jersey Elementary School Certificate** and have completed all the requirements necessary to teach. More importantly, my teaching experience has provided a **strong background in both whole-language and phonics reading instruction. I am sufficiently familiar with diagnostic and remedial methodologies** to work with students who have a diverse range of abilities. **Substituting at the Upper Snoot Academy** has provided valuable experience in dealing with elementary school children. I further intend to enroll in two urban education courses to further enhance my abilities as a teacher for all students.*

You can see how both formats clearly identify you as a fully qualified candidate. By demonstrating the one-to-one match between the ad requirements and your background, you maximized the probability of an interview. Other applicants may have failed to make this connection clear and committed a deadly error.

THIRD: *Request an interview*
Once your credentials are established, request an interview and the opportunity to explore your qualifications in depth. In this paragraph, re-indicate your high interest in the position and the need for further discussion of your candidacy. End by providing an indication of the best time for someone to reach you and pertinent information on your availability. Here is a sample of how this might look.

> *As you will see by my resume, I possess many of the qualities you seek for this position. Your advertised position is precisely what I seek, and I would like to meet with you to discuss my candidacy in full. I know that it is often the match between a person's qualifications and a district's specific needs that may determine a candidate's final suitability. I am available*

for an interview at your convenience. Should you need to speak to me by phone, I am home most evenings after 5:00 PM or you can leave a message on my machine, (732) 555-1234 at any time. I will return your call as soon as possible. I look forward to hearing from you in the near future.

This closing paragraph tells the interviewer you are qualified, available for an interview, and when you can be best reached. It will get results and you have done everything necessary to establish your candidacy.

THE DO'S AND DON'TS TO CREATE A GREAT COVER LETTER:

Now that you know what needs to be included in your cover letter, you should consider a few other items of importance. Attention to these matters will help prevent potential mistakes and provide a professional style to your letter.

- **DO** personalize the letter to the district and include the name of the person to whom you are writing. A blanket or form letter can be spotted from a mile away and it lacks impact. Avoid the deadly, "To Whom It May Concern" salutation at all cost. Do your homework and find out the name of the principal or superintendent.

- **DO** use short hard-hitting paragraphs written in simple, straightforward language. A cover letter is not the place to demonstrate your vocabulary and facility with a thesaurus. Excess verbiage only makes your cover letter sound contrived and unnatural. The intent of your cover letter is to make the reader say, "Here is someone we should see."

- **DO** present a positive image. It is unwise to complain about previous employers, supervisors, principals, or other situations that were not to your liking. This comes off as sour grapes and underscores a possibility that perhaps *you* were less than a team player.

- **DO** word process your letter! This is not a personal note to a pal; it is a business letter. Handwritten letters can be difficult to read and they fail to provide the professional appearance you are trying to create. **CAUTION:** *When you use a word processor to send multiple letters, be sure to check your dates, personal information, and all specific references to insure they are correct.* There is nothing more damaging than letters with the wrong names of people, districts, or dates in the text. It can kill your candidacy before it gets started.

- **DO** place your name, address, and phone number in the heading for easy access.

- **DO** use a slightly heavy bond (24 lb. works well) paper with a high quality luster (90 or "brighter"). Off-white, buff or cream can make a nice appearance, but white is considered the standard. You can find good quality paper in any office supply store. Lightweight, white duplicating paper will look like all the rest. Why not stand out a little?

- **DO** identify your ability to work on extra-curricular activities. The details can be saved for the resume, but a one-sentence indication that you are qualified and interested in working beyond the classroom will be noted and well received. Most candidates leave this out and your attention to the matter may provide just the edge you need!

- **DON'T** get folksy or cute. I have seen letters that included a quiz, down-home humor and other casual, off-message paragraphs. Believe me, this is not appreciated and places you in an unprofessional light. The reader has no time for games or humorous side-trips.

- **DON'T** offer an indication of weaknesses or negative points. For example, if your teaching experience in language arts is different than what the district seeks, omit mention of it. Find the areas where you meet the district needs and underscore those.

- **DON'T** make boastful statements such as, "I know exactly how to make your fifth grade team the most successful team in the school." Such statements are rarely well received. Moreover, they may antagonize someone and you need to avoid that possibility.

- **DON'T** use clichés. Avoid statements like, "You'll never find a better candidate than me." or "I'm a real child-centered teacher." or the proverbial, "I'm a genuine team player." These statements are overused and generally ignored by the reader.

To demonstrate how you might write a good cover letter, I've used an actual ad and written a corresponding sample letter. You may also wish to review one of the many books on cover letters in your local library. Although most are written for business, you might find specific features in their examples for your use.

> **Middle School Social Studies**
> *Upper Utopia School District*
> *Upper Utopia, NJ 09999*
>
> *Septermber opening. Must have NJ certification, knowledge of team process and NJ Core Standards. The district is suburban with strong commitment to student achievement. All inquires to Dr. Ruth Jones. No phone inquires.*

Look at what this ad tells us about the district and what it seeks in its candidate. First, the *opening is for September.* Can you be available then? If you are just finishing college or you are between positions, the answer is probably yes. You will want to focus on this attribute. If you are under contract and will need to provide notice, you will not discuss the topic of availability until the interview.

Certification is a <u>must</u>. Preferably you already have state certification. If you are applying from out-of-state, you need to make a statement about your certificate qualifications and the status of your application. Certification is an essential area to address in the cover letter because it is the number one criteria used to eliminate unqualified candidates. It will not be appreciated if you reach an interview and then disclose you do not yet hold a certificate to teach in that state. **NOTE:** *If you are applying to schools in a state where you are not yet certified, the minimum requirement is that you have already established your eligibility and submitted an application to the proper agency.*

"Knowledge of team process" means that you have worked on a teaching team with two or more teachers to organize instruction for a group of students. If you have this experience, underscore it and provide a brief example of how that team worked together. You might highlight such things as interdisciplinary units, the planning process, or other team activities. If you have not been on a team, you can speak to your understanding of the team principle and how you have worked with other teachers on team-type projects. In this case, you should emphasize your understanding of the philosophy.

"Knowledge of NJ Core Standards" is a very specific set of State requirements, but you can substitute any state's graduation requirements in this phrase. As such requirements are generally accompanied by student competency tests, it is essential that you know the specific expectations for your subject area. If you do not already know this information, you need to get a copy of your state's requirements before you go to the interview. This is another "must" and will be discussed in greater detail in later chapters.

"Strong commitment to student achievement" suggests the district gives significant attention to student scores on the various normed achievement tests. It might also suggest students are expected to achieve above average class grades. High failure rates are rarely acceptable. Your letter should identify how you will focus on student learning and attainment.

The advertisement finally provides *the name of the person to whom applications should be addressed* and alerts you to avoid directly phoning the district. This is common in districts where they receive a large number of applications. FOLLOW THE DIRECTIONS! You can be sure the secretaries will take note of your name should you ignore the ad and call for an interview.

Now that we have distilled the key information from the ad, we can prepare a cover letter for the **well-suited applicant.** Our second letter will be for a candidate that may lack one or more of the required criteria.

SAMPLE COVER LETTERS:

James T. Hopeful

38 Deer Path Lane
Clearbrooke, NJ 07777

Work: (908) 555-1212
Home: (908) 555-8513

Dr. Ruth Jones
Upper Utopia School District
Upper Utopia, NJ 09999

May 14, 2011

Dear Dr. Jones,

I noted with great interest your ad in the *Newark Star Ledger* for a middle school Teacher of Social Studies. As you will see in my resume, my qualifications are suited to the advertised position, and I would like to personally speak with you about how I might fit your school team.

The following summary highlights some of my qualifications for this position:

September opening for middle school social studies	*I hold a BA from The College of New Jersey and possess an Elementary Teaching Certificate with emphasis in Social Studies. Available September*
Knowledge of team process	*My student teaching experience was at the Hopewell Middle School where I was an active member of the sixth-grade team. As part of that team I assisted in the planning of units, design of field experiences, and running team meetings.*
Knowledge of NJ Core Standards	*I have reviewed and constructed numerous lessons to teach key indicators of the Core Standards and Proficiencies in Social Studies.*
Strong Commitment to Student Achievement	*Student mastery is a primary criterion by which each of my lessons is evaluated. Alignment to required proficiencies is made during planning and each student's progress is continuously evaluated against those desired outcomes. My class performance on the ITBS was two stanines above the national average.*

I am a highly motivated teacher who has a proven record of results with children. In addition, I am anxious to work on building initiatives and school committees as well as extra-curricular activities. I am available for an interview and can be reached at the above address and phone. I look forward to meeting with representatives of your district to explore my candidacy.

Sincerely,

James T. Hopeful

Enclosure

James T. Hopeful

38 Deer Path Lane
Clearbrooke, NJ 07777

Work: (908) 555-1212
Home: (908) 555-8513

Dr. Ruth Jones
Upper Utopia School District
Upper Utopia, NJ 09999

May 14, 2011

Dear Dr. Jones,

I noted with great interest your ad in the *Newark Star Ledger* for a middle school Teacher of Social Studies. Your profile of the desired candidate appears to be an excellent match with my qualifications and your district is one in where I would like to build my professional career.

The following are highlights of my qualifications that match your requirements:

- I hold a BA from The College of New Jersey and possess an Elementary Teaching Certificate.
- I have worked with colleagues on grade-level projects and read numerous articles on middle school teams.
- I have been part of several in-service workshops regarding the NJ Core Standards and incorporated them in my teaching.
- Student mastery is an important part of all lessons. Students are continuously monitored and provided before or after school assistance if they require additional support.

I am a highly motivated teacher who is anxious to produce results with children. In addition, I am eager to work on building initiatives and school committees as well as extra-curricular activities. I am available for an interview and can be reached at the above address and phone. I look forward to meeting with representatives of your district to explore my candidacy.

Sincerely,

James T. Hopeful

Enclosure

As you can see, the letters are very similar, but the second one is less targeted than the first on the topic of team teaching. Did you see the differences? The first letter provided direct work experience while the second was more general. Although the second teacher has not yet worked on a teaching team, the requirement is addressed in other ways. Both letters provide assurance that the candidate meets the stated requirements and would be worth the time of an interview.

It cannot be too strongly stressed that anything you place in your letter must be accurate *and verifiable.* If you say you know the Core Standards, you will need to be fully conversant on that topic at the interview. If you say you worked on a team, then that *must* be the case. Assume that anything you place in your cover letter or resume will be explored in depth at your interview.

A last word of advice is to have your cover letter read by at least one other person to insure it is clear and well written. If you can find someone who is qualified to check grammar, that is always a worthwhile step. Double-check all spelling and be sure to sign the document with an original signature. Now you are on your way and have everything you need to write a cover letter that will receive notice. Write it and good luck!

"He who wants to persuade should put his trust not in the right argument, but the right word."

—Joseph Conrad
A Personal Record, **1912**

BUILDING THE DYNAMIC RESUME

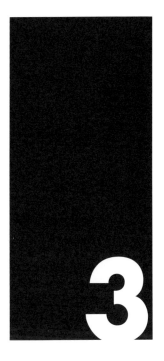

The primary purpose of your cover letter was to establish a clear link between your background and skill sets to the needs and values of the prospective school. If a cover letter is successful, the reviewer will want to know more and examine the more important document, your resume. It is a compelling resume that will win you the interview. Basically, it is an advertisement for you! It describes what the district will gain when they add you to their teaching staff. A good resume will convince the employer that you are someone special; someone who brings the specific competencies, ideas, and energy to more than meet the needs of the posted position.

Write your resume with the intention to create interest and build a sound set of reasons the hiring director should bring you to the school. A great resume will be so targeted and so pleasing in its appearance it almost compels the reader to put it in the "call this person" pile. If you write your resume with these purposes in mind, it will look vastly different than all the rest and be much more than just a catalog of experiences and job histories. It will sell your story!

SOME GENERAL CONSIDERATIONS:
THE MAIN OBJECTIVE OF YOUR RESUME

Because the first and primary objective of your resume is to place you on the must interview list, it must persuasively link your skills to the culture and vision for each school to which you apply. The resume should tell your story in a way that the reader can see how you would be an asset to his or her school. Keep in mind that most applicants look at writing their resume as simply a necessary evil they need to address in order to "apply for the position." They approach the task with no more enthusiasm than they have when filling out an application for a car loan. Even worse, the vast majority of the people write one resume and use it for every position to which they apply. No thought is given to what a school district needs or might look for in a candidate. As a result, most resumes simply recite the employment history and give a list of miscellaneous accomplishments with no particular focus. This is a major mistake and will almost always diminish, if not eliminate, your chances of making it to the interview round.

> **FATAL ERROR OF RESUMES:** *The resume fails to clearly and attractively identify the ways an applicant's background, competencies, and philosophies match the district's needs, values, and vision for the future.*

Your resume needs to stand out in its message of how you are a match to the district's needs as well as its future direction. This emphasis will move your resume ahead of all the plain vanilla, historical resumes that seem to populate most application piles. Remember; the reader needs to see exactly how you will improve his or her school and make a better candidate than others.

HOW TO MATCH YOUR RESUME TO THE DISTRICT NEEDS

We now know the most effective resumes focus on matching your background to the district needs. The difficult piece is how to identify each school's priorities. Often, you will not be able to speak directly with someone in a leadership position prior to an interview. However, there are ways to obtain the necessary information from other sources. Many districts publish an annual report or newsletter. In most states there are school report cards and annual reports that are part of the public record. These documents have valuable information about schools. Individual schools might publish a brochure. Most schools now have their own web page with a complete view of all the things taking place. These websites usually contain calendars of events that identify many elements of the school culture. If you research these items, you will learn about their student activities, grade level projects, school mission statements, school goals, and other important programs. Once you identify the priorities that stand out most, you can select corresponding elements from your background to use when you build your resume.

Add power to these matches on your resume by adding bullets and highlights to the specific qualities of your background that target school priorities. Although we will discuss in detail how this can be accomplished later in the chapter, for right now, let's say that you note on the website that the school recently invested in SmartBoard classrooms.

You might either have used this technology or are at least familiar with its purpose. On your resume you would highlight this match:

- Developed and implemented lessons that *incorporated SmartBoard components* to aid visual clarity, student involvement, and excitement to the daily lessons.

OR

- Have researched ways to increase lesson effectiveness and visual clarity through the *use of SmartBoard technologies*. Anticipate participating in a future workshop to improve my use of this teaching tool in future lesson design.

As you can see, both statements identify you as someone who is anxious to put the district money to good use as well as an excellent match to the direction in which the school is moving. **WARNING:** *If you put something like this on your resume, you must be prepared to speak to it during the interview.* If you suggest you are familiar with how SmartBoards are used, you will potentially need to explain this when you are in front of the interview committee. If you say you will attend a workshop or take an online seminar, then you need to be able to specify how and when that will take place. It will be fatal if you are quizzed about this information and cannot clearly speak to what you have written.

MAKE THE RESUME COMPACT AND POWERFUL

There is nothing that will dim your chances for an interview more than a fifteen-page blockbuster resume. The reviewer only wants to know what makes you a potential fit for the advertised position. He or she does not have time to wade through your life history and pull out the important information. The most powerful resumes I have seen are only two to three pages long. If you are particularly experienced, you might go a bit further, but generally anything beyond 3 single pages is not well read. WARNING: Do not reduce the print to less than 10 points in order to squeeze in information. This will overcrowd your resume and make it difficult to read.

WAYS TO ADD POWER AND GET NOTICED:

- *Replace the job objectives portion of the resume with the name of the position for which you are applying.* School districts often have multiple openings and they need to easily identify which applicant is applying for which position. Some books on the subject suggest that you lead with a more general employment objective, but this is not necessary on resumes for teaching positions. It occupies

31

precious space that would be better used to tell your story. A job objective that trumpets, "I am looking for a rewarding teaching position" will do little to place you at the head of the line. Instead, help the district and use this space to identify the precise position for which you are applying.

- ***Use language that will create impact:*** Wherever you communicate a special accomplishment, it is made stronger when you cite the evidence of that work. Quantitative results can be added to create impact. For example, which of the following statements is more effective?

"Improved student ability to read."

OR

"Average student achievement in my 3rd grade reading classes rose by 1.4 years in 2010-2011. All 26 students tested at or above grade level."

Obviously the second example makes a much stronger statement. Your entries should use action verbs and specific examples wherever possible. Words like "implemented, designed, and employed" effectively underscore your deeds and accomplishments.

- ***Avoid the use of personal pronouns:*** Repeating the phrase, "I did this," and "I did that," becomes redundant and reduces overall impact. The reader will make the logical assumption that you are speaking of your own work. Personal pronouns can also make your application sound boastful whereas a list of activities and accomplishments usually does not.
- ***Eliminate unnecessary information:*** Do not bother to tell the reader about a hobby or how you spent last summer unless you feel the item has some relationship to your qualifications. Experience you gained working in a real estate office for the last two years does not qualify you for a teaching position. In fact, references to numerous business positions, no matter how good you think they were, can have the negative effect of making a reader wonder if you are serious about a teaching career. Avoid business references unless they have a clear connection to the teaching position for which you are applying.

ALTERNATE ROUTE CANDIDATE: If you are coming from a business field and hold alternate route certification, then past business experience will be impossible to avoid. The interview committee will want to know a little about what you have done prior to making this career change. When you create a paragraph to describe what you have done for your more recent job history, there is a preferred methodology. We will provide greater detail when we discuss later how to write your resume, but for now the below paragraph is an example of a way you might link your work background to the teaching profession.

Before pursuing my passion to teach, I was a manager at a local real estate office. In that position, I was charged with the responsibility to train and develop new agents. I was directly involved in teaching seminar sessions, mentoring, evaluating performance, and developing a success mentality in my students.

The objective is to explain what you have done in a way that you draw attention to any experiences that would transfer to the teaching process.

- ***Don't overstate your case!*** Honesty is not the best policy on your resume – it is the only policy. If one fabrication or half-truth is discovered at the interview, you will not likely survive as a candidate. You might be forgiven for almost anything else, but dishonesty will not be tolerated. Even if the interviewer does not initially catch the dishonest statement, it may cost you the job if it is discovered later. Believe me; you already have sufficient positive qualities to be an attractive candidate.
- ***Pay attention to details:*** Use proper grammar, correct spelling, and correct syntax. I once reviewed applications for the position of school superintendent where an applicant had misspelled the word "superintendent." The result was swift and predictable. Check your dates to insure they are correct and there is no overlap of time that places you in two locations simultaneously. If you are applying to multiple districts, make certain that you do not include "cut and paste" mistakes that identify the wrong school, dates, or individuals. Errors such as these can reduce or even eliminate your chances of moving to the interview round.

WRITING AN ATTRACTIVE RESUME THAT WILL STAND OUT FROM THE CROWD:

- ***Never, ever send a handwritten resume.*** If you have weak computer skills, let someone prepare your resume professionally. The most commonly used program in schools is Microsoft Word. In over twenty years of hiring, I never saw a handwritten resume move past the initial review.
- ***Do not include a picture.*** Legally, employers are not permitted to consider information gathered from a picture in their hiring decision. There are many districts who now discard any resumes with a picture just to avoid the possibility of legal impropriety or allegations of discrimination.

- *Make the resume easy to read and follow.* Use standard margins, do not make paragraphs too long, and allow for space between sections. Keep in mind your resume is likely to get an initial review that lasts sixty seconds or less. Lengthy paragraphs with crowded information will often remain skimmed or unread. Use bold face type where there is something the reader must see. **CAUTION:** *Bold type can be effective when wisely placed, but it can also be easily overused.*

- *Keep your paging clear.* If your resume is two or more pages, be certain to number and place your name on every page except the first.

- *Do not skimp on the stationery.* If you are sending hard copies, I recommend you use a white, ivory, or very light buff paper of bond quality. The slightly heavier 24 lb. weight will stand up to harsh handling and still look good. Take care not to use a paper that is too heavy because it is difficult to handle and may not photocopy well. <u>Never</u> use bright or phosphorescent paper. The reader should not require sunglasses to review your resume. Such paper may stand out, but it does not present a professional image.

- *Use shading in your resume very sparingly or perhaps not at all.* Although shading can add visual impact when done well, if a school scans your resume into their computer, that section can come out much darker and make it difficult to read. If you choose to use shading, be sparing and make it very light. Use your own discretion, but you should scan and duplicate your document first to be sure it will get the results you intend.

- *Supply appropriate references.* Avoid the popular "references on request" phrase. Principals do not have time to dig this information out. Provide the name, title, and relationship of at least two references on the resume. *Be sure you include the name of the person who directly supervised and evaluated you.* Do not list relatives, other colleagues, or people who were not in a supervisory position. The lone exception to this is your cooperating teacher during student teaching. If you are an **alternate route candidate** and did substitute teaching, the name of a teacher for whom you substituted and who is familiar with your work will be satisfactory. If there is a problem or delicate situation with someone at a former place of employment, discuss this situation at the interview. Very few principals or superintendents will call references unless you are being strongly considered for the position.

BUILDING THE DYNAMIC RESUME BY SECTIONS:

Now it is time to put this information together and construct a resume that will command attention. It is best to first divide the resume into neat, identifiable sections.

This will provide easy reference for those conducting the interview. At the outset, let me **strongly advise you to put your email address** right at the top of the page in your heading. On that topic, ahem….it is prudently advised that you use a professional or neutral email address for your school contacts. An address like, partyanimal@hotspots.com is not likely to help your candidacy. Almost every school uses email as a preferred way of communicating and having this information clearly displayed will be to your advantage.

Now let's take a look at our recommended sections and how to build each one.

OBJECTIVE: As mentioned earlier, this is where you will place the exact position to which you are applying.

CERTIFICATIONS: List any and all certificates you hold. If you do not yet hold a certificate, but have made application, list that certificate by name and provide the date on which you applied. If you hold certificates in other states, they should also be listed. If you have certificates in subject areas or job categories that are not directly applicable to this position, you might list them as well. **Alternate Route Candidate:** You must place the certification standing that you hold for that state. For example, if you have a *Transitional or Provisional Certificate with Advanced Standing*, you list that. The essential ingredient for you is that when the screening administrator looks at your application, he or she can see that you are qualified to be employed in the district by the date for which they would need you to start.

EDUCATION: It is only required that you identify your college experiences. Generally, your high school is not relevant unless you are an alumnus of the school to which you are applying or there is some other direct connection. Place the college name and city on the left with your dates of attendance on the right. If you received a degree from the listed institution, identify it along with your major. If you graduated with honors, be sure to indicate that next to the degree. If you have advanced degrees, list the highest degree first and work down to the lowest.

Indiana University   2006-2007
Bloomington, Indiana
MAT, Elementary Education

Bethany College   2000-2005
Bethany, WV
BA, Cum Laude, Early Childhood Education

If you are an **alternate route candidate**, you use the same format because the content of your major area of study often connects to your area of teaching. In addition, if you are enrolled in a professional studies program as part of your alternate route program, you list that first and then your undergraduate degree institution under that.

Educational Experience: This is perhaps the most important section of your resume. Here you will list all relevant teaching experience along with a few important elements of your work while in each position. This is where you will begin to specifically link your background to the stated needs of the school. Let us assume you know the school uses block scheduling for some classes and has a pull-out program for basic skills students. Your resume can clearly reflect where and how your background matches those aspects of the prospective school. Look at the following example to see how this relationship is drawn.

Forest Hills Elementary School   2007-2008
4th Grade Teacher

- Planned and taught Language Arts and Math in 90-minute blocks four
  days per week. Utilized multi-path lessons and learning centers
  to maximize student involvement and learning activity.
- Developed individualized learning packets for 17 pull-out students to
  maintain their standing when classes were missed. Also worked with
  the BSI teacher to coordinate student schedules and workload.

Notice how each bullet targets an item the school will see as important. Although there were numerous experiences and skills in your background from which to choose, your resume must focus on those that meet the needs of the prospective district. Include a few high impact bullet items for each school you list on your resume. They add power and they *will* receive notice!

In listing your experience, begin with your most recent employment and work backward to the earliest teaching post. Unless you have two or more school districts and six years of experience to cite, you should list your student teaching. Each listing should include the dates of service, teaching duties, and specific school information. If there are gaps in service, this is not necessarily a negative point. Simply be ready to discuss what you were doing during that time. A good explanation is generally accepted.

Other Pertinent Educational Experience: This section describes any special workshops, in-service training sessions, summer courses, or other relevant training you have completed. **REMEMBER:** *Include any and all clubs you advised, sports coaching, or other extra-curricular activities.* Principals are looking for teachers who involve themselves in the full school program. Wherever possible, indicate an interest in activities or programs where the prospective school has an advertised need. Review the many in-service days you attended and select those that complement your new school's agenda. For example, if the school to which you are applying recently conducted in-service training on brain-based learning and you once attended a seminar or have specific course instruction on that topic, highlight that matching experience. The following is an example of how this can be done.

- Attended an evening PDK workshop with David Sousa who described his book, <u>How the Brain Learns,</u> and how it can be directly applied in the classroom.
- Participated in a ½-day in-service that taught the means to create instructional activities that improve retention. Used this information to revise future classroom lessons.
- The college course, <u>Teaching Strategies for Secondary Teachers</u> at Indiana University included extensive coverage on the means to relate teacher actions and lesson design to brain-based theory.

You can see how the second item might not be a perfect fit, but it is close enough to reflect your continuing growth in a relevant field. It is unlikely that everything in your background will be a perfect fit to district's initiatives, but you can include entries if there is a reasonably close match. Use this section of the resume to build those all-important connections. It will pay big dividends!

NOTE: *To help you indentify the places where you might make an effective co-curricular connection, look in the newspaper or wherever you originally saw the position advertised. Were there also coaching vacancies or other openings listed for which you might be qualified? If so, announce them prominently on your resume and get to the front of the interview line!*

References: As pointed out earlier in the chapter, it is important to include specific references on your resume. Principals will appreciate your consideration in this matter. Anyone you intend to include as a reference should be alerted in advance that he or she is on your resume. It also makes sense to suggest what specific information you would like him or her to provide if contact is made. Whenever possible, obtain a written reference from the people you list on the resume. Some candidates attach reference letters directly to their resume. If you choose to do this, only include one letter. You can bring the others to the interview and offer them at the proper time.

SUGGESTIONS FOR THE ALTERNATE ROUTE CANDIDATE:

Understandably, not everyone has a wealth of teaching experience and background from which to draw when they are preparing their resume. If you recently graduated from college or are an alternate route candidate with no student teaching experience, this can present a special challenge. But do not overly concern yourself with this matter as there are ways to minimize its impact. The key will be to draw on related experiences in your pre-teaching professional life while simultaneously seeking new experiences now that will add to your background and resume.

The first and best advice for someone who is limited in actual classroom experience is to become a substitute teacher as quickly as he or she can. This will provide numerous experiences and a background context to use in building a resume. In most cases, you will begin as a daily substitute and cover for teachers in a variety of teaching disciplines. Take advantage of every one of these opportunities! By working in classes with students of different abilities, teaching a variety of subject areas, and covering multiple grade levels, you will be able to present yourself as someone who has a sound understanding of the wider role of a professional teacher.

If you do become a substitute teacher, keep a journal of different activities, classroom events, and teaching experiences. Identify any class management issues you faced and what you did to solve them. Note other professionals in the building with whom you work and any projects where you might have been involved. If you were part of faculty workshops, meetings, or planning groups, identify what you did and any results that were attained. It is easy to forget or overlook important experiences after time has passed. This journal will help you remember and become an invaluable tool when writing your resume!

Even better than being a daily substitute, you might try getting a **permanent substitute or replacement substitute post.** The difference between these two positions is that the first is simply someone who is asked to come in every day and the district will assign you the class schedule for a teacher who is unavailable. As a replacement teacher, there is a staff member they expect to be absent for an extended period of time and you would assume all of his or her duties until he or she returns. This is the best of all options and usually given to only the better substitutes. Districts do not select a person for a replacement post unless they are familiar with her and confident in her work. The value of such a position is that interviewers also know that only the better teachers are given such appointments.

If substitute teaching is impossible, then you will have to draw on whatever professional training you have had in college or through the alternate route program where you are studying. You can also use experiences you have had through things such as recreational programs, coaching, church school, scouting, mentorships, tutoring, or other areas of instructional contact.

A final area where you can gain valuable experience is the private or charter school. Many churches operate their own schools and may have full time openings for classroom teachers. These generally do not require a formal teaching certificate, and you can gain a wealth of experience while waiting for that right job to come available. Similarly, charter schools sometimes have higher than usual turnover rates and new teachers are readily considered.

It is important for you to keep in mind that, if you take advantage of the available opportunities, you can build a very respectable resume in a short period of time.

This is a good time for us to review a sample resume and examine its key features and differences. In the example offered at the end of this chapter, it is sectioned into columns and a quote is placed to the very left. Whereas the quote will help the aesthetics, the power is in the message content. Select your quote carefully so that it loudly speaks to your personal philosophy. An added value of this tactic is it will make the appearance of your resume somewhat unique so as to stand out from the others. It also offers the hiring director one more insight into what makes you a special individual.

Like the traditional resume, your first sections will identify the position to which you are applying and specify precisely what kind of certificate or state authorization you have at the current time. Because states have so many different ways of naming and describing their programs, I did not specify a particular name in the sample; you will need to identify the one you hold. If your application to the state has been submitted but is still pending or you are only in the process of obtaining your license to teach, then you must identify exactly when you expect to receive it.

For the work history and experience section, it is recommended that you use a paragraph format. This allows you to highlight the portions of your previous work that will make the most positive impression while downplaying or remaining silent on the less compelling aspects of your background.

It is important to at least describe what you have been doing over the course of your career. Ignoring five or ten years of employment history on the resume will often give the impression that you are either less than forthcoming or perhaps even hiding something. You can see that we have added paragraphs for each time period that tell where we were, briefly what we were doing, and any reason for leaving. If you were fired or let go, it is best to remain silent on the issue at this point. Note too, that any experiences you had in the workplace that might have a positive translation to the classroom can be highlighted. I have shown how that is done in the sample. And oh by the way…"Collected Unemployment Benefits for 13 months" is not the kind of "work experience" we would like to share at this time. Even if such was the case, find a better way to describe that period in your life. It may surprise you to know I once saw that exact statement on a resume. Keep in mind, these paragraphs are designed to highlight your positives and eliminate the negatives.

Because you have either limited or no experience with regard to classroom teaching, do not assume you will have only limited things to include in this section! Try to pull from your background those specific places where you did work in a teaching or related capacity. You have had some degree of professional training as part of your alternate route program, and this is a good place to begin. For example, if you designed and taught practice lessons in front of your class, those will demonstrate that you understand the principles of lesson design. If you did field observations in a school, you can use those experiences to underscore key skills you have seen or assisted with in practice. If you were part of a planning team either in class or at your place of work, that might translate to being part of teaching team. Even though you may not have had a great deal of *actual* classroom experience, you can underscore your preparation and the places where related experiences add to your qualifications. These will count!

A powerful addition to your resume is the last portion that tells the reader that you would be interested in assisting with the co-curricular aspects of the school. These could be clubs, sports, mentoring, tutoring, or anything else you can identify that the school offers and you have some interest or qualification. If you see that this school is advertising for specific co-curricular openings, target these. Look at this section in the sample resume and you will see how to effectively add this to your list of skills. Understand, it is not always necessary that you have previously been directly involved in any of these activities. If you have no direct experience, you can simply announce your interest and/or willingness to become involved should the opportunity exist. In a competitive process, this section can often be the difference between either securing the interview or being placed in the non-interview pile.

As you can see from this sample, it is possible to present yourself in a very positive light by using the paragraph format. By spotlighting only the areas of strongest impact and identifying your ability to work in a variety of ways that match the school's needs, you can make a very strong impression. As with every candidate, regardless of background, the more the resume matches teacher background to school needs, the stronger the probability of reaching that next round. With a hard hitting cover letter and this resume, you have an excellent chance of getting that interview!

ELECTRONIC FILING AND THE NEW TECHNOLOGY:

In today's technology driven schools, it is becoming almost the standard for districts to require that the application and resume be completed electronically. Some schools might even have specific online application pages that will need to be completed in order to apply. If this is the case, there is no need to also send hard copies. In fact, sending a hard copy when the district requires electronic submission will diminish your chances for an interview.

Districts tend to prefer the electronic submission because it cuts down on filing, lost documents, and the need to photocopy. In addition, they can electronically send the resumes of the candidates to members of the interview committee more easily.

When you go to the interview, you should bring a few extra hard copies of your resume. It is unlikely that you will be asked for them, however, if someone unexpected arrives, you will have a copy for them to review.

POSTING RESUMES ON INTERNET JOB BOARDS:

The Internet has a growing number of sites where you can post your resume in the hope that a school searching for a teacher with your background will find yours. In fact, there are indeed a few districts that use such sites; however, it is not their primary or favored source for teacher applicants. The probability of a school in your target area contacting you because they saw your resume on one of these job boards is low. The research suggests that of those who have resumes on job boards, less than 10% are ever contacted, and this statistic is for *all* types of positions (Beshara, 2008). For only teachers, that number is likely to be even lower. There is no way to fully quantify any of this information, but it is safe to assume that job boards are not the best place for your resume.

In addition to the low probability of success, there is an added danger. Once your email address is out in the public domain, you can expect spam, unwanted job offers, and bogus opportunities to over-populate your inbox. Even worse, these unwanted emails are likely to continue well after you have already secured a good job! Once your address and resume are placed in cyberspace, they can stay there indefinitely. You can go back

41

and delete the information or remove your name from the board, but it will be too late; the address was already captured, and you are on thousands of lists.

In brief, my recommendation is to skip this kind of job search entirely. There are far more effective and less dangerous ways to get your resume noticed.

ADVICE ON THE USE OF SOCIAL NETWORKS:

It is popular today to stay connected to friends and relatives through the use of social network sites such as **Facebook, Twitter, and personal blogs.** Be aware that a growing number of employers look at the material posted on the Facebook pages of prospective employees. In speaking with a number of principals from around the country I asked if there had been times when material on Facebook had influenced their opinions. In almost every case where someone had looked, they answered that at least one person's pictures or writings on their Facebook page had created a negative impression. Whatever you post, or whatever others post to you, might be visible and create the wrong picture of you in the mind of a school official.

Because of the above, my best advice is to either take down your Facebook page or make it inactive during the entire interview process. Should you get a position and want to have a Facebook page at a later time, make certain that whatever you post will be something you would not mind a parent or employer viewing. You read of cases every month of teachers who are involved in some kind of difficulty over things they have posted on their Facebook, emailed, tweeted, or blogged. Be very careful with what you put online.

A last item is your home or cell phone recorded answer when you are not available. Be sure the message someone hears, if you do not pick up the phone, is something neutral or professional. We do not want the principal to be treated to a message like, "Hey there, whaddup? I'm not here right now, must be out on the town partying so leave a message, and I'll get backatcha." Informal, humorous, and wiseacre messages can make you appear immature and you can bet will not be well received. Update your phones accordingly. Technology is a great thing, but it can represent some risks that, during the interview process, are best not taken. Act wisely.

SAMPLE RESUMES:

Your resume and cover letter are the only documents to represent you when applications are first being considered. The extra time you spend to research the district and align your credentials will be well worth the effort. You cannot afford to submit a bland cover letter and boilerplate resume similar to everyone else's. Follow the directions provided in these last two chapters and you will have first-rate documents that get an employer's attention. There are literally hundreds of resume formats and samples on the open market. Entire books are given to just this task. You might find specific elements of resume writing from other sources that you like. I urge you to look for the best way to make yours attractive and compelling. A few sample resumes follow for your review. You should choose the one that reflects your style and personality best.

RESUME FOR TRADITIONAL CANDIDATE:

RESUME
JANE B. WRIGHT

1095 Lake Front Drive
Bear Lake, TN 07777

WORK: (908) 555-1212
HOME: (732) 555-8513
Email: jwright@uten.org

OBJECTIVE: High School Special Education Teacher

CERTIFICATIONS: Tennessee Elementary Teacher Certificate
Teacher of the Handicapped Certificate

EDUCATION: EAST TENNESSEE STATE UNIVERSITY 2009
Johnson City, Tennessee
MAT Special Education

TUSCULUM COLLEGE 2007
Greeneville, Tennessee
BS Science Education
Oliver Gray Scholar

**WORK
EXPERIENCE:** **RESOURCE TEACHER GRADES 9 - 12** 2010 – present
NORRIS ELEMENTARY SCHOOL
Norris, Tennessee (1 year replacement teacher)
• Case manager for 11 students
• Member of Child Study Team
• Assisted in developing inclusive science
  education program that **received best
  practice award**
• Assistant coach for Girls Soccer

STUDENT TEACHER   2007
GRADE 3
DOAK SCHOOL
Doak, Tennessee
- Established Writing Laboratory
- Co-developed thematic unit on "Preserving Our Environment."
- Eight of our students recognized in Character Counts program

OTHER PERTINENT EXPERIENCE:
- Attended a summer institute on "Writing Workshop."
- Participated in the "New Teacher Workshop; Beyond Madeline Hunter."
- Taught 3rd grade Sunday School
- Teacher representative to PTA

REFERENCES:

Dr. James Cost, Director Pupil Services
Norris Schools
(999) 555-1010

Mrs. Sally Bible, Cooperating Teacher
Doak School
(999) 555-1907

RESUME FOR ALTERNATE ROUTE CANDIDATE:

RESUME

Arthur Goode

777 King Hill Road, Pleasantville, VA 09999 | 555-555-1212

Agoode@gmail.com

OBJECTIVE

Eighth grade science teacher

The quality of a person's life is in direct proportion to their commitment to excellence, regardless of their chosen field of endeavor.

Vincent T. Lombardi
(1913-1970)

CERTIFICATION

YOUR STATE Teaching Certificate Title

Secondary Physical Science

EDUCATION

EVANSVILLE UNIVERSITY	1999
Evansville, IN	
BS Chemistry	

JOHNSON COMMUNITY COLLEGE	1999
Kokomo, IN	
AS Business and Finance	

WORK EXPERIENCE

2010 - Present
Crown Point Public Schools
Pleasantville, VA
Substitute Teacher

Taught general science, biology, and chemistry classes from grades 7 through 11. Responsibilities were to **prepare lessons**, participate **in middle school team meetings**, **supervise activities**, and evaluate **student performance**. Created **multi-media science excursions** for 6th grade team and **assisted with class trip** to Williamsburg, VA.

2002 – 2009
Chemco Laboratories
Tarrytown, NY

Operated a testing laboratory involved with environmental biohazards, water quality, and general ecosystem quality control issues. **Some of my responsibilities included training, supervising, and developing field investigators.** This involved **classroom teaching, field observation, and student evaluation.** Laid off when company downsized.

RELATED EXPERIENCE

- **TAUGHT SUNDAY SCHOOL** at Faith Church in Pleasantville, VA for two years. Worked with both the 5th grade and the Confirmation classes. Assisted in the **development of the Confirmation Class curriculum** and developed a complete home and church outreach program for the students.
- **ASSISTANT SOCCER COACH** with the sixth grade recreational girls soccer team. Organized practices, assisted with game day preparations, and completed the required first aid courses.

CO-CURRICULAR INTERESTS

- **School Store:** Given my background in business, I would welcome the opportunity to work with students in operating a school store or other similar school based enterprises.
- **Science Club:** Would consider initiating a school Science Club or assisting with any similar club that may be in place.
- **Sports Coach:** Although my previous experience in coaching involved recreation soccer, I played softball and basketball in high school. I would enthusiastically welcome an opportunity to assist in those areas should a need arise.

REFERENCES

Mr. Paul Taylor, Principal   555-555-1000
Crown Point School
Pleasantville, VA

Dr. LouAnn Peabody   555-555-9999
Alternate Route Certification Director
Old Dominion University
Norfolk, VA.

"A well-written life is almost as rare as a well-spent one."

—Thomas Carlisle, **1827**

HOW TO BUILD AN INTERVIEW PORTFOLIO

4

THE NEED FOR AN INTERVIEW PORTFOLIO:

So you made it to the interview. But, so did a number of other candidates who also have good resumes and what seems like the right qualities for this district. Although we have no idea how they might have fared with *their* interview, we know we need to do better. This puts the onus squarely on your shoulders to insure you close the deal. You need to leave that interview committee with something that will last in their minds well after you are on your way home. *That* is precisely the role of the interview portfolio; it's the deal closer! It must be something visual, powerful, and memorable that will back up every claim we made and put an exclamation point on the end.

An interview portfolio, if well designed, will accomplish this important goal. But the key to success lies in just how you constructed your portfolio and how it captured the interviewer's interest. Make no mistake, there is an art to this, and a badly constructed portfolio can actually detract from the viability of an otherwise good candidate. So be aware, there is a set of do's and don'ts that we must closely examine in this chapter.

The first thing to understand is that an *interview portfolio* is different from a *professional portfolio*. First, let's consider the comprehensive **professional portfolio**. Every professional teacher, regardless of the path he or she took to arrive, should build a portfolio that begins with their earliest teaching experience and continues on throughout his or her career. In the professional portfolio you include a wide variety of artifacts, mementos, testimonials, photos, and other documents to provide a moving chronology of professional vision, work, and achievements. It is meant to be comprehensive in scope and reflective in construction. An **interview portfolio**, on the other hand, is much smaller and has a *definitive focus and* *purpose*. The content of your interview portfolio is dictated by the specific goal you want to achieve.

In building an interview portfolio you must first consider the limited amount of presentation time you will receive. Bear in mind that the purpose of this portfolio is to accent and give life to the points you have made during the question/answer portion of the interview. It is to close your time with the committee on the strongest possible note. Therefore, you will present your materials at the end of the interview when there might be other candidates waiting, and brevity will be valued. The principal and committee will want to move onto the next applicant in a timely way, however, they are usually willing to spend the additional few minutes to see and review the work you have done with children. As a rule of thumb, portfolio reviews should not take more than four or five minutes and you need to let the committee know it will take no longer than "a few minutes." Its purpose is to enhance your resume and visually highlight the things that tell the committee you are the kind of teacher they want on staff. This means your portfolio strategy must be dictated by what you know about the district and its values.

With time at a premium, include only items that add high impact to your presentation. The more closely the items match the school's values, the greater the impact. For example, you may think photos of your class experience on a local nature excursion demonstrate your ability to motivate students with a "hands-on" approach. However, if you are interviewing in an urban district with no such facilities and where outside experiences are unsafe, the impact of your photos will be limited. You should consider a different piece to demonstrate the hands-on approach you provided in your class.

Look at the in-service topics for teachers. If specific initiatives are underway, photos of work that match your teaching to those initiatives will be well received. For example, if two million dollars was recently invested in technology to facilitate interactive learning and online courses, pictures of your class working on an Internet enrichment project will be meaningful to the committee. Note that, in this case, your picture is perhaps not a perfect match to the district's "online course" direction. BUT, when you display the picture you can speak to how excited you would be to now have that added capability to integrate and use the Internet as you go forward! Such matching activities resonate with committee members and can move you toward the top of the committee's "most desirable" list.

Most candidates will not even have a portfolio and those who do have likely failed to do the necessary homework to link their credentials to specific district goals. This oversight provides you the opportunity to tell a more compelling story. *Attention to details gives you the advantage!*

WHAT TO INCLUDE IN A WINNING PORTFOLIO:

- *A copy of your teaching certificate:* This should not be the original certificate. A copy will serve just as well. If you are an **alternate route candidate**, then you would post the certificate offered by your state. If you have not yet received a certificate at the time of the interview, you can omit this page. For most candidates, the certificate is their lead page.
- *An innovative unit or lesson plan:* The plan must be described on a single sheet of paper. Be sure to include your broad objectives, the main activities and timelines, student involvement, assessment strategy, and any other information you determine the district would see as important. Additional components might include interdisciplinary elements, real world connections, technology, use of webquests or SmartBoard technology, or enrichment activities. In sum, you can include any design features that fit the district profile.

WARNING: *It is easy to overdo the unit plan section of your portfolio. Plan your design so that key aspects and innovative features stand out. Include a few elements that, when explained, will <u>most fit</u> your plan to the culture and direction of the school.*

- *Student work samples:* Work samples can effectively highlight the results students can achieve under your direction, but consider a few guidelines when putting this section together. First, always delete any names or identifying information on the work sample. Confidentiality is essential. Select a cross-section of student work. The committee will be interested to see how a variety of students perform in your class. It is important to show that you are proud of all your students, not just the top few. As a principal who has viewed many portfolios, I was always favorably impressed when a candidate showed me work samples from a struggling student who had risen to a higher level. Almost every teacher can produce good results when they have the brightest student, but success with limited ability students connotes a higher level of teaching skill. Use a highlighter to bring out elements of a student's work that demonstrate critical learning. Do not underestimate the power of this section; student performance is something every administration wants to see.
- *Student surveys:* If you are currently teaching, design and give the students a 'teacher survey form" that requests some honest feedback about their views of the class and your teaching. Include two open-ended questions of the following type.

1.   *What did you like best about this class?*
2.   *What did I do that most helped you to be succesful?*

To focus student thinking on specific teacher actions or classroom events that will help build a strong portfolio, you need to "seed the pot." To accomplish this goal, provide suggestions or ideas that will help students start their thinking. You might write on the board, for example:

"In question #1 you can think about things like the field trips we took, activities we completed in class, our circle discussions, the computer centers, or special help sessions."

By identifying a few specific areas, you almost insure students will write about some of the things a prospective school might value. (Yes, yes, I realize some will consider this to be some form of cheating. Too bad! We're trying to get a position here and we're going to do what it takes! Are you with me on that?)

Once you have the surveys, make copies of those you think will have some value. When constructing the portfolio, select surveys that fit your needs and use a highlighter to *underscore items* you want the committee to see. *Do not* rely on committee members to pick the important points out for themselves because that rarely happens. Do it for them! It is important for the committee to see how students enjoyed your class and were well supported by your teaching stance. Student comments have a very persuasive voice in verifying your teaching expertise.

- **Selected photos:** This section is another one that can easily be overdone. Only include photographs that specifically exhibit a quality of your teaching you feel the committee will see as important. A half-dozen well-chosen photographs with a purpose is more effective than a potpourri of forty to fifty meaningless snapshots. Besides, you have limited time and cannot give attention to a photo extravaganza. With regard to photographs, there is often a question about the use of student faces and the need for release forms. If you do not plan to show the portfolio in a public setting, it is not generally necessary to have signed releases.

When thoughtfully chosen and arranged, photographs can make a powerful statement about your work in the classroom. Pictures of interactive bulletin boards, field studies, project fairs, group work, and laboratory settings effectively show innovative teaching. Think about why a photograph is included and what story you will tell about it. A last tip on style is to include people in your photos. Bland snapshots of your class or decorations are tedious and create scant visual impact. Photographs of happy students engaged in learning will be far more effective in stimulating a positive discussion with the committee.

A suggestion that will add impact and value to your photos is to place a brief narration next to each one. A sentence or two, no more than three, to explain precisely what is taking place or why this snapshot is included will have better effect than just pictures on a page where the viewer is left to figure out their importance.

- *Copies of parent communications:* If you have sent out parent newsletters or information letters to launch new units and involve parents, you might place samples of those in your portfolio if the district places a high value on parent involvement. If students made special presentations to the class and parents were invited, such expositions also exemplify a commitment to involving parents in the education of their children.

- *Copies of evaluations:* Some districts have begun to ask that you include copies of your evaluations along with the resume. If you have done this, then you would not include one in the portfolio. If you did not already submit evaluations to the district, then some might advise that you put one of the better ones in your portfolio. Although this is not a terrible idea, you should be aware that they *are not usually* the most effective way to verify your instructional competence. Most interviewers are smart enough to know you will only include puff pieces that say good things. As a result, the credibility of such documents has limits. This can be improved if you yellow-highlight statements in your evaluation that compliment teaching skills the district values. For example, if the prospective district has a strong interest in innovative assessment and your evaluation identifies innovative assessment as your lesson's strength, highlight those remarks for the reviewer to see. Do not include more than one evaluation no matter how glowing the others might be. Checklist evaluations are superficial and have no impact; eliminate them altogether.

- *Letter(s) of reference:* A good letter of reference is somewhat more effective in speaking to your qualities as a candidate.   As with evaluations, interviewers know you are likely to only include good letters, but when they are from respected members of the school community, they can serve a useful purpose. If possible, when you ask for a letter of reference, ask the writer to directly address those elements of your professional background you want to underscore at the interview. Again, use a yellow-highlighter to make the pertinent passages stand out. No more than one letter should be included in your portfolio. Others can be offered if requested. **TIP:** *Make a number of copies of each reference letter.* Multiple copies will allow you to use one for each portfolio and accent the valued areas for each school. Always keep your original fresh and unmarked.

- ***CD's and DVD's:*** Classroom teachers should leave CD's and videos out of their portfolio. Oh, while on the topic? Do not use anything about yourself held on YouTube for any reason whatsoever! Interviewers will not have the necessary time or inclination to view a CD or watch YouTube clips. If you are a music teacher, however, you may be asked to supply a CD/DVD of one of your concerts or marching band performances that the committee can review at a later time. For this reason, you may wish to create well-edited CD/DVD sample of eight to fifteen minutes in length. This CD is only likely to be reviewed if you are a candidate under serious consideration.

- ***Copies of musical programs:*** If you are a vocal or instrumental music teacher, you should include a copy of two or three typical music programs you have presented. Principals will definitely want to see examples of your work in this area. If you are a new or **alternate route teacher**, then put together a program you might like to deliver if hired. Again, do some homework. Find out what kind or programs have been traditionally presented in the school. Were they well received? If so, this provides good information on how to craft your program. The public aspect of concerts makes these documents an important part of your portfolio.

HOW TO MAKE A POWERFUL PRESENTATION:

My suggestion is that the portfolio be held in a plain, ¼ to ½ inch, three ring binder. You might choose a dark color like blue, burgundy, or black. For every page, use a clear page protector, it makes a much better appearance than just a stack of pages in a book. You might also want to use labeled section dividers. The reason for these is not to separate multiple pages, it is to make finding important items easy. Be sure your name is prominently displayed on the outside. Use a label maker or computer generated label as opposed to scrawling it on the front in magic marker. Don't laugh, I've seen it! By using this bound edition, you will have something that makes a positive statement about you, your organizational ability, and your professionalism.

As you enter the interview, carry the portfolio in your briefcase or some other unobtrusive way. It is best to produce the portfolio only after the committee has indicated their willingness to review the contents with you. At the conclusion of the questions, the interviewer will generally ask if you have any questions or additional things you might wish to add. *This is the moment where you close the deal!!!* You can alter this if you like, but you might want to say the following.

"Yes I do. We have talked about so many things here today and I have brought a very brief portfolio that will give a little additional insight into my teaching. It will only take a few added minutes; may I show it to you?"

Now, two things can occur. First, they will say yes and you can get started on the presentation. Or, in a few cases, they might actually decline. Try not to take this personally or as an indication you did not do well. From time to time the committee is so far behind schedule they just want to get on to the next candidate. If that should occur, all is not lost and here is your fall-back position. (Good strategists always have a Plan B).

"I understand. If you will allow me then, I will just leave the portfolio with you and you can look at it at when you have more time. Most of it is self-explanatory, and I will not need it back."

This last statement regarding the need for the portfolio's return is important. People are hesitant to accept something they have to take care of or where it will be a nuisance to return. You have eliminated that objection. In addition, it is not unheard of that the committee chair might even reverse his decision and say, "Oh, let's just look at it now." Halleluiah! In that case, you get a second bite of the apple.

Now on to the important step....showing the portfolio. <u>Do not</u> just hand over the book and sit back humming happily while the committee leafs through the contents – you must guide and narrate the process. As you show your portfolio, provide a brief oral explanation of each section that underscores and draws their attention to the important matching details.

If you plan to have power in your presentation, you will need to plan the key points you want to make. Go over each item and make note cards outlining details you need to emphasize. Rehearse your presentation a few times, preferably with someone who is able to provide constructive feedback. Make sure it stays inside the recommended timeframe. Interviews are stressful times, and it is easy to leave important things unsaid. Keep that smile and your enthusiasm up. You will be amazed how polished you become after you have rehearsed your portfolio presentation a few times.

CONCLUDING THOUGHTS:

The good portfolio is not a scrapbook or trophy case. It is a testament to the teacher's ability to create a passion for learning in his or her students. With a little effort and planning, the visual images along with a persuasive commentary will be an excellent close to your interview. It will make a powerful and lasting impression the committee will find hard to forget. When the portfolio review is over, your committee will have seen your professional commitment to children, enthusiasm for learning, instructional skill, and planning ability. The portfolio will have demonstrated your ability to relate to children and insure their success. Try these ideas and ***end your interview with a portfolio that slams the door on the competition!***

DRESSING FOR A SUCCESSFUL INTERVIEW

MAKING THAT GREAT FIRST IMPRESSION:

There is a saying: "You only get one opportunity to make a first impression." The moment a candidate walks into the interview, minds begin to make judgments regarding his or her suitability. It was once said that, "You might not be able to win the interview in the first fifteen to twenty seconds, but you can sure lose it." If you do not present a neat, professional and well-groomed appearance, be sure your chance of success just went down. The visual image, confidence, handshake, and demeanor you project will be well noted by each person on the interview committee. You will be measured against the other candidates and any subjective expectations the interviewer has regarding the school image. Keep in mind that dress and grooming affect behavior and self-image. When you look great and have impeccable grooming, your confidence improves and you become a more formidable candidate.

REGIONAL DIFFERENCES AND STANDARDS:

The advice provided in this chapter is appropriate for almost every area of the country. With that said, there will be some variation between regions as to how conservative and buttoned down the good candidate will look. For example, if you are interviewing in Texas or a number of other more western states, boots or more casual attire might well be the norm for that geographic area. In a state like California, casual attire is accepted, even expected, in many school districts. I will suggest, however, that even in states or areas where more casual or unique attire is not uncommon, the more conservative approach recommended in this chapter will continue to serve you well. At a recent ASCD conference,

I interviewed over 30 principals and superintendents from all areas of the country on this topic. Without exception, they were of the mind that the well-dressed candidate made a solid impression and likely helped themselves to be seen as serious and professional. My recommendation is to strongly consider what is offered in this chapter and then make your own decision.

PERSONAL GROOMING ADVICE FOR MEN:

A FACT: *Personal grooming directly affects the impression you make.* Men should have a recent haircut. Excessively long hair on men is not generally well received. Also, research has shown men with ill-kept beards have a significantly lower chance of being hired. Whereas the ponytail may have been fine in college or at the beach, it is not generally accepted in the professional world. Here again, you can find some regional variation with regard to just how long you might wear your hair, but whatever length you choose, be certain that it is clean and well fashioned. Gentleman; pay attention to your nails! Dirty, uneven or badly cut nails will be seen every time you show your hands and they can undermine your entire appearance; be sure they are cut, filed and clean for your interview. Use a good mouthwash before you leave the house. It is a good idea to carry breath-freshener or mints in the car and take them just prior to entering the interview site, but you should not eat them in the office or during the interview.

It should go without mention that body odor is guaranteed to be less than well received. Controlling this problem is unique to each person. Take whatever steps are necessary to prevent it. Keep in mind that the added pressure and anxiety of an interview can add to this concern unless you have taken precautions.

PERSONAL GROOMING ADVICE FOR WOMEN:

For women, much of the above also applies to you; however, a few additional special areas require comment. Your interview is not the time for the ultra-deluxe, fancy, designer nails. You know the ones – inlaid jewels, pictures of kitties, candy cane stripes, or other complicated treatments. Have a good manicure with a nice coat of fresh nail polish in a subdued color. Nail length, although ordinarily a matter personal preference should be considered. If they are long enough that they draw a lot of attention, it is possible to are too long. Keep in mind that your hands are generally on display for the entire interview, and you want to avoid them becoming a focal point. For hair, it is best to spend a little time at the salon and have someone provide a good styling to fit the business image you are going to present. By taking the extra time to present yourself as a professional who understands the importance of her image, you are telling your prospective employer you respect his or her time and school. The visual image you leave in the minds of each person on the interview committee can be long lasting.

GENERAL NOTES ON PERSONAL ATTIRE:

No matter what region of the country you reside, for both men and women, a conservative look will serve best. This does not mean to infer plain vanilla. Many fashionable outfits make a positive statement, so it is not necessary to assume you are limited to only the traditional plain blue suit. The most important thing is whatever you select should be neat, well pressed, and well fitted. It is not necessary for either men or women run out and buy the latest thing on the pages of a fashion magazine; just insure that your attire sufficiently reflects current standards.

CREATING THAT CONSERVATIVE LOOK FOR MEN:

SUIT OR JACKET?

Many authorities strongly suggest men wear a contemporary suit to a first interview. Most experts also recommend a color in the blue or gray family, and that is considered safe advice. If you already own a pinstripe or light chalk-stripe suit, this can provide the conservative look you need. If a suit reflects your taste, then by all means go with it.

For school interviews, however, a well-chosen sport jacket with neatly pressed slacks can also be quite serviceable. Contemporary men's fashions feature many well-designed jackets with a traditional look. A well selected, sport jacket can offer a high quality appearance when thought goes into the other items you will wear to compliment the coat, but a word of caution is in order. In recent years, it has become somewhat accepted that a sweater or neat open collared shirt complete the sport look. You can use your own judgment on this, but my preference for you remains a tie. The open shirt is perhaps a bit too laid back and casual for an interview where you are trying to impress.

To maintain a conservative look, avoid the more flamboyant color combinations. Plaids and big bold stripes are too flashy and draw too much attention to your dress. Save those for the country club or casual party. If you choose a sport jacket, make your matching slacks a solid color to compliment the jacket. **WARNING:** *Never ever, ever wear white slacks or white belt no matter how warm the weather.* The yacht club is a nice place for these, not a professional interview.

Pay attention to fabric and fit. Although there are many fabrics available, conventional wisdom suggests wool or a wool blend is often your best choice. If it is summer or you are in a hot climate, a lightweight cotton fabric is a good choice. Well-made clothing maintains its neat, fresh look and makes a nice appearance. The bottom line is to wear something in which you feel comfortable and look good.

WARNING: *Pay attention to fit!* The sleeves should extend to about two inches above the top of your thumb. If you have a few pounds to hide, make sure the chest size on your jacket is correct. You may have worn a 44-long all your life, but if it is a bit tight when buttoned and the lapels do not lie flat, allow a competent tailor re-measure and refit the garment. Better yet, purchase a new one. The right size will make you look and feel a lot better. Suits that are too small can make you look like a stuffed sausage, and we do not want that, do we? Suits that are too large hang all over you, and it appears you are wearing someone else's clothes. The sign at a local, upscale men's store says this best. "Approximately – is *not* your size!" Any questions?

Here are some last minute thoughts to consider before you leave for that important interview. Make sure your interview suit was professionally dry-cleaned and pressed just before the big day. If you are wearing an older suit or jacket, be sure it has *all* the buttons (yes, including those along the cuff), is not frayed, and is in style. Think ahead about your drive to the interview, how long will it take? I like to hang up my jacket in the back of the car. Sitting on your jacket for a long drive can ruin the freshly tailored look you worked so hard to achieve. When hung in the car, it will be sharp and ready to wear when you arrive. A last thought pertains to wearing a topcoat or raincoat. If the day calls for one, make sure it has been recently cleaned and pressed. The "just came in from the rain" look is not what you want when you first enter the office.

CHOOSING AN APPROPRIATE SHIRT AND TIE

When selecting a shirt, choose one that compliments your suit or jacket. Many stores now feature dark colors and they are considered "in." Perhaps this is true for some occasions, but not an interview. Avoid the mistake of wearing a dark colored shirt that makes a "big statement." When in doubt, follow the rules given by almost every writer on the subject and take the safe route with a white, off-white, buff, or light blue shirt. Also, when wearing a suit, straight collars should be worn. A button-down is fine with a sports jacket ensemble, but the more conservative presentation offered by a suit makes the button-down shirt contradictory.

I always suggest a new shirt, but if you have a recently purchased shirt in good condition, that will be fine. If you must use an older shirt, make sure there are no frayed collars or cuffs. Check to insure all the buttons are present and in one piece. Look at the collar; does it have some dirt around it that cleaning no longer removes? If so, it is not for this interview. Invest in a new one. Take my word for it, such imperfections *will* be noticed. I prefer to wear a 100% cotton fabric that has been professionally cleaned, pressed and starched. Cotton looks and feels better than a blend or synthetic and, unless you are an ex-marine who really knows how to press a great uniform, spend a little extra money and let a professional makeup your shirt. Avoid anything that is "wash and wear." You can be sure, there is no such thing. Finally, a long-sleeve shirt is an absolute must, no matter what the weather. It is the standard in the professional world.

A final thought is to double-check the fit of the shirt you choose. If you have a 16-½ -inch neck, please do not try to squeeze into a 15 ½ -inch shirt. It looks positively ghastly to see someone's neck overlapping the collar and straining at the button. And for heaven's sake, do not try to get away with just leaving the top button unbuttoned so you have "a little" breathing room. Likewise, if your arm has a 35-inch length, a 34-35 inch sleeve *will not* do. A 36-37 inch sleeve that extends three inches past the end of your jacket to cover half your hand also provides a very poor image. Proper cuff length extends slightly past the end of your jacket sleeve; see that it does or buy a new shirt.

Men should take care in the selection of their tie. A good tie can make an ordinary suit or sport jacket look very sharp. Conversely, a tie that is too loud or contains clashing colors can ruin an otherwise good appearance. The tie must provide the complement to your suit or jacket. A conservative stripe or print will wear well. This is the one place where a little color can be a nice accent to your look. If you are unsure, go to a good men's store and seek advice from one of the salesmen (I said the salesman at a *good* men's store, not the kid at Wal-Mart). Avoid the more modern ties with large, bold patterns and nouveau designs. If you are going to wear a tie that has been worn before, check its cleanliness. The knot area tends to collect grease and dirt from your fingers and can become discolored. There is nothing more unsightly than a tie with a soiled knot area. Remember, the neck area is a focal point during the interview and everyone will see this oversight for the entire time. Your best bet is to buy a new tie for your outfit. There are numerous discount men's stores where you can purchase good, name-brand neckwear for an affordable price.

DON'T FORGET YOUR FEET

If you wear a suit, then a matching pair of tie shoes should be considered. Loafers present too casual a look with your suit, but with a sports coat loafers are perfectly acceptable. Stick with the brown or black color and, unless you will be attending the race track after you fail the interview, avoid two-tone shoes. Another important point is that your shoes must be well shined with good soles and heels. For goodness sakes, do not wear a shoe with a hole in it and think you will just keep that foot on the floor so no one will notice! You may laugh, but I actually interviewed that person! Over the years, I have seen a good number of candidates arrive wearing scuffed shoes and/or worn heels and soles. It made their entire appearance shabby and did *nothing* to improve their chances of success. Do not be misled; your interviewer will look at your footwear at some point during the interview, so make the impression positive.

COMPLETING YOUR IMAGE

Men should be sparing with jewelry and accessories. A nice leather briefcase for your portfolio and other materials is fine. If you bring a briefcase, some additional words are in order; be sure it is organized and not overstuffed. You do not want to release the catch and have it blow open to disgorge its contents all over the principal's conference table. This is considered poor form, indeed.

Let us review other items such as watches, rings, hankies, and cologne. A conservative watch can add to your appearance, but stay away from flashy or fad watches. Even if you are now the proud owner of an original "Mickey Mouse" watch, this is probably not the time to show it off. A wedding ring is fine, but be careful of gaudy rings that attract too much attention. (You know; the big horseshoe one with all the zirconium diamonds that you wear to Las Vegas sometimes.) Also, do not wear the fashion hanky in your jacket pocket. They may look fine on game-show hosts, but they say all the wrong things about a professional teaching candidate. A final thought is cologne. My best advice is, forget it. You are not going on a date and the presence of strong cologne does nothing to enhance your appearance or chance of success.

CREATING THAT CONSERVATIVE LOOK FOR WOMEN:

A BUSINESS SUIT, SKIRT OR SLACKS?

As with men, women should first consider the primary aim of their attire. A lady requires a professional appearance that compliments her purposeful approach to the school and organization. Your outfit should be conservatively tasteful. This does not mean you have to limit yourself to dull and uninspired attire in drab colors. As more women have entered the work force, fashion designers have added business suits, pants outfits, and skirts for the workingwoman of today. Martin Yate in his book Knock 'Em Dead Interviews 2011 offers some excellent suggestions for women on this topic. Many large chains such as Nordstrom, Belk, Macy's, or Black and White have also established excellent areas for the businesswoman to shop.

In selecting your wardrobe, a simple suit is always safe. As with the men, there are attractive jackets with matching skirts that also work well. It is really a matter of taste and what fits your style and personality best. Conservative color selections in the blue and gray families are a wise choice because they coordinate easily and carry the traditional look we seek. Nonetheless, I must admit I have seen very smart outfits in other colors as well. If you should choose a color, take care that is not too loud or bold.

The suit or jacket should be chosen to suit your shape and style. Comfort is important and you should take care regarding fit. Clothes that are too small strain in all the wrong places when you are seated and can be quite uncomfortable. A poor fit can be distracting and upset your concentration because you are trying to keep that blame skirt in place. By the same token, don't wear oversized clothing that hangs like a potato sack. One certainty in life is that fashions in skirt length change. But no matter what the current style, shorter skirts do not generally serve well at an interview. This suggestion is not intended to limit you to only skirt lengths of which our Puritan forefathers would be proud, but a length that extends just to or below the knee would be more fitting.

FANCY FOOTWORK

A wide range of footwear styles is available to women, and this can be a challenging decision. My recommendation is to choose a leather shoe that matches the color of the skirt, either the same color or slightly darker. The closed toe is the style of choice, but I have seen a few conservative open toe shoes that will suit as long as they are carefully chosen. The interview is also not the place for 5-inch stiletto heels. Heels are fine if they are not too high, but flats are also acceptable. If you are already tall, you may be more comfortable in flats or low heels. After all, there is no sense in towering over the poor principal. Sneakers are inappropriate at all times – even if you *are* the PE applicant.

COMPLETING THE LOOK WITH JEWELRY, ACCESSORIES AND MAKEUP

Accessories are an important part of a woman's presence and should not be overlooked. As with men, I suggest a good leather briefcase where you can keep your portfolio, a pad, pen, and folder with extra copies of documents you are bringing to the interview. (See the warnings provided to men on this subject. The same applies to the ladies.) Leave your purse in the car and just bring the briefcase to the interview. Having both can make you look as if you are coming for the weekend, plus shaking hands can be awkward if all of your hands are full.

Jewelry should be kept uncomplicated. A simple necklace, small earrings, and wedding or engagement rings are sufficient. Avoid gaudy or oversized costume jewelry. Long strands of pearls, multi-band bracelets, or other jewelry can be a distraction and should generally be avoided. A good rule of thumb is, "When in doubt, leave it out."

Regarding makeup, my grandmother used to say she could not go somewhere important without "putting on her face." This is wise advice. Makeup is a key part of a lady's preparation, and we understand you want to rise above the "Plain Jane look." Still, keep things simple. A light coating of lipstick or gloss is fine, but the bold, high-impact varieties are probably not a good choice. Caked on foundation or heavy eye makeup is also best left for another occasion. If you need a little mascara, fine, but keep it light. If the interviewers are likely to take sharp notice, it is probably too much. Similarly, if you feel the need for eye shadow, keep it light and subdued. Perfume, particularly one with a strong scent, is not necessary or desirable. Save those for that grand evening at the ballet or opera.

CONCLUDING THOUGHTS:

It is critically important that you are well attired and prepared for your interview. Obviously, you are going to spend more time putting this ensemble together than you might for just an ordinary day at the school or office. You want to make a positive and lasting impression on those who will be conducting the interview. I would suggest that you put this outfit together in advance and have someone look at you. This person should be able to be objective and provide constructive criticism (We love Mom and Dad, but they are rarely objective with their beloved crown jewel children – no matter what the "child's" age.).

As a general goal, you want to look professional but not flashy. Have some fun with this. Everyone likes to shop and select things in which they look good. Try things out and see how you look. I wish you luck, and now we are ready to move onto the next phase – the interview.

GENERAL INTERVIEW FORMATS AND STRATEGIES

The first thing to know is that, over the years, schools have begun to use more than one interview format, and in many cases, there may be several rounds of interviews before an offer is extended. The most common interview formats include the phone interview, group interview, individual interview, and performance interview or demonstration lesson. In addition, many school districts now send prospective candidates one or two written questions to submit as part of their application package. This chapter will examine each of these formats and provide specific suggestions as to the best ways to deal with each.

RESPONDING WITH POWER TO THE WRITTEN QUESTION:

School districts have come to increasingly rely on a requirement for all candidates to submit written answers to one or more posed questions. This is generally done as part of the screening process and prior to the district's decision on who they will invite for a face to face interview. The primary goal of these questions is to assess your ability to write and your approach to a special problem of interest to the school. The educational areas for written questions might include such things as your philosophy of teaching, classroom management, or problem solving skill.

GUIDELINES FOR THE WRITTEN RESPONSE

- *Follow the directions as to length.* If the district indicates a particular word count or page length, be certain you do not exceed the direction. Excessive length does not improve your chance for success.
- *Read the question carefully* and decide what it specifically asks. Stick to that topic with a few hard-hitting paragraphs. Where possible, include a specific example

or anecdote to illustrate your point. The answer is always made more effective by a concrete example to accent your position!

- *Look for places to include ideas or thoughts that will be congruent to district goals or initiatives.* As we have repeatedly said in this book, the more you are able to underscore where your philosophy and skill sets are a match to the district needs, the stronger your application.

- *Be certain of your grammar, spelling, and clarity.* Bear in mind that the primary objective is to see how clearly you write and think. Awkward sentence construction, writing errors, or poor spelling is very likely to prevent you from reaching the interview round of the process.

- *If at all possible, have a qualified person read and edit your response.* It is always wise to have a knowledgeable friend or professional proof your response before you send it or include it in your application portfolio.

Below are a few examples of questions that have been included in district writing requests.

1. *The Long Beach California Schools have many science and exploratory classes at or near their student enrollment cap. These courses also possess a unique curriculum that involves tools and materials that can cause serious injury to the learner. Because of this distinctive design, these classes offer a teacher diverse challenges in monitoring and managing student behavior. In light of this information, please provide a complete description of your classroom management philosophy toward dealing with this kind of classroom environment.*

2. *Recently you have read of the increased accountability placed on Wisconsin schools to have all students reach minimum proficiency in reading by the end of their eighth grade year. What role do you see for the middle school Social Studies teacher in that mission and what specific strategies would you employ to help students in your class reach this goal?*

3. *Your principal has advised you that a parent of one of your students was most annoyed at the amount of homework you are assigning and the overall difficulty of your class. It was suggested that they meet with you this afternoon to discuss the matter. What will be your meeting goals, and how will you deal with this parent concern?*

As you can see, these are thought provoking questions. The exact nature of your answers will depend on your own teaching philosophy, your decision making process, and what you know about the school profile. None of the questions have a specific right answer. Your goal is to craft a response that demonstrates clear writing and the ability to problem solve. Within this book you will find answers for many of the specific questions or scenarios a district might pose. If you couple this information with your own teaching philosophy and craft a few good paragraphs, you will be well on your way to the interview.

EFFECTIVE STRATEGIES FOR THE PHONE INTERVIEW:

The school's purpose in a phone interview is to efficiently determine if a candidate is someone they would like to bring in for a more extended face-to-face meeting. In only the rarest of circumstances will this type interview result in a job offer. Phone interviews tend to be more conversational and include only a few questions. Because you are unable to see the interviewer, special problems need to be considered. Many good candidates do not reach the next step in the process because they failed to make the right impression over the phone.

MEETING THE INITIAL CHALLENGES OF YOUR PHONE INTERVIEW

There are a few very effective ways to make your phone interview a success. Below are a few suggestions to help you reach that goal.

- *Begin on offense.* You need your phone interview to begin on a positive, upbeat tone. To do this, keep your message and voice cheerful and inviting. Your initial greeting might be something like, "Thank you so much for calling. I appreciate your taking time to speak to me today as I have really been looking forward to our getting together to talk." If your voice has enthusiasm in it, your interview will be off on a great note!
- *Keep control of your voice and energy throughout the call.* It is quite easy to fall into a bland, low-energy tone of voice once you have been on the phone for a few minutes. Take care to vary your tone of voice and keep a smile in it. Yes, I realize that the caller cannot actually "see" a smile in your voice. But take my word for it, the listener can "hear" a happy voice. Maintain a speech pattern that is a normal pace. Speaking too fast or cramming eight ideas into one sentence will lose the listener. Maintain a simple conversational pace.
- *Don't overdo it.* It is one thing to be positive and have energy and yet another to be gushing and soupy. You want to exude confidence without sounding overinflated or cocky. Don't try to be glib or over-personal with the interviewer. Although a light tone is desired, keep in mind that you are on this call for professional reasons and you need the bulk of the conversation to maintain that tone.

- ***Listen. Listen. Listen.*** I cannot tell you how frustrating it is to interview someone who is so intent on talking that they fail to even properly hear the question. Keep a pad right in front of you and <u>listen</u> to the question and directions without interruption. When you are certain the full question has been asked, you can then target your answer to its specific elements. Sailing off on an answer that does not address what the interviewer asked is one of the cardinal sins of the phone interview.

- ***Keep your answers on point and don't over answer.*** Provide what you think is a good answer and stop. Repeating yourself, rambling with long-winded and convoluted dialog, or wandering off topic will steal power from your answer. If you are not fully certain that your answer is complete, then you can ask, "Did I fully answer your question, Mr. Jones?"

- ***End with a positive feeling tone.*** Once the interviewer indicates that he or she has finished, you should take that opportunity to put a positive light on the interview. You should say how pleased you were to have this opportunity to speak together. Let your interviewer know that, based on the conversation you just had, you are more convinced than ever that you and this position are a great mutual fit. Be proactive and indicate how you look forward to meeting him or her in the next step in the process. Be sure to tell the person about your availability and desire to accommodate their schedule on the visit to his or her school. **The finishing touch is a short thank you note or email to express your appreciation for the school's interest.** Do not omit this last step!

AVOID THE PITFALLS OF THE PHONE INTERVIEW

Now that we know the ways to make the phone interview a success, we need to consider the ways to avoid things that might damage your chances of reaching the interview round.

- ***Do not underestimate the power of a positive appearance.*** Even though the interviewer cannot see you, it is still a good idea to be dressed and ready for the day. Lounging in a housecoat or sweats is not the way to be mentally prepared. What you wear and how you look, DO affect the way you think and behave. Wear something comfortable and groom yourself as you might if you were on the way out for a luncheon.

- ***Avoid using a cell phone to take this call.*** Cell phones are a wonderful convenience but they are notoriously unreliable for maintaining the connection and clarity.

Arrange for this conversation to be conducted on a landline where you will not have connection concerns.

- *Avoid taking the call in a noisy atmosphere.* Find a quiet place that is free of distractions to host this call. There is nothing worse than trying to conduct an interview with a dog barking, crying infant, or loud TV in the background. It is distracting to both parties and you will not advance your candidacy for the school interview. Have a nice quiet room with the door closed, and let everyone know you are not to be disturbed *even if* the fire trucks are outside.

- *Do not become overly casual and comfortable.* Lying on the couch with a beverage is great for watching TV or listening to the stereo. It is deadly to a phone interview. Either sit at a desk or, if you prefer, stand near the desk. Your physical position will come across in your voice and energy.

- *Do not eat or drink during the interview.* This goes along with the previous suggestion and should not even have to be mentioned. Yet, I once conducted a conference interview where a candidate for a supervisor's position consumed a sandwich as the four of us sat at the conference table listening to her try to chew while simultaneously answering our questions. Needless to say, our group was *not* impressed.

- *Do not forget to use resources!* Since you cannot be seen, it is perfectly acceptable to have a pad with a few talking points listed. Have a few reminders of school characteristics where you can see them. You might even want to have the school website up on your computer. (I caution you not to try and look things up during the course of the interview as it distracts you and is easily picked up by the interviewer.)

WHAT KINDS OF QUESTIONS CAN I EXPECT ON THE PHONE INTERVIEW?

Every candidate wants to know what to expect during an interview. Even though the phone interview is generally less intensive than the onsite meeting, it is sure to include a few questions designed to determine if you have the skills and cultural fit necessary to move you to the next stage of interviews. There is no sure way to identify all the potential questions because every school is unique, and its leaders will craft their interview accordingly. However, below are two general areas that research has demonstrated to be somewhat common for the phone interview.

YOUR INTEREST AND REASON FOR APPLYING TO OUR SCHOOL

This is a relatively common subject for the opening question of a phone interview. For the unprepared candidate, they will simply talk about how wonderful the school

69

is, how it is a community in which it would be so nice to work, and so on. This is all fine and lovely; *however*, it does absolutely *nothing* to advance one's name to the front of the onsite interview line! As the prepared candidate, you will have a much stronger answer. You will talk about how you see a great match between the vision and specific initiatives of the school and your philosophy and skills. Speak to how you want to be part of their plans for one or two of their stated goals. Exude confidence in your ability to fit into a culture that values (insert a key mission of the school). Keep this answer sharp, crisp, and to the point by just ticking off one item at a time. Take my word for it, the interviewer will be favorably impressed, and you will have started with a home run!

EXAMINE SPECIFICS ON YOUR RESUME

If there are any questions or areas of the resume where the district has a further question, it is customary that they address this during the phone interview. Have your resume in front of you and mark anything where the caller asks a question. There is no need for lengthy explanations or in-depth, life story scenarios. Simply answer the questions in a straightforward and honest a way.

THE ALTERNATE ROUTE CANDIDATE. If you have previously been involved in a different career and are now an alternate route candidate, you should expect this interview question to be more intensive and important. In your case, you will want to listen carefully to any resume questions and seek opportunities to describe positions or work that might translate well to school needs or goals. What clinical observation experiences have you had that can be included? Where did you do your practicum work and how has that added to your qualifications? If you have done substitute teaching, be ready to give an overview of the valuable impact those experiences might have had. It is essential that you have already pre-thought these connections and have them listed on a piece of paper in front of you. It is almost impossible to think of these things on the fly. Most of all; do not be defensive or apologetic about your past! Instead, **portray your work history and decision to teach as a strength.** Talk about how much your work experiences will help you to provide purpose and color to all of your teaching; how speaking with students about the real world after school can be of immense value as you work together to help them craft their own skills. You have a lot to offer this school, and your answer will let them know exactly what those things include!

If you handle your phone interview in the way this section describes, you will be sure to stand out from the other candidates and be on your way to the school interview.

COME OUT AHEAD IN THE GROUP INTERVIEW:

When districts decide to screen large numbers of applicants, they will sometimes hold a group interview. Although it is somewhat less common, it is possible to come to your interview and find four or five other candidates sitting in the room with you. If you are not prepared, this can throw you off and make for a very stressful situation.

Like the phone interview, this session is often designed to simply identify which candidates they would like to invite back for a more in-depth interview. It is unlikely that the final decision of a school's final candidate will be determined as a result of the group session. There are a number of important things you should know and steps you can take if you are involved in this interview format.

TIPS TO HANDLE THE GROUP FORMAT

- ***Establish a professional image and use your interpersonal skills.*** The interviewers will begin to compare you to others from the moment you walk into the room until the moment you leave the room. There are a number of very subtle but effective ways to make your impression positive. First, shake hands with everyone on the interview team and make eye contact. If you have a tendency to have hands that perspire, be sure to dry them before shaking hands. People are favorably impressed when you use their name. It is *always* Dr., Mr., or Ms. and their last name. If possible try to have the names of your committee in advance and write them, along with their role or position, on a pad. If you do not have them, the secretary can sometimes give them to you while you are waiting. When I enter the room, I make a little diagram on my pad that identifies where each person is sitting so I can address the questioner by name when it is my turn to answer.

- ***Watch your body language and posture.*** Body posture is important. If you are sitting at a table, leaning forward with your hands folded on the table in front of you is a good base position. If you are openly seated in circular fashion, then your feet on the floor with hands on your lap is a sound base. DO NOT slouch, lean back, or slump. Such postures convey disinterest and detachment. When you leave, shake everyone's hand a second time and bid them good day, preferably by name. These may seem like small items, but it is this collection of small items that will often make the difference between success and failure.

- ***Do not engage any of the other candidates in the room or try to "one-up" an answer.*** Direct all of your responses to the committee and target the question asked not the answer given by someone else. It is the interview committee who must hear and appreciate what you have to say. Maintain a frame of mind whereby you see the other candidates as of little consequence.

71

- *Maintain eye contact with the committee and keep your smile, energy, and enthusiasm directed toward them.* Focus on the committee and not the competition. Be sure to watch your body language and facial expressions when others are answering questions. You do not want to give any indication that you agree or disagree with what another candidate says; it is irrelevant to what you might say. A good way to handle this is to have a pad and take a few notes while others are speaking. This shows interest but not validation.
- *Answer the interview questions with precision and provide a practical example whenever possible.* The best way to describe this is by example:

Q: *Tell the committee what you do to keep students actively involved when teaching a class where there are students of wide ability ranges.*

This is a reasonably common question, but also one that is easy to mishandle unless you know how to attack it! First, you must quickly decide which *specific* principles of learning the question explores. This question clearly asks about two things: "active involvement" and "motivation." You must target your answer to address those two items in a clear and compact way. Separate your answer from the pack by adding an example of either how you have done it in the past OR, if you have not yet begun teaching, how you might do it in the future. It could sound something like the following.

A: *When I have a diverse group, my lesson design always includes a good balance between teacher instruction and student involvement. Because student attention span is limited, especially in classes with a wide ability range, I structure the lesson to have two or three different student-centered activities. By keeping the amount of teacher-talk and student activity varied, I maintain the momentum of the lesson and student attention. In order to motivate student involvement during their activities, I usually add some level of performance or reporting to each segment. For greater accountability I stay actively moving so that students know I will check on their progress. In a class I recently designed on a public debate issue, I included a paired-sharing segment to brainstorm the various arguments, a small group activity that produced a student made chart, and a public presentation of each group's findings along with their supported position. By varying the ability levels of students in each group, I was able to keep everyone invested and involved.*

This answer takes less than a minute to provide and yet it really gets to the heart of the question. It speaks to good lesson design, active participation, and motivation. By providing a specific example, the committee can see that you not only know the theory of student involvement but you can apply it as well. This kind of response *will* get the attention of committee members and quickly identify you as a practitioner who knows how to handle a class similar to the one they described. Let the other candidates try to top that one.

We realize it is unlikely you will get that exact question, but group interviews often include questions on lesson design, motivation, class management, or student participation. Think about these topics ahead of time and be prepared to speak about them. You will almost assuredly be able to weave whatever advance ideas you have into the interview at some point.

- ***Don't panic if everyone gets the same question and the person answering in front of you steals your answer!*** I think this is the fear of everyone who has ever been involved in a group interview, and it *can* happen to you. If it does happen, just keep that smile and act as if nothing is amiss. Go right ahead and hit the key points of the answer you had in mind. It will not matter if they are similar to what has been said because you are going to add the one thing that will make your answer stand out from the others. As mentioned earlier, *you* are going to add the concrete example and anecdote from your own experience. You are going to add the practical information that others have likely left out. This piece cannot be duplicated. So maintain your smile and composure; be confident you will prevail and stop worrying.

Confidence, energy, and preparation will carry the day for you. You now have everything you need to be the most formidable candidate in the room. So, go into that interview with confidence and blow the competition away!

CREATING AND DELIVERING THE GREAT DEMONSTRATION LESSON:

In many districts today, they will narrow the field to two or three final candidates that they bring back to do a demonstration lesson in a live class. This performance interview is generally observed by two members of your original interview committee who will analyze everyone's teaching segment and decide which candidate is the best fit for the position. Handling this lesson can be very stressful unless you are confident of your strategy and lesson preparations.

To plan our lesson, the first thing we must know is the teaching topic. In that regard, there are only two possibilities: (1) it is a topic or guideline the school gives you, or (2) you are allowed to choose your own subject matter. If we assume the school will lay out some parameters for your lesson, they will likely provide a general set of guidelines and let you choose what to teach within those limits. If you are an elementary teacher applicant who will have a self-contained class, you might expect the subject area to be mathematics, reading, or written communication. Districts like to watch you teach something from one of the areas on which students will be taking the state test. If you are teaching in a secondary school or a separate discipline, the school will usually require a lesson within one of the standard curriculum units for the vacant position. Whatever your assignment, the teaching lesson will need to embody some very important elements. Those elements need to be carefully examined as we construct a hard-hitting thirty to forty minute lesson.

THE FIVE TEACHER CHARACTERISTICS FOR WHICH EVERY COMMITTEE LOOKS

The most important question you might have is just what is it observers want to see when they observe your lesson? First, the observers will carefully look to determine if you will be a good fit for the culture of the school and the students you will teach. Second, do you actually have the skills you spoke about when you were interviewed?

To answer those two central questions, observers most often look for five general teacher characteristics. Of the five teacher qualities I list below, there are numerous variations. With that said; these general statements are among the most common observation goals for a model lesson.

1. How do you interact with the students, and can you command their attention and respect?
2. Do you exhibit a passion for teaching and make the class a safe, enjoyable place to be?
3. Are students actively engaged in the lesson and learning what you intended?
4. Is the lesson flexible enough to provide success opportunities for all learning levels?
5. How did you assess student progress during the lesson?

Now look at a simple design to achieve all five of these goals.

Characteristic #1: *Tips on developing observable student relations and respect*

There are a few ways to develop great connections with students and do so in a short period of time. It will be important for the committee to see that you work towards building interpersonal bridges to the students during your time in class. Look for ways and places where you can employ some of the following strategies.

1. ***Use student names where possible.*** If you can get a seating chart to keep on the desk in front of you, this will be a big help. If no chart is available, you can always have the students put their first names on an index card that they can fold and place on their desk.

2. ***Keep your smile and sense of humor.*** When interacting with students, a smile and pleasant demeanor is a great communication device. At times answers or interactions will occur that have a humorous nature. Take advantage of these opportunities to add a positive and enjoyable atmosphere in the class.

3. ***Involve a wide variety of students in your questions and interactions:*** It is easy to begin focusing on just a few students. Do your best to physically move through the class and deliberately reach out to involve a wide number of students from around the room. This keeps students on their toes and also provides for their active involvement.

4. ***Provide positive but accurate, specific feedback.*** When students answer questions or perform well, always let them know how they did. If the answer was correct and on target, tell the student what made the answer right. If the student is not right, DO NOT fall into the trap where you say something good to make a poor response sound right. Instead, you can provide a different cue or add more information. Once the student has the additional information, you can ask if they want to "rethink" their point. Do not say, "good answer" when it is not.

5. ***Demonstrate courtesy and respect:*** Words like "thank you" and "please" convey the idea that you are treating students with respect. You will be surprised by how such small courtesies are noticed and returned.

6. ***Be supportive:*** You will find numerous opportunities in class to help struggling students or provide words of encouragement. Use those moments to demonstrate your care for each student's individual success.

If you use these strategies, you will see how quickly students respond to your efforts. The committee will also notice, and you will be seen as someone who both fits the culture and works in a positive way with students.

Characteristic #2: *Exhibiting passion and making the class a safe, enjoyable place*

Your committee will take careful note of your professional demeanor and the level of energy and enthusiasm you put into the lesson. The best advice to achieve this goal is to make your lesson a little fun for both yourself and the students. When you have limited time, two suggestions make the most sense. First, include an anecdote or story to punctuate important information in your lesson. If the story has a little humor, this is all the better. A good anecdotal tale can bring color and vitality to otherwise bland information. Listen to any good speaker and you will find that he or she uses related stories and humor to great advantage. A second vital step is to add a few innovative and enjoyable student participation segments. You can find ideas for such activities on the many Internet planning sites for teachers. Throughout the lesson, you should find places to model enthusiasm, inject energy, and exude a sense of enjoyment in what you are doing. Use your smile and body language! Your liveliness will transfer to the students and the atmosphere of the room. This enthusiasm and passion, along with the combination of your stories and innovative activities, will dramatically impact student interest and the feeling tone of the class.

Characteristics 3-5: *Designing a powerful lesson with student involvement, success, and ongoing assessment*

Now it is time to put together a tight, well organized teaching episode that will make a lasting impression on the committee's observation team. Because this is a short teaching segment, it is essential to choose a target objective that can be effectively taught, mastered, and evaluated within the given period of time. Too often, teacher candidates will try to cover too many things for the time allowed. We will not make that mistake.

Once we have a clear and precise idea as to what we will teach, we must identify the essential instructional pieces, the activities that will engage the students in meaningful work, and how we will monitor both group and individual progress throughout the lesson. The basic lesson design I recommend has just four specific components and we will examine each one. If you choose, this model can be later used to construct your own demonstration lesson. Let's get started.

DEMONSTRATION LESSON COMPONENTS

Assume the district gives us a fifth grade class and asks for a lesson from the poetry strand of Language Arts. It is not uncommon to be provided a topic that has little natural interest to students and poetry might be such an example.

1. ***The Lesson Objective:*** We need to create an objective that contains two elements. First, exactly *what will students learn* and be able to do at the end of the lesson? *Second, how will I evaluate this* and know students have mastered the concept? **KEY TEACHER ACTION:** Before the lesson even begins, let the students know exactly what they will be expected to do by the end of the period. Put this information in easy to understand student terms.

EXAMPLE: *Today's lesson is on the poetry of music. You will need to <u>identify a rhyming pattern</u> and then create your own rhyming poem. You will <u>identify the rhyming pattern in a popular song</u> and then <u>create new rhyming lyrics</u> for a two to four line song of your own.*

2. ***The Teaching and Information Segment:*** With fifth grade students, you will need to keep the length of any teacher input to about 12 minutes or less. Teacher talk that extends beyond this timeline causes loss of momentum and reduced student attention. Here are the pieces for this part of the lesson.

   - ***Initial Hook:*** *I'd like you to raise your hand if you have listened to music and noticed that it has a lot of rhymes? Who can give me an example? (allow for responses) Those are some great examples, and I bet everyone here has one of their own. Today we are going to learn about these rhyming patterns, and everyone in here will have an opportunity to write a little song of their own! Let's get started.*

   - ***Necessary Information:*** *Select a sample song from contemporary music students would be likely to know. Play either a short music video of the song or its audio track. Put the song lyrics on an overhead or PowerPoint and underline the rhyming patterns together. Demonstrate the way to label each pattern such as AABB or ABBA. Once you have evidence everyone is comfortable with this process, introduce a second song but this time ask the class to label the rhyming pattern themselves. By using a combination of individual and "chorused" answers, you can check for overall group understanding.*

   - ***Student Activity #1:*** *To promote everyone's involvement, provide the students a few sets of four line stanzas that leave the rhyming words blank. Ask students to work in pairs and fill in a rhyming word for each line but use a common pattern for musical rhyming such as ABBA. Monitor, monitor, monitor.*

   - ***Teacher Information Segment 2:*** *Explain a process to help students move from a musical topic to creating a few lines of poetry that can be turned into the chorus for a song. Demonstrate use of an online Rhyming Dictionary. Tell an anecdote about a well-known song-writer and how he/she went about writing a song. Demonstrate how this is done for everyone to see and duplicate.*

   - ***Student Activity 2:*** *Give students several song topics along with a few starter lines (most students cannot yet start with a blank piece of paper and complete this task). Working in groups of 3, ask them to produce the four lines of a chorus for their own song. They <u>must</u> identify the rhyming pattern they choose.*

3. *Check for understanding:* Go to each group and assess whether they are able to complete the closing task. Provide support, clarification, or assistance as necessary. As you travel among groups, you can determine everyone's level of mastery and build in specific individual or class correction wherever necessary.

4. *Student Closure on the Learning.* It is important to make sure students can tell you what they just learned. To do this, have a final closing question ready that asks everyone what they now know about song writing and rhyming schemes.

CLOSURE QUESTION: *Before we go home for today, let me ask a question. We now know that song writers use poetry for their lyrics. What rhyming patterns did you learn today? How did you use those patterns to make your own song? Pick a partner and share what you have learned.*

As you can see, this is a very simple lesson that can be taught with a lot of enthusiasm, fun, and student success. It has all the features of a solid teaching episode and can be accomplished by teachers of almost any experience level. Through the addition of a story, a little technology, and good student activities you have maximized both student interest and mastery. Now when you are asked to teach a demonstration lesson, you can use this same model to write your own power-teaching segment and leave a great impression with the review committee. Frankly, I *like* your chances!

WHAT TO DO IF YOUR LESSON CONCLUDES BEFORE THE END OF THE PERIOD

Unless you are a very experienced teacher, it is not unusual that your lesson might conclude prior to the actual end of the class period. If that happens to you, do not try to do some kind of "soft-shoe" routine and fill up space with mindless comments or spur of the moment activities. Such attempts can often undo the good impression you worked so hard to obtain. Just simply look directly at the committee and say, *"This concludes the lesson I brought for today and the students were simply terrific."* At that point, you can count on the regular classroom teacher to reassume control of the class, and you are done. It is professional and conveys an high level of comfort on your part.

THE DRESS REHEARSAL

Do yourself a very large favor and DO NOT try and teach this lesson without a practice run or two. Very often what looks great on paper does not quite come out the way you intended when you teach it live. Would a great singer or performer even think about going onstage without a dress rehearsal? I don't think so. So why should you imagine you can approach your big day without at least a trial run of your lesson. When you teach this lesson, it is important to teach it to *someone* and not just in front of a mirror. You want to have the feedback from your teaching subjects as to whether your instructional pieces were clear and easy to follow. Were the activities enjoyable? Did the activities work to solidify the learning? Was the timing right? Did you actually have *observable evidence* that your trial students learned what you were trying to teach? This is all important feedback that will let you know what needs to be strengthened, altered, or even discarded BEFORE you face the committee observers. Who the students are is not especially important. You can use family members, your children, neighborhood children, friends, or even a spouse. Yes, spouses are good! Why should they escape the torture? If you can do two trial runs, you will be ready. And I assure you that with just a little practice you will enter that room with confidence and a rock solid, tight lesson sure to impress. So go design that lesson, try it out, and WOW the committee!

CONCLUDING THOUGHTS:

Today's school districts have become increasingly selective in their hiring practice. This often necessitates multiple rounds in the interview process. You may not encounter all of these different interview strategies with the specific school or district to which you applied. With that said; it is more than likely that you will have to navigate at least one of these interview formats in order to reach the face-to-face interview we will handle in the next chapter. The good news is that you now know *exactly* what to expect and the best way to deal with each format. With this knowledge in hand, you have the advantage over your competition, and *you* will be the more formidable candidate. So good luck and we will see you at the school for the next interview!

"The want of education and moral training is the only real barrier that exists between the different classes of men."

— Susanna Moodie, **1853**

GENERAL QUESTIONS AND INTERVIEW STRATEGIES

MASTERING THE FACE TO FACE INTERVIEW:

One of the most important steps to secure that desired teaching position is a good in-person interview at the prospective school. It has traditionally been this interview that determines the suitability of a candidate, and it is one where you *must* do well. Because of its importance, this chapter is designed to arm you with the most successful interview strategies and answers to some of the most difficult general interview questions. Once you have this information, you will be able to study and use it to become one of the most confident, well prepared candidates the committee is likely to meet.

In over twenty-five years of interviewing experience, I have seen scores of good candidates falter at this stage of the selection process. Their lack of success was not always the result of weak teaching skills or their passion to teach, it was often the lack of preparation and readiness for the interview itself.

There are distinct and learnable interview strategies that can help you distinguish yourself from the many other good candidates who applied for the same position. These interview skills can be separated into two categories: Skills to (1) handle the interview process itself and (2) respond to the questions with memorable, hard-hitting answers. This chapter examines each skill set and provides strategies for both the traditional route teacher as well as the **alternate route candidate**.

The sample questions included in this section are taken from actual interviews or were given to me by administrators with extensive interview experience from around the country. Items from a variety of sources provide a wide base of information. Included are questions that will explore a candidate's philosophy, organizational suitability, and understanding of the teaching-learning process.

MAXIMIZING THE BENEFITS OF OUR SAMPLE QUESTIONS:

This and each of the following chapters will provide a variety of sample interview questions. Unless otherwise noted, your approach to the answer will be relatively the same whether you are a **traditional route** applicant or an **alternate route candidate**. Their primary objective is to provide advance opportunities for you to see how interview questions are worded and help you pre-think a sensible, power-laden answer to each. Do you remember this adage? "To be forewarned is to be forearmed." That works for us.

For each question, the discussion will describe those elements of a candidate's qualifications and training most commonly sought by interviewers and principals. It is important to understand, however, your answers at an interview will need to be shaped to your own individual background, experience, and philosophy. One cannot simply memorize the discussion information and recite it at an interview. Look at what each question tries to uncover and then select items from your background that highlight your strength in that area. At the end of each question you will find a set of **"KEYS TO YOUR RESPONSE."** These present the essential answer components in an abbreviated format. When you are preparing for an interview, these keys will provide quick reference to refresh your thinking.

THE FIVE THEMES OF INTERVIEW QUESTIONS:

In deciding how to phrase your answers, it is helpful if you understand how to shape your answer around one of the five central themes of successful teaching. You will not try to address all five themes inside one answer; however, each interview question is likely to explore your knowledge within at least one of the five themes. Here are those themes:

- *You are a child-centered teacher and recognize your chief goal as the promotion of individual achievement and growth in students.* In public education you are required to teach children who possess a wide variety of ability levels, degrees of motivation, and educational backgrounds. In a single class there may be gifted students, special needs students, and so-called "regular" students. An important concern shared by every principal is that teachers show a genuine care for *every* student. Most teachers will tell you they entered the field because they love children or enjoy helping them learn. Fine, but that platitude does not count until it reaches an individual level and becomes, "I genuinely care about Devon or

Sarah." Principals need to know you have the understanding, skills, and motivation sufficient to reach out and touch every child.

- *You have clear mastery of content knowledge in the area(s) you intend to teach.* If you are applying for a science position, there are a variety of subjects subsumed in that discipline. You will need to demonstrate competence in the areas you expect to teach. If you are applying for a language arts position, the committee will want to see strong evidence that you understand the most current strategies to teach writing and communication. Knowledge of the content you intend to teach is essential to your success.

- *You have the instructional skills required to convey a body of knowledge to students of all backgrounds.* It is one thing to have a child-centered approach and another to have the teaching skills necessary to insure learning in the diverse classes of today. Principals want to know you understand the principles of learning necessary for successful teaching. Will you effectively plan instruction? Will you have strong, clear presentation skills? Will you be able to diagnose and remediate learning problems? Will you employ effective assessment strategies? Teaching is an art and a science; you must demonstrate a comprehensive knowledge of both.

- *You possess sufficient classroom management skills to organize curriculum, control student behavior, and manage resources.* You cannot teach anything to a class that is disorganized, off-task, or lacking sufficient materials. There are specific skills teachers employ to maximize their efficiency in these areas. The interview committee will want to know your approach to each management skill. What are your discipline strategies? How do you manage space and time? How do you maintain materials? Can you manage the curriculum? These are all questions you will need to answer.

- *You possess personal and professional characteristics that will enhance the teaching staff and culture of the school.* The interview committee will continuously assess the degree to which you embody the qualities of professional behavior they seek in their teachers. These qualities include, but are not limited to, teamwork, reliability, dedication, integrity, loyalty, passion, and pride. You need to clearly demonstrate how you will add to the good chemistry of the school, department, or grade level team on which you will serve. It will be important to identify yourself as someone who is a self-starter, motivated, and persistent seeker of excellence. You will need to show how your character and skill combine to make you a teacher with the potential to command respect from students, parents, colleagues, and administrators.

As you are asked each question during your interview, try to identify which of the above theme areas is addressed. You should see opportunities to demonstrate your attributes within most or all of the areas at some point during the interview process. You may even find that more than one theme can be addressed within a single answer. In any event, it is easier to organize a response when you know what the committee seeks.

> **KEY PRE-INTERVIEW STRATEGY:** *Before you ever go to that first interview, it will be to your advantage to conduct a self-assessment for each central theme and write down specific teacher qualities, ideas, or background elements you possess that will establish your qualifications.*

This exercise will be extremely valuable as you try to promote clarity in your phrasing when the interview questions begin to fly. If you have done no preparation and attempt to develop your ideas as the interview proceeds, you will find it a difficult and anxiety ridden experience. **Alternate route candidates** will need to take extra time and care to address this task. One of the main concerns and questions that school officials will have regarding your candidacy is whether you are as qualified as other more traditionally trained applicants. The fact is that you do have specific course training and experience in your background to effectively teach. Whether you are involved in a more traditional college, an online institution like the University of Phoenix, or even come to teaching directly from another field, you have a completed body of coursework and clinical experience to draw upon. You may even have been in the classroom and directly worked with students. Go through your background and conduct a careful analysis to identify your strengths. Once you have done this, you stand an excellent chance of demonstrating your *capacity to fill the position* and holding your own in any forum.

Keep something important in mind; the interview committee or principal is interested in you. If you were not a candidate they thought might fit the position, you would not be in the seat you now occupy. As this is so, your only task is to clearly and confidently address the key issues raised by their questions. **KEY POINT:** *Do not concern yourself that every element of every answer needs to be a solid 10; it does not.* This is equally true for the **alternate route candidate**. None of the interviewees, no matter what their skill and background, will answer every question to perfection. *Your approach simply needs to be professional, clearly articulated, and designed to highlight your strengths and minimize any weaknesses.*

By its very nature the interview is a time when nervousness is common. Because of this anxiety, it is a time when flaws can easily creep into your responses. Therefore, before we specifically look at what you might be asked, let's review a few general rules you can use to frame your answer to any interview question.

RULES TO FRAME AN ANSWER FOR ANY QUESTION:

- *Listen carefully to the question and answer what is asked as precisely as possible.* One of the most common flaws in providing a good answer is what I call "question avoidance tactics." The candidate talks and talks but does not address the question asked. A clear example occurs when a principal asks the candidate to identify any recent workshop experience, and he or she talks at length about his or her summer reading and college coursework. The conclusion of the principal is there was no workshop experience or the person did not listen well. Either way, the candidate made the wrong impression. If you are not certain what the interviewer asked, then by all means get a clarification, but answer the question and do it truthfully.

"You ask an interesting question, but I want to be sure I understand. Would you be kind enough to explain it again?"

If the question probes an area that is not your strength one of the worst things to do is "wing it" or dodge the issue. You might simply say something like:

"As I was not recently in a position to take advantage of workshop opportunities I haven't any to share at this point. I would like to say, however, I think workshops are a valuable part of every teacher's continuing growth. I would be very interested in attending workshops about technology in the classroom, teaching diverse student groups, or diagnostic teaching strategies. Does the district have some specific workshops they would like me to attend if I am selected for this position?"

This answer is on target and shows you understand the value of professional development. Look at the last sentence of this answer. It is especially strong because it opens an avenue for the principal to link his or her priorities to your agenda. To add even more power, if you already know the district is involved in a specific staff development initiative, this is a great time to insert that as one of your areas of interest! In any case, you have been clear and honest. This will be noted and appreciated.

- *Be concise! Direct your answer to the question and make a few powerful points.* Every interviewer's nightmare is the candidate who takes five or six minutes to answer a simple question. Rambling answers that are convoluted and repetitive steal potential impact from your response and diminish your effectiveness. A good rule of thumb is to limit an initial answer to an absolute maximum of two minutes. If the question is complicated or has multiple parts, you may have to exceed the two-minute time limit, but these questions are not the norm. Also, if you hear yourself repeating information, draw your answer to a close. Repetition generally means you have exhausted the good ideas.

KEY INTERVIEW STRATEGY: *Two or three strong points make a better answer than a half dozen off target ideas. The length of an answer has no relationship to its quality.*

- *Provide specific examples or points to underscore and add power to your ideas.* When you give a specific example of how you would apply a principle to a real situation, you add power to your answer. For example, a common interview question asks how one would deal with off-task students. The ordinary candidate will simply talk about a few strategies he or she might try. This is not necessarily a poor approach, but it lacks power and will sound like almost all the other candidates. A better candidate will provide a specific example from his or her experience that explains how he or she has successfully dealt with this common problem.

"Although this has not happened often, your question does bring one student to mind. In that case I did three things, and they proved so successful I have used the strategy several times since."

Then go on to detail the three steps and their effect. This answer is stronger because it shows how you *applied* the classroom management principles you outlined.

The **alternate route candidate** may not have as rich a set of experiences on which to draw; however, you may well have various clinical or substitute teaching experiences. You would define your answer around strategies you have used to this point or even those where you may have been a co-teacher. If you have no real classroom experience but have been involved as a trainer or mentor in your job history, you may be able to describe a similar situation from that setting.

- ***Do not be afraid to take a moment of time to reflect and frame your thinking before answering a complicated question.*** Candidates often feel obliged to begin their answer immediately at the end of the question. For more complicated questions, you might need a little time to mentally organize your response. If you have a pad in front of you, you might even wish to jot down a few key words to help you stay on target and hit the important points you want to make. Whereas there cannot be a full minute of dead silence, five to ten seconds of organization and thinking is not unreasonable. You may even explain what you heard the question to be and ask if your understanding is correct. This provides both clarity and needed processing time.

SAMPLE GENERAL QUESTIONS AND THEIR ANSWERS:

There will be other suggestions to discuss as we proceed, but now we are ready to look at a few of the tough interview questions you may encounter. These questions are a representative sampling, and I selected those items that were the most common, difficult, or interesting.

> *Describe the aspects of your background that best qualify you for this position.*

This question, or a variation of it, is often the lead question in an interview. It is also one of the most commonly mishandled questions! This is the perfect opportunity for you to sell yourself and your skills, but too often a candidate will just review the same information contained in his or her resume. Worse yet, he or she embarks on a long narrative that wanders aimlessly all over the lot and never addresses the substantive issue posed in the question. There is a substantive piece of this question. Did you see it? *"...aspects of your background you believe <u>best qualify you</u> for this position."*

This is the perfect place to target your answer to what you know about the district and its students! Forget the resume they already read and focus the committee on specific teaching skills you use that match the needs of their student body. Tell them about projects you designed that fit their vision, extra-curricular work that improved student life, or any other item in your background that matches the district's needs. If you have not researched the school, it will be impossible to match your background to its specific values, so be sure to complete this important step before the interview day.

A good conclusion to your response will outline your commitment to student achievement and personal dedication. You might say,

"Finally, one of my most important strengths is a commitment that every child in my class should leave school at the end of the day saying my class was one of the highlights. To that end, I will direct my best efforts all day, every day!"

KEY UNDERSTANDING: *Put the ending in your own words, but keep in mind that **your ending statement is often the most lasting in the memory of the committee.***

KEYS TO YOUR RESPONSE:

- Be specific and stick to the question. DO NOT WANDER.
- Target the elements of your background that *best fit* what the district values.
- Include information about your teaching style, special projects, or ideas that relate to school initiatives.
- End with a statement about your dedication and energy. Let them know you will be an impact teacher from the first day.

> *Describe a difficult classroom challenge you confronted and how you addressed the problem.*

This is another common question. Its purpose is to evaluate your problem solving ability and how you think on your feet. The committee wants to know what approach you will take in dealing with the tough situations that will confront you. Here is a possible approach.

"I first recognize that a difficult problem in <u>my</u> class is my problem, not someone else's. But that said; there are always others who can provide insight and assistance when necessary. I generally use a four-step process to determine my best course of action. One, I identify the specific elements of the problem and who might be able to help. Two, I outline some possible steps that might be employed. Three, I discuss those steps with a colleague or administrator to see if they have other insights or suggestions. Four, I take action."

With this approach, the principal knows you do not just take a trial and error approach to difficult problems. You are a deliberate problem solver with a plan. But this does not fully answer the question and, as you know, that is one of the serious flaws we want to eliminate. Now, give an example of a problem and what you did. This question is common enough to warrant the time you will devote to a pre-thought answer. In the heat of an interview, your mind may not land on a problem that will effectively demonstrate this key skill. The following is a good example given during an interview I held some years ago. It should provide insight as to how you might prepare your own answer.

> *"When I took over a class as a permanent sub, the class had had five different teachers in two months. There were no classroom routines, and student behavior was unruly and hostile. I determined there were two root problems. The first was the lack of a classroom structure, and the second was the presence of a group of alienated students. As a class, we decided to suspend all academics for two days. We used the first day to identify problems and some possible solutions. The students developed three classroom rules we would all follow, and posters were made for placement around the room. The second day, we examined the course of study, and I listed some things we could study that fit into our curriculum. We decided which of the areas the class wanted to pursue. We began our work with an improved, although not perfect, level of participation and energy. Although it took over a month to establish a good routine and mutual respect, the cooperative approach to decision making was a sound strategy that we all made work."*

This answer was a perfect practical example of the described strategy! We hired this teacher. Think about what you will say and similar results may well follow.

KEYS TO YOUR RESPONSE:

- Begin with a specific problem-solving design.
- Provide a specific story or example of how that design worked in a difficult situation.

Outline how you assess student performance and how you address differences in student backgrounds and abilities.

This is a double-barreled assessment question and one you may well encounter in your interview. Begin by identifying the components of the question. The first part wants to know how you determine student progress while the second wants modifications you will make for students with unique problems or abilities.

With the increase in the number of special needs students in classes and a host of diversity issues, assessment has become increasingly complex and now encompasses a variety of practices. You will have to choose those that best fit your style and what you know about the school's student population and philosophy. If you know a school is involved in authentic tasks, problem-based learning, or some other initiative, then by all means learn about it and be ready to use that information in your response. To prepare yourself for questions in this area, you will do yourself a big favor by reviewing the book, <u>Understanding by Design</u>, by Grant Wiggins and Jay McTighe (Wiggins and McTighe, 2005). Both are recognized experts in current assessment theory and practice.

To approach the first portion of the question, how you assess student performance, begin with a statement of how you recognize the different roles assessment can fulfill. Discuss the ways you see assessment as having changed over the years.

> *"When I was in school, the only use of assessment was for the teacher to figure out your grade at the end of the marking period. Teachers gave us quizzes and tests, added in our homework, and gave us a grade. Now, we know there are many ways to use the assessment process."*

Go on to describe the numerous roles assessment will have in your class. Specifically talk about how you might use assessment to make teaching decisions and guide student learning. Describe the distinction you make between diagnostic assessment and grading practice. If you use self and/or peer assessment strategies in your class, be sure to describe them.

From this foundation, move to the second portion of the question and state how you will account for different educational backgrounds and abilities. Describe the way you alter your grading practices to meet individual differences. The principal will want to know if you intend to use differentiated testing practices, multi-level homework, extra-credit, self-selected projects, peer tutors, cooperative learning, technology, or other techniques to insure the success of struggling students and while continuing to challenge the brighter students. Which strategies you choose are not particularly important. Choose those that best fit your teaching style. *What is important is that you have specific plans to use a variety of assessment practices and have a sound rationale for their employment.*

This is one of the more important questions and the committee will want to know how you will use your knowledge of assessment to promote student success. Are you a teacher who knows how to reward the exceptional student and maintain his or her challenge? Do you have the flexibility and strategies that will insure strugglers, poor readers and below average students have opportunities to succeed when they put forth a fair effort? Most administrators fear they will hire an inflexible, dogmatic teacher who has a narrow grading philosophy such that it promotes settings where the strong survive and the weak are left to fail.

KEYS TO YOUR RESPONSE:

- Do your homework on the district and identify any information they have on their assessment practices. Select assessment strategies in your style that match the district philosophy.
- Identify a few purposes of assessment and describe how you will use them to design instruction and to help students learn.
- Outline how you might vary your assessment patterns or make modifications to meet challenges presented by students of different abilities.
- Tell the committee about your grading practices and be sure to let them know you recognize the need for both individual grade success as well as student mastery of course goals.

> *Tell us what qualities you believe are essential to being a good teacher. Of those qualities, which is your strongest?*

This is an excellent question for you to separate yourself from the pack! It is an open invitation to talk about your knowledge of teaching and underscore your strengths. Take a moment to see how this might be done. First, just *what are* the essential qualities of a good teacher? Qualities to include will be similar to the five central themes we spoke of at the beginning of the chapter. Those included the ability to relate to students and inspire their learning, possess the instructional skills necessary for inspired teaching, understand class management, and manifest a high sense of professional behavior. Whichever personal strengths you identify, provide a practical example to add impact to your point.

The question further asks which dimension you feel represents *your* greatest strength. A good approach to this answer might combine two areas.

For example:
> *"One of my strongest qualities is an ability to relate instruction to the world of children and design activities that interest and motivate their involvement."*

KEY POINT: *Whatever qualities you identify as strengths, they should be supported with short anecdotes.* It is from this connection the answer draws its strength. A good answer to this question can set a positive tone to the entire interview.

KEYS TO YOUR RESPONSE:

- Describe the qualities that are essential to being a good teacher.
- Use practical examples showing that you possess those qualities.
- In describing your personal strengths, try to use an anecdote to tell your story.
- This question is asked often enough to make it worthwhile to pre-think an answer. If you are not prepared, your examples are likely to be less effective.

If we were to speak with your students, what would they tell us about the educational experience they had with you?

This question can be phrased in different ways. Sometimes you will be asked what your supervisor, department head, or principal would say. Each question asks the same thing: How do others perceive your work? Even if there have been some problems in your background, it is in your interest to remain positive and focus only on the good things that might be said.

If you are currently teaching and can conduct a student survey, do this and include a question that asks students to write what they like about your teaching. From their responses, select a few comments to share in an interview. Even if there has been criticism about a few elements of your class or teaching, focus on the qualities students said they liked. Do not forget to select a few student response forms to include in your interview portfolio.

If you have never conducted such a survey, it is acceptable to relate things a student may have told you. You may also talk about the things you did in class that students responded to best. Your goal is to convey the fact that students liked your class and responded well to your teaching efforts.

ALTERNATE ROUTE CANDIDATE: This is the kind of question that is more difficult to answer because you have not had a great deal of classroom experience. If you have been substitute teaching, you will have some student feedback that can be useful. Where that is not the case, you will focus on your clinical experiences and any student teaching you have completed. Ordinarily, if an interviewer knows you are an alternate route candidate, they will phrase the question differently and will substitute the word "supervising teacher or employer." In all cases, you will want to talk about such things as your ability to get along with others, problem solving, planning skill, taking direction, or some other characteristic that would translate well to a school environment. If you are coming from a different profession or field, you want to avoid highlighting a skill that only relates to the workplace. *"My previous boss would tell you I was one of the best people in the office for evaluating the cost effectiveness of our benefits packages."* Great, but how would that help you be a better teacher? Here is a more worthwhile response.

> *"My previous boss would tell you about my human relations skills and ability to create great team effort. We had a number of new employees with very low knowledge of our system, and I was charged to organize and mentor them as we built a new sales team. It took some time and training to put everyone on the same page, but in three months our team was one of the top units. These very same interpersonal skills I used with adults will help me work with students to motivate and challenge them to become successful learners in my class."*

The strength of this answer is in how it ties a key strength for which you have already been complimented to a useful skill that will serve students in your class. If you want to make it even stronger, identify one of the specific strategies you employed that made the system work. There are many skills like this, and you need to think about which ones you have so that you can effectively insert them into your interview when the time comes.

Be aware that the committee may offer a follow-up question that asks, "Was there anything your students disliked?" **WARNING:** *This is a loaded gun waiting to go off.* There is no need to bare your soul and convey every complaint. On the other hand, telling the committee it was all peaches and cream and there was nothing students did not like will not play well either. There are many things students can dislike about a class that do not reflect poorly on the teacher. Examples include weekend homework, resubmitting papers that were not up to standard, too many tests, and so on. You know your classes and what students may have found less enjoyable. Select something you feel will meet the needs of this question. If you have an ability to add a humorous tone to this area, it can be very effective. If not, just be honest and open without making the segment an exposé of unhappy students. The committee will respect the candor.

 KEYS TO YOUR RESPONSE:

- If you are now teaching, do a student survey. Select a few responses that highlight your better qualities and have them ready. Leave the committee with the knowledge that students liked your class and responded positively to your work.
- Be ready for the reverse question, "what didn't your students like?"

Motivating students of today is a difficult task. What do you do to inspire your students to actively learn in your classes?

Many interviews include a question on what you know about student motivation. Students do not thrive in boring, uninspired classes. Moreover, those classes are exactly where discipline problems and public relations nightmares go to spawn. **TIP:** *I do not wish to raise your anxiety, but you <u>must</u> do well on this question.* Let us begin by examining some of Madeline Hunter's ideas found in her book, <u>Mastery Teaching</u> (Hunter, 2005). Each of the items listed below has a proven influence on student motivation. Once mastered, these variables can be woven into an outstanding response.

VARIABLES OF MOTIVATION

- *Classroom atmosphere:* Is the class a warm, safe place for children to learn?
- Level of *active student involvement:* Is this a class where there are lots of activities and engaged student experiences?
- *Pace* of class: Do you have a variety of daily activities and events that move the class swiftly towards the learning objectives?
- *Interest:* Is the instruction and designed activities interesting and connected to the real world of students?
- *Personal success:* Do students feel they are learning and attaining good grades? Do they enjoy a sense of accomplishment?
- *Recognition/Reward:* Do you recognize students for good work and effort? Do the rewards have both intrinsic and extrinsic value for the student?
- *Level of concern:* Are students held accountable? Do students have to meet reasonable expectations on a consistent basis?
- *Engagement in purposeful*, *worthwhile experiences:* Do students see a reason for what they are studying? Is the effort they are putting forth seen to be worth it?

This is not the all-inclusive list of motivation variables and you can find other ideas discussed in the literature. In your answer, select two or three of these variables and describe how you utilized or manipulated them to achieve positive results. Feel free to tick off the entire list at the beginning, but you only have time to expand on a couple. Again, supply practical examples wherever possible. This answer can be made even more powerful if you cite an instance where you had a poorly motivated group and used your knowledge of these variables to reverse the situation. Under-motivated classes are a common problem, and the committee or principal will be favorably impressed if you demonstrate you can deal with those issues when they arise.

KEYS TO YOUR RESPONSE:

- Learn the variables affecting motivation before the interview.
- Begin your response by providing a short list of variables that impact motivation.
- Select two or three variables and provide a more in depth discussion of how they were used in your teaching OR how you intend to employ them in your teaching.
- Provide classroom anecdotes to strengthen your points.
- If you can provide an example of a poorly motivated class and what you did to turn that situation around, your answer will be complete.

Today's classrooms often have a number of special needs students with a wide range of identified learning disabilities. How will you alter your instruction to meet the needs of these students?

Schools want to be confident that you know how to handle special needs students who may be placed in your class. If you plan a career in public education, it is a near certainty you will encounter students with a classification such as ADD/ADHD, OBD, or perhaps even a medical challenge such as Down Syndrome. If questions are permitted, you might ask about the district's inclusive education policy and how it is implemented in your prospective school. The interviewer will often give you valuable information about his or her expectations and the school model. You can use this information when crafting your answer.

In providing your response, there are several important points you will want to make. First and foremost, note that since all special education students have *an Individualized Educational Plan (IEP)*, this will be the controlling document you use to design *any* aspect of a student's program. Describe the ways you try to individualize assignments, class-work, and tests. Explain how you modify class activities to meet the specific needs of students. It is wise to add that you do this for any child who might be struggling and not just identified students. Discuss your reliance on the *case manager* who can provide valuable direction and assistance. Additionally, there is usually a support class for

95

identified students. Describe how you might work with the support teacher to mutually guide a student through your class and towards successful learning.

Finally, with respect to Attention Deficit Disorder (ADD)/ Attention Deficit Hyperactivity Disorder (ADHD) and Oppositional Behavior Disorders (OBD), you understand that such students might have a history of impulsive or even defiant behaviors. Sydney Zentall has an excellent reference book on this topic, _ADHD and Education: Foundations, Characteristics, Methods, and Collaboration_ (Zentall, 2005). This reference has a wealth of proven classroom strategies for the difficult learner and explains how a teacher can build positive interpersonal connections with such students. It is suggested that you seek opportunities to reinforce the good behavior so it increases in frequency. Whichever strategies you employ, always add that you plan to work with other building professionals to minimize those behaviors that can disrupt the learning environment for the class.

When you have concluded this answer, you want the committee to recognize you as a teacher who will be responsive to individual needs and ready to use a range of professional services on behalf of students. Flexibility in both your teaching practice and assessment is an important quality to demonstrate because it lies at the heart of your ability to respond to the needs of special education students.

KEYS TO YOUR RESPONSE:

- Ask the principal to describe the program for mainstream students in his or her school. Use this information to frame your response.
- Explain your knowledge of the IEP process and how it will be used to shape student programs in your class.
- Describe program or class modifications you have made for students and where you felt such individualization was appropriate.
- Talk about ways you will try to build positive student relations and mutual respect over the course of the year.
- Convey your willingness to assume a collegial approach and use the case manager, support teacher, and other professionals to craft student programs.
- Illustrate your ability to be flexible and adapt your teaching to the special needs of students.

What is the role of homework in your teaching and how do you organize it to support the learning process?

Homework has many purposes. With this question, the interviewer wants to know how you design and use homework in your class. Begin by asking if there is a school or grade level homework policy already in place. If there is, ask for a description and use this information in your answer.

A sound answer will begin with how you intend to use homework. Most candidates simply answer this question by describing their homework frequency, length of average assignments, and the grading practices. This is not wrong and should be included, but it lacks uniqueness and will sound like too many other candidates. We will do much better and provide an answer interviewers rarely hear. Your approach will frame the use of homework around a significant piece of *research information*. **RESEARCH TIP:** *Research identifies a variety of homework purposes and suggests that when teachers make outside assignments, they should* <u>identify to students in advance</u> *the homework's purpose if they wish to maximize its effectiveness.* Below is a synopsis of this research to use in giving that answer sure to capture the attention of the committee!

USES OF HOMEWORK
- The **application of learning** outside the class.
- The **enhancement of speed and proficiency** on new learning.
- The **reinforcement** of the degree of original learning.
- **Preparation** for new learning.
- The **development of a home and school connection**.

Use these ideas to frame the opening of your answer and illustrate the variety of ways you have or will use homework. For each use, give a practical example that clearly demonstrates your point.

EXAMPLE: *One of the underused purposes of outside assignments is its ability to help construct stronger connections between what happens in the classroom and the home. I will often add a component to the assignment that will allow students to involve their parents or some other adult in the house. An example might be if we were working on measurement, to use a standard recipe for something like mac and cheese. The student is asked to work with an adult at home to make the measurements and compute any measurement conversion. Not only do they learn…they EAT!*

Include two or three examples like this, delivered with a little humor and happiness, and you will go a long way to move you to the front of the candidate pool.

A second punch will be to describe a method that provides **ability modifications** to your homework so every student can be appropriately challenged. When you have an assignment to reinforce new learning, you are likely to have students at a variety of places along the mastery continuum. For that reason, you should consider a practice where you offer several different levels of difficulty and allow the students to choose the one for which they feel most ready. Because each level has an appropriate but different credit value, there is an incentive to choose the higher value assignment.

For example, if the class were reading a specific book or story in their literature strand, you might have three different levels of tasks. (A) In your own words, list the main events of the first chapter. *(4 points)* (B) Construct a story board of the first chapter. *(7 points)* (C) Construct a story board and analyze the relationship between the two main characters. *(10 points)* As you can see, the rising complexity of the assignment adds both challenge and reward.

As mentioned above, you need to briefly outline the homework routines you commonly employ such as the frequency, typical length, and late policies. If the school has specific policies on homework, expect that interviewers might ask you to expand on specific elements of your practice as it relates to the school's philosophy.

Keep your answer upbeat and convey the idea that homework is a vehicle you use to promote student success and measure their understanding. By including the research design and homework modification plan, your answer is sure to stand out as one of the best!!

<u>KEYS TO YOUR RESPONSE:</u>

- Ask if there is a homework policy in place and, if so, use its key points to shape portions of your answer.
- Cite several ways you use homework. Where possible supply examples.
- Include a plan to use homework modification strategies.
- Outline your standard homework policies and practices.
- Describe to the committee how you use homework to promote student achievement and shape future instruction.

Our community is very involved in the education process and schools. What are your thoughts on parental involvement? What relationship would you want to establish with the parents of your students?

If there is one skill where principals want to be sure of a teacher's competence, it is in how he or she deals with the parents and community. In my review of hundreds of interviews, a majority had at least one question concerning parent relations. It is critical you prepare yourself to address the important goal of keeping parents informed and involved. Describe specific steps you will take to reach that goal and your answer will resonate well with the committee.

This question asks for two specific reactions. First, what is your opinion regarding parental involvement? Second, what will you do to establish a sound relationship with the parents of your students? Be certain to answer both parts and not just the latter. Unsuccessful candidates often answer the last part first and then fail to address the other essential question.

In this case, begin with the initial question on philosophy. It is the easiest and shortest of the two. You must use your own ideas here and not mine, however, open with your understanding that historically, where parents placed a high value on education and involved themselves in positive ways with their child's schooling, such has had a positive affect on achievement results. To that end, every teacher has an important role to play in promoting strong parental support. Add in your own thinking, but that is a workable core for your answer.

With the second part of the question, you will need to communicate *specific* steps you have taken, or will take, to promote that productive parent involvement. Do you send out newsletters or notices at the beginning of units? Do you call student homes to provide positive reports rather than just call when there is a problem? Are parents invited to special events in your class? Do you provide parent guides to help students succeed? If you have any well-received parent newsletters or other communications, you may wish to include an example in your interview portfolio.

Many textbook publishers have now included entire programs in their <u>Teacher Manuals</u> to promote home involvement. If you can obtain a copy of one of these manuals, you will find a wealth of ideas you can incorporate into both your answer and future teaching. Paint a picture for the committee of just how important enlisting parent involvement will be in designing the unit introduction and ongoing instruction. At the end of the day, the committee must see you as a person who invites parent participation. Identifying this kind of specific information on your invitational practices will be just the way to leave that impression.

 ## KEYS TO YOUR RESPONSE:

- Address the philosophy portion of the question by talking about the positive impact parent involvement has historically had on achievement.

- Inform the committee that a central goal is to keep parents informed of the progress of their children and aware of any major events that will take place in your class.
- List specific strategies you have or intend to use to open lines of communication.
- Describe how you use materials provided by the publishers of textbooks and their Teacher's Manual to introduce units and design communication.
- If you have prior substitute or regular teaching experience, do not forget to put sample copies of any newsletters, information flyers, or other forms of parent communication in your portfolio.

We have both school scheduled and parent requested conferences. How do you approach parent conferences?

Parent conferences, when they do not go well, often end up in the principal's office as an even bigger problem. Successful conferences, on the other hand, result in increased parent confidence toward both the teacher *and* the school. Begin your answer by showing your understanding of this reality and your intention to take deliberate and effective steps to maximize the probability of successful parent conferences.

The first question a professional teacher must address is who initiated the conference and for what purpose. With this information in hand, cite the necessity of good planning. You might start your answer with the following phrasing:

> *"With all parent conferences, I want to establish a purpose for the meeting, identify a few outcome goals, and think of a means by which we can cooperatively work towards the attainment of those goals."*

Also, let the committee know you are a *good listener* who uses conferences to open dialog and promote communication. Show that you recognize parents as the ultimate consumers of your services and state how you would want to do everything possible to insure their satisfaction.

A key to a successful conference is the ability of the teacher to enter the meeting with an open mind and willingness to *hear what the parent is saying.* The one thing you want to avoid in any parent conference is extended confrontation. It is very likely that you will encounter a combative parent at some point in your career. Let the interviewer know that should that situation present itself, your strategy is to allow the parent to fully explain their concern without interruption. Then ask the parent to suggest ways you can both work together so the solution goal is successfully met.

> **CONFERENCE TIP:** *Too often, teachers are more interested in letting parents know why they are right. That may be a teacher's goal, but I can assure you it is not the parent's goal. If you let the committee know you are aware of this problem, you have taken a large step forward.*

Consider ending with this idea: When parents come with a problem, what they really want to know is whatever that problem might be; you are willing to work with them to improve the situation and make the class better for their student. Sometimes this means both sides must do things differently, but if everyone is willing to work together, great results can be achieved. *With this approach you will be right and will have taken a long step in the direction of a new position!*

 ## KEYS TO YOUR RESPONSE:

- Begin by exhibiting your understanding of the importance of successful parent conferences.
- Describe how you will plan for a conference and determine the conference goals.
- Be sure the committee sees you as a good listener and cooperative problem-solver.
- Convey the understanding that you are willing to work with the family to make adjustments on both sides that will improve their child's experience.

> *Each year our students must take the state proficiency examination. It is of critical importance that students perform well in such areas as mathematics, language arts, and reading. Tell us how you see your role and some ideas as to what you will do to maximize student achievement.*

Teachers! *You can almost count on hearing this question or its first cousin during your interview!* Every state has its own required proficiency test, and you will be wise to make certain you are fully aware of the specific requirements in your state. These tests are federally monitored and publicly reported. Perception of overall school quality is closely linked to student performance and test results have become priority #1 in almost every school district. Questions on this topic can be very pointed and *a lack of understanding can be fatal to your candidacy.* The interview committee will want to certify that you are a teacher who knows the test's requirements, standards, importance of student success, and best practices to maximize that performance.

In this example the committee asks two questions. First, how do you see your role and second, how will you promote student performance? The candidate who enters an interview with just general knowledge and minimal forethought will almost assuredly fail to impress the committee. The tendency on questions like this is for candidates to over-talk and under-clarify their answer. As the better candidate you will have done the advanced planning necessary to have a concise, well researched response.

The first part of the question asks about how you see your role. Begin with a statement that you recognize the teacher as one of the central players in each student's test performance. For that reason you need to stay abreast of (1) best practices, (2) school initiatives, and (3) individual student needs. As the teacher, it will be your job to incorporate the essential skills and understandings students will need into your lessons and essential that you rehearse students on the kinds of questions they are likely to encounter on the test. Let the committee know your philosophy is underpinned by the knowledge that, "who stands in front of the class is the prime player in future student performance." These simple ideas make a very positive statement regarding the question on your role.

The second half of the question asks you to identify the *specific practices* you will use to promote the student performance suggested in the opening of your answer. Your approach will depend on the specific state test in use. In Texas for example, you have the *Texas Assessment of Knowledge and Skills (TAKS).* This is used in the primary and secondary schools to assess student attainment in reading, writing, math, science, and social studies skills. If you have an interview in Texas, then go to the Internet and look up information about this assessment on the state website. The source will supply the required standards by grade along with numerous links to support material. With a little research, you should find a wide variety of research-based, best practices to use in your answer. You want to identify from three to five practices that will fit your style of teaching and have been shown as effective. If you are an experienced teacher, it is likely that you have already extensively dealt with this issue. Select those classroom ideas and techniques you have used that were most effective. Craft an example or two that will exemplify the good results you obtained. Most importantly, if your students have been successful and you have statistics to cite, do so. Performance data will make your answer a huge success!!

ALTERNATE ROUTE TEACHER: If you are new to the profession or traveling by way of an alternate route, you will not have the specific examples an experienced teacher might offer.

Do not be concerned. In your case the committee wants to insure that you have thought about this and have sound ideas as to how you will approach the issue in your class. There are many articles, websites, and even books written on exactly this topic. You do not have to read everything, but you *must* read something. Being well read is essential to being well prepared. You need only a few class tested ideas to cite, but because it is unlikely you have actually used these strategies, you will need to do something more. You need to increase the legitimacy of each idea by adding an ingredient unsuccessful candidates omit; *the source of your idea and its validity.* **Consider the sample response below.**

> *"Let me speak to reading because that is such a gatekeeper to almost all academic success. Erin Schreiner in her article, "How to Improve Reading Scores in the Middle School," lists six different ways a good classroom teacher can improve reading performance. One of her suggestions that I intend to use is to make certain that students are familiar with reading terminologies such as metaphor, simile, and personification. An in-class practice will be to post such terms on a bulletin board and identify them in our own class readings. To reinforce understanding and retention, students will be encouraged to add their own examples to the bulletin board as they encounter them. A second strategy that impressed me is from a Harvard report that suggested that the best way to improve student vocabulary is to study words in context. Many commercial readers such as Kindle now have imbedded dictionaries that allow students to see the definition of a word they do not understand as soon as it is encountered! I can connect my Kindle to an LCD and make it a truly powerful classroom tool. This strategy is dynamic because, in the past, most readers simply skipped words they didn't know. Now my students will have on the spot definitions and in context, just as the study suggests. I would also encourage every student to keep a journal of four or five words a week they find interesting. If they highlight one of those words in their own writing, I will give them extra credit. There are many other strategies out there, but my intention is to stay focused on those that show the most results and use them in my class."*

You can see how this answer provides only a few examples but has a powerful delivery with that one, two, three approach: **(1) state the source, (2) give the strategy, and (3) provide an example of how you will use it**. It is so simple, but rarely heard and will separate you from the pack!

The final touch to your answer comes by way of a commitment to staff development. Nearly every school district includes staff development workshops and in-service training on the topic of test scores. Be sure to make it clear that you anxiously await the opportunity to learn more about how the district wants teachers to proceed and any classroom strategies they want employed. With this ending statement, you demonstrate how you are a team player and one who wishes to take an active role in the student preparation process.

KEYS TO YOUR RESPONSE:

- Describe a philosophy that identifies *you* as the central figure in promoting strong student achievement.
- Briefly talk about the state test and demonstrate your knowledge of its requirements.
- Experienced teachers should cite a few strategies they have successfully employed in their classes AND any data that points to achievement results. Give specific examples.
- **Alternate route teachers** or new teachers should identify classroom strategies they intend to use along with any research sources. Provide a solid example of how each will be employed.
- Identify yourself as someone who is interested in staff development opportunities that will add school-endorsed, cutting edge practices to your skill sets.
- End with a statement about how this work was important to the students and benefited the school.

In looking at your resume, I see that you have a degree from a good college. Tell me, how were your grades and just how important do you think they are in predicting your success here as a teacher?

Interesting question, no? At first glance, you might think it is about whether you were a good student and academically up to the standard required for this school. *It is not.* The real quality being investigated is whether you believe previous grades are always an indicator of future performance. The committee's underlying motive is to see whether you have the capacity to be a great addition to their teaching team. Interviewers will be listening to your answer to decide if you are a good "fit" for their staff. This is the topic that should be the main substance of your answer.

The exact nature of your answer regarding college performance will obviously be influenced by what grades you received during your academic training. If you were an honors student, then by all means point this out and speak to how this attainment is an indicator of just how hard you are willing to work; the importance you place on meeting required standards. If your academic history was good, but not necessarily at the honors level, then you will frame your answer around such things as the outstanding preparation for your field, a well-rounded set of experiences, and so forth. The desired message should be that you worked hard as student, received outstanding preparation for this position, and developed work habits that will contribute to success in any field.

To address the more fundamental reason the interviewer posed this question, you should point out how grades rarely tell the entire story of a person's prognosis for future success. In fact, you can and should say that grades are actually "progress indicators" as opposed to final results. Predictors of future results do not come from a single source, and you might phrase a bolder answer in the following way.

> *"Although I am proud of my accomplishments throughout college and what I have done through my post-graduate years, the most important things that will determine my success in this or any other position is more broadly defined. It will be a combination of the skills I learned throughout my course preparation, the work ethic I have developed over that time, and my passion for becoming one of the most productive and respected teachers on your staff. My grades notwithstanding, I still consider myself to be learning and growing. I intend to continue to improve my skills as a professional teacher. I don't believe for a moment that anyone can move forward on the road to a great career by focusing on the rear view mirror. You become a great contributor by focusing on the road ahead and preparing every day to be better than you were the day before."*

Oh yes. I think that will do nicely! The message you just delivered tells this committee in no uncertain terms that you are someone who will be a great worker, great team player, and lifelong learner. Grades provide some information, but you are someone who has the technical skills *and* professional passion that will translate to success. If you can speak to this philosophy with some passion, you have provided a very strong response.

 KEYS TO YOUR RESPONSE:

- Begin by speaking to the highlights of your academic experience, the excellent preparation it provided, and the important things you might have learned.
- Move your answer ahead by outlining the limitations simple grades might have as predictors of future success. Point out how there are several other equally important elements that influence a person's potential value.

- Paint yourself as exactly the kind of person who has outstanding qualifications, but intend to continue to grow and will passionately pursue the kind of professional excellence this school needs and demands.

> *Tell us about the most significant professional article or book you have read in the last year. What was its impact on your approach to teaching?*

WOW! *What a question!!* I have seen this one stump some of the best applicants. It has literally stricken fear into the unwary simply because they never anticipated it would be asked. Fortunately, you will have read this book and will be ready to sparkle with a sharp, well thought out answer.

One of the important professional qualities a school seeks in their candidate is a current understanding of pedagogy. They want to know he or she is a learner who constantly seeks improvement. This question helps identify that quality, yet it often strikes with such surprise the candidate cannot even offer an answer. Although not generally a knock out question, do not let a question like this take *you* by surprise. Begin now to read some of the journals and books that are available. As the question allows you to choose a book or an article, you may be best served by a current article. Look at people like Grant Wiggins, Roland Barth, Madeline Hunter, Jon Saphier, J. Howard Johnson, or others in your field. Journals like the <u>Kappan</u> or <u>Educational Leadership</u> have many articles and are available in most libraries.

Remember to answer the second part of this question, "*…how did it affect your teaching?*" If you have an actual example of how you have read and used an article in your teaching, then by all means use it now and go to the head of the class! Application is the most important element of this question because it tells the committee you are a teacher who can put ideas to work. If you are an **alternate route teacher** or new teacher, simply turn this into a "how it *will* impact my teaching. You are at no disadvantage on this question.

A last thought to consider; there are interviewers who only ask for *books* you have read. Articles are not an option. To avoid that problem, read a book as well. Yes, yes. I can hear all of you moaning now and saying, "WHEN?!" It is worth the extra effort, just do it. Some good choices would include, <u>The Passionate Teacher</u>, by Robert Fried; <u>Awakening Genius in the Classroom</u>, by Thomas Armstrong; <u>The Courage to Teach</u>, by Parker J. Palmer; or <u>Teach Like a Champion</u>, by Doug Lemov. All of these are just great books with lots of classroom ideas you can use. I assure you that if you can speak intelligently on any of these books your committee will be most impressed!

KEYS TO YOUR RESPONSE:

- Stop making excuses and read some books and articles!
- Decide how the ideas presented by the author could be used in your class.
- **BEWARE: *You cannot bluff this answer,*** so use candor and, if you have not done any recent reading, just tell the committee this is an area where you should do more and intend to do so in the future. Honesty will be far superior to a shallow, ring-around-the-rosy answer that does not stand up to inspection.

Describe the ways you would include technology in your classroom to make the teaching/learning process more effective.

Many districts have invested substantial sums of money in upgrading their technology. They will want to know the teacher they plan to hire recognizes the significance of technology and can put these tools to good use. It is the second half of this question, however, that embodies the essence of what the committee seeks. Did you see it? It asks how you, *". . . make the teaching/learning process more effective."* The interview committee is not interested in your course background, familiarity with MS Office, or other personal skills *unless* you can draw a direct link between those skills and the teaching of students.

Before you attempt an answer, you might want to ask the interviewer what kinds of technology are commonly available to classroom teachers and if specific district initiatives are in progress. This will do two things; provide an opportunity for the principal to trumpet some good things he or she has to offer and further identify the kinds of technology he or she wants to see used. With this information, you can outline how you might use Internet resources and teacher planning sites to research student activities and proven lesson designs. Identify where you might use test preparation or Computer Assisted Instruction (CAI) programs in the class. Bring yourself up to speed on the use of such teaching designs as WebQuests, Virtual Field Trips, and virtual science labs. If you are not familiar, find out about SmartBoard technology and what it can do for your instructional style. Ask if there are LCD projectors in the classroom for teacher use. These can be used for Power Point or multi-media teaching segments.

Bear in mind that your classroom may have a limited number of computers. If this is the case in your prospective school, you might offer ideas as to the use of computers to create learning centers. Go on to explain how such centers can extend learning or provide remedial instructional segments. If you can talk about how you have designed lessons to include technology, the power of your answer is dramatically increased. **WARNING:** *Do not talk about a technology unless you are able to discuss it in some level of depth.* There is often a follow-up question based on your response, and you would not want to get caught name-dropping. This is a good question for you to display your creativity and resourcefulness. Go for it and let the principal know you are the kind of teacher who is ready for the modern classroom.

 ## KEYS TO YOUR RESPONSE:

- Ask what technology is available and if there is a specific training program you will be expected to complete.
- Provide information on any technology you have already successfully used in class. **Use concrete examples** that show where you used technology to inspire children and add impact.
- Describe the power of online teaching resources and how you use them to add interest and imagination to your teaching.
- Get familiar with SmartBoard technology. This has become a more common tool in today's classroom. Explain how you would incorporate this into a solid teaching lesson.
- If you have used learning centers, include information on how they were designed.
- Identify at least one interactive learning opportunity such as WebQuests. Describe how it has been, or will be, used in your class.

 Every school wants teachers who are great team players. Tell us about the personal qualities you have that make you a good team player.

There are two goals you want to achieve in your answer. First, establish the fact you have sufficient human relation skills to work in a variety of collaborative settings and with various groups – fellow teachers, administrators, or parents. Second, show you are the kind of professional who has the energy, dedication, and drive to serve on a variety of committees and school initiatives. You are ready to be that person who can help the school bring about its vision.

Some of the characteristics that make a person a good team player include personal initiative, problem-solving, listening skills, leadership, persistence, task orientation, and communication skills. Choose three or four of the above areas and describe what you see as your qualities in each. If you can relate a specific anecdote or example to demonstrate your point, that is all the better. If all of this can be done with a small amount of humor, then try to add that element. Make these points and you will have answered the question well.

KEYS TO YOUR RESPONSE:

- Begin with a personal commitment to the collaborative process. Talk about how you have successfully worked in the past with superiors, coworkers, and parents (or clients).
- List a few important qualities of a constructive team player and describe how you embody those characteristics.
- Discuss a practical example of your collegial approach or team leadership. (If this question is asked and you have something in your evaluations to underscore the skill, highlight it during the portfolio review.)

> *You spoke to why you are a good team player, but suppose you are on a committee with someone you don't like or someone who does not like you? How do you make that work toward a productive result?*

When this question comes at you out of the blue, it can really cause interview anxiety. Yet, this is precisely the kind of follow-up question good interviewers are likely ask! So be ready. What the group wants to know is just how you deal with uncomfortable human relations. The political landscape of today's schools often place individuals together who are not on the best of terms. You need to convince the committee that such circumstances will not adversely affect the committee's work or results.

This answer need not be long, and it is one time when perhaps a specific example will not serve you well. There is no need to bring a past problem or negative hue to the answer. You might want to try an answer similar the one offered by Tony Beshara in his book, <u>Acing the Interview</u> (Beshara, 2008).

"Because I give a lot of respect to everyone regardless of the situation or my personal feelings, I seem to get a lot of respect in return. I try to use as much courtesy as possible and keep things on a very professional level. I always give credit where it is due and listen

carefully to ideas no matter which person is speaking. By doing this, the overall working environment of the committee is maintained on a high plane and personal issues never enter the equation."

This answer is more than sufficient to establish you as a collegial person. The one thing I would caution is that whatever you tell the committee your style might be; that *needs to be* your style. Honesty and accuracy are required of every answer.

KEYS TO YOUR RESPONSE:

- Keep negative examples out of your response.
- Describe your ways of providing courtesy and respect to all parties on the committee.
- Talk about keeping everything on a professional level.

If you are the person we hire, tell us what extra-curricular activities you would be willing and able to advise or coach.

This question is becoming more common. Anyone who believes the role of today's teacher is defined simply by what he or she does in the classroom is mistaken about the expectations of principals or the needs of today's schools. A good school cannot run unless teachers are willing to involve themselves in the daily life of students and overall school program.

This question provides a golden opportunity to demonstrate your utility and increase your value. All other things being equal between candidates, the person willing to coach, advise clubs, mentor the after-school groups, or run the yearbook will see his or her stock rise above those who offer only limited involvement. Make a point to ask the principal which activities need help. Even if you have never been involved with the identified activities, you can indicate a willingness to try. If the principal does not specifically name areas of need, let him or her know of your interest in a few general areas. School officials like to know an applicant is a team player. **INTERVIEW TIP:** *If this question is not asked, be sure to provide the information at the end of the interview.* Do not leave the room without putting everyone on notice that you enthusiastically wish to participate in school activities.

KEYS TO YOUR RESPONSE:

- Begin with a brief statement to demonstrate you understand the wider range of responsibilities expected of today's teacher.
- Be ready to identify a variety of extra-curricular activities where you have been an advisor, a coach, or had other experiences.
- List areas where you have an interest but not yet had an opportunity to participate.
- Do not limit your answer to student-oriented activities. Building level committees, district initiatives, teacher workshops, enrichment teaching for parents, or anything that benefits the school or community can be included.

> *As a new teacher, what kinds of support would you need from the administration and teaching staff to help you adjust to the new position?*

Here is the **WRONG ANSWER**. *"Oh, I'm very self-reliant and won't need much assistance at all."* Unfortunately, it is an answer too often given by the uninformed candidate. Quality teachers are not loners, and to suggest you need only "minimal" assistance generally fails to win points or enhance your standing.

This question affords you a perfect avenue to introduce your interest in working with other teachers or building leaders. It is an excellent time to ask a few questions of your own and find out more information on departmental or grade level expectations and routines. Use it! Tell the committee you want to learn more about school initiatives and how you can involve yourself in workshops or other in-service activities. Talk about things you did to adjust to your last teaching or student-teaching position. If you have not taught before, you can focus on your adjustment to a work organization. Do not forget the students. You want help to learn more about the students in your class. Guidance will be an important resource. You may want to speak with the library staff or a technology coordinator if the school has that role.

Whereas you do not want to present yourself as a high maintenance pest with a question for every situation, you need to appear enthusiastic and interested. Choose a few areas where you feel help would be legitimately welcomed, identify them and move on. If you have done your homework and become familiar with a few district initiatives, now is a good time to indicate your interest in learning more in those areas. Let this

111

committee know you are interested in professional growth and would be anxious to work with others in the school.

KEYS TO YOUR RESPONSE:

· DO NOT portray yourself as a loner in need of no assistance.
· Identify support members of the school who will be able to help you be a more effective teacher.
· Describe how you look forward to the staff development opportunities of the district and your future work together to improve your craft.

It has been stated that good classroom management is an outgrowth of good teaching. What does that mean to you, and how do you intend to put that maxim to work in your teaching?

What the district wants to know is do you understand the relationship that exists between well planned, successfully delivered lessons and the management of student behavior. Use this question to outline how you plan lessons to command the attention and involvement of students. There are numerous classroom strategies relevant to this goal, and you will have to select those best fitted to your philosophy and practice. A few ideas to consider include: multi-level activity lessons, real-world connections, innovative uses of technology, discovery lessons, increased novelty, multiple assessment strategies, and other designs that lead to high interest and student involvement.

An important principle of learning that helps increase student attention is something Jon Saphier in his book, The Skillful Teacher, calls **lesson momentum** (Saphier, 2008). When students are interested and busy, there is little time for management problems to present themselves. Similarly, poorly designed lessons lacking vitality and activity will invariably invite off-task behavior. Robert Fried in, The Passionate Teacher, underscores the idea that a great classroom experience engages students quickly and maintains that interest through the lesson (Fried, 2001). Fried explains that once we get students started on an interesting activity, we need to recognize it has a limited life span. Eventually, children will tire of the work, lose focus, and become restless. **Momentum** is skillfully maintained when the teacher **moves students through a variety of activities of short duration** and has something worthwhile for them to explore when they complete their task early.

SAMPLE RESPONSE: *In my opinion, good classroom management flows directly from active student engagement in an interesting lesson. I think this works best when I keep the momentum and flow of the class moving in a positive direction. To do this, I always include a few high interest or high involvement things for students to do throughout the period. I then actively walk through the different work groups to make sure they are still on task and involved in the work. If I see the engagement winding down, I know that it is time to change the format and move on to something new. An example of this was a science lesson I designed on characteristics of living things. In this case I used birds. The first activity had small groups of students use pictures of birds where they had to write down as many distinguishing features as they could find. The bird pictures were posted around the room and each group gave their defining characteristics to the class and everyone tried to point out the bird they were describing. When this began too lose momentum, we went on to a short teaching segment on bird songs. The activity that followed had students listen to a song and then point to the correct bird posted on the wall. It was a lesson with a lot of fun, and students remained involved from beginning to end.*

This short answer and lesson example provides the committee an excellent idea of how you will include high impact activities to reduce class management problems. By giving a description of the lesson's activity, you will have demonstrated what you meant by the term "momentum." Now, you will need to think this through and formulate an activity driven lesson of your own. Again, if you experience a little mind block, go online to one of the teacher planning sites and find a good idea you can steal and *make your own.*

As long as you describe your awareness of how class activities must move and how you plan for transitions, you are a light-year ahead of most candidates. Use your knowledge of good teaching to convince the interview committee you can create great lessons and go right to the head of the class!

 ## KEYS TO YOUR RESPONSE:

- Convince the committee you will be well planned and have a variety of activities each day.
- Give examples of innovative, engaging teaching practices and activities. Use an anecdote to provide meaning and impact to your discussion.
- Illustrate how you will maintain class momentum through the use of innovative activities, smooth transitions, and an instructional pace that maximizes student interest.

We will be interviewing a number of candidates. Why do you feel we should hire you as opposed to one of the others?

This is one possible end question for your interview. It is also another question where a lesser candidate might drop the ball with a weak, self-conscious response.

"Gee, I don't really know the other candidates and I wouldn't want to say I'm the best, but I'm sure I could do a good job, etc., etc., pap and blather."

Poppycock!!! We go for it right now! And your answer will be concise and memorable. Avoid a reprise of the entire interview. Everyone will go to sleep, and the sight of interviewers snoozing at the conference table is never a good sign. Go right back to what you know the district values and tick off a few of the skills you already shared to match those needs. You only need two or three of your better points.

"I know this school only wants outstanding professionals who can motivate students and competently deliver instruction. I have described my training in this area and outlined a number of strategies I know will make my classes a place students look forward to each day. We're going to learn and have fun doing it!"

Use a targeted approach and deliver short, compact points to **underscore your match** to this job. Convince the committee right now that you are a child-centered, team player with instructional competence and high motivation. You have already given complete, meaningful answers to each of the committee's questions, so you need only a few well-chosen refreshers at this point. A good conclusion to your answer might highlight your dedication and work ethic.

"Without knowing anything about the other candidates, I can only promise that you will not interview anyone who is going to work harder or be more concerned with the success of every child than I. I know I have the right skill sets to meet the needs of this position, and I am the right teacher for this job."

Why is this, or something like it, an important last statement? What you say last is the one thing that *will* last. Last statements, if carefully crafted, linger in the air well after you have left the room. This committee must know and remember they *will not* meet a more dedicated or enthusiastic candidate than YOU!

KEYS TO YOUR RESPONSE:

- Your goal is to ensure the committee recognizes you as a child-centered, instructionally competent, motivated team player.
- Provide short powerful statements on each of the above qualities.
- Remember to **match your answer to what you know are district needs wherever possible.**
- End with a strong message that will be remembered.

> *Is there anything else you would like to say that we haven't already discussed? Do you have questions for us?*

This is the other possible last question. Candidates often take a pass on this and say "no." **THAT IS ANOTHER MISTAKE!!!** *You have a last chance to make an impression, use it.* If you did not have an opportunity to talk about your extra-curricular work during the interview, describe it now. If you did not see a place to use the closing outlined in the preceding question, this is a great place to include that statement. Always use the last moments of an interview to make lasting and memorable statements. Leave thoughts in the minds of committee members that will help you stand out when discussions begin regarding which candidates impressed them most. Make that candidate you!

Note how the phrasing of this question provides an opportunity for you to ask questions. If you choose to ask a question, take care that you do not fall into an open manhole and ask one that might diminish the good impression you worked so hard to create. Here a few questions you should avoid.

- *Could you tell me how much sick time I am allowed each year?*
- *If I have to stay past the contract, will I get paid?*
- *What is the district's position on non-tenured teachers becoming a part of the Association?*

There are many other questions that convey the wrong impression, but I think you can see the point we are attempting make. **WARNING:** *Avoid asking any question that may suggest you are more interested in the contract requirements than you are the teaching of students.* Questions regarding your contract are best left until an offer is made. Inquiries about the district benefit package and salary are expected. Principals will not mind providing this information. In many cases, if you are to be strongly considered, the committee may discuss these topics without prompting.

A last caution is to limit your questions to one or two. Choose what you feel you need to know now, and save the other questions until an offer is tendered. One question you definitely want to ask is:

> *"Based on where you are and the vision you have for the coming year, what would be the one or two most essential skills or characteristics you want to see in the person you hire for this position?"*

There is an excellent reason to ask this question now. *This may not be your last interview session.* That's right; it is entirely possible you may need to see someone at the central office level for a final review before a contract is offered. If that becomes the case, you will attend that interview with the full knowledge of exactly what this interview team sees as most important to the school. That gives you time to prepare and a relative advantage to any other candidate. You just gave yourself the potential winning edge!

Once this is complete, the interview is over and you are ready to **close the sale!** This is the time to invite the committee to take a few minutes to review your portfolio. Be sure to tell them you will only take a few minutes and stick to that limit.

> *"I have put together a short portfolio for you to see some of the work I have done with students. Would you like to take just a few minutes to look through it with me?"*

Lead the committee through this portfolio and leave everyone in the room with the knowledge that they have just interviewed a first-rate candidate – YOU!

 KEYS TO YOUR RESPONSE:
(See last question)

CONCLUDING THOUGHTS:

There are an infinite number of questions an interview committee might ask; however, the number of topics is more limited. This chapter has provided a variety of questions and offered sound direction as to how you can phrase strong answers. Between these suggestions and your experience, you have an excellent foundation for almost any question.

I strongly suggest you read this chapter a few times. Take the time to sketch out a few ideas and points you want to make in your interview. You have undoubtedly noticed a number of places where it was suggested you pre-think an answer. My advice is that you write those answers on an index card. Keep the question on one side and the answer on the opposite side. Before you attend an interview, review these cards and refresh your memory. Even if you get questions we have not covered, it will surprise you how often you can use the same information on a related topic during your interview. Most interviews have between six and ten questions and rarely last longer than thirty to forty minutes. If you articulate even a few of the sound responses provided in this chapter, you will be a very strong candidate. Now go to that interview with confidence and take the committee by storm!

""In this age, which believes that there is a short cut to everything, the greatest lesson to be learned is that the most difficult way is, in the long run, the easiest."

—Henry Miller, **1951**

THE ELEMENTARY SCHOOL INTERVIEW

8

GENERAL ADVICE ON THE ELEMENTARY SCHOOL INTERVIEW:

Interviewing for an elementary school position is different from middle and high school. Beyond the age difference, elementary school teachers are usually required to teach multiple subjects and manage the core curriculum in a self-contained setting. This carries a wider requirement for him or her to display subject area competence. In addition, class management, momentum, and subject transitions are more complex issues the committee will want to explore in depth.

Within the academic curriculum, interviewers tend to focus on mathematics, reading, and language arts more than science and social studies. The reason is twofold. First, these are the essential process skills that underlie the academic success of all students. Second, they are core areas assessed annually by every state with results reported to the public. Those scores are often used as a barometer to gauge the overall effectiveness of the school and its teachers. You should prepare yourself to answer in-depth questions in these important areas.

Classroom management also receives a great deal of interview attention. There is a little publicized fact you should consider:

SCHOOL FACT #1: *More teachers lose their position due to poor classroom management than sub-standard teaching.*

Of course the areas of classroom instruction and classroom management are interrelated. Good teaching materially reduces management problems, and management difficulties interfere with good teaching. Prepare for questions about your classroom procedures, discipline, and student rules. Identify a few of your better strategies before the interview and have ideas ready to share with your committee. When questions come rapidly from several directions, it is difficult to do your best thinking and craft high quality answers.

Elementary school teachers tend to be more involved with parents and community matters than do teachers at other levels. The interview committee will want to explore your feelings about parental involvement and how you might handle various situations. This is a subject where you should read a few journal articles and listen to what others have to say. Sound thoughts on this topic can go a long way toward placing you at the top of the candidate pool.

Now that you know where school committees and interviewers might focus their attention, take a look at some possible questions and how they can be approached.

SAMPLE ELEMENTARY SCHOOL QUESTIONS AND THEIR ANSWERS:

There has been a continuing debate regarding the whole-language versus phonics approach to teaching reading. Which of these do you support and why?

If you know the prospective school has already adopted and made a large investment in the whole-language approach, you must be prepared to speak on the strategies and advantages of whole-language. Conversely, if you know the school uses a basal, phonics, or literature-based approach you need to speak about these programs with clarity and confidence. Before attending your interview, it will be wise to refresh your mind on the philosophies and instructional approaches of contemporary reading strategies and their reputed strengths and weaknesses.

If you are not certain of a school's specific position regarding reading instruction, it might be best to take the high ground and provide an answer that incorporates more than one school of thought. You might also just ask the principal about the school's preferred approach before you begin your answer. Someone on the committee will probably give you useful information. Your question to the committee might sound like this.

"In approaching reading, I know every child is different and has a learning style that may be benefited by one or both of these teaching approaches. I like using the whole-language approach in some instances because of it... (list two or three strengths), but I also know how a strong understanding of phonics has been shown to help students with essential decoding/encoding skills. Is there a preferred approach here at this school?"

After the committee has provided additional information on their program, you are ready to fashion a more complete answer around the teaching approaches they identified.

Make no mistake, this is an important question, and you need to demonstrate your knowledge about current reading practice. You can expect one or two follow-up questions to more fully explore elements of your answer. Do not be thrown off by such questions, it is a good sign and generally indicates interest in what you have to say.

KEYS TO YOUR RESPONSE:

- Investigate your prospective school and learn whether it is using a whole-language, phonics or blended approach. If you cannot get this information, begin by asking a question that identifies the school's practice.
- Discuss the relative strengths and weaknesses of each reading approach to demonstrate your understanding.
- ***Answer the question.*** Tell the committee which approach to reading you support and give two or three reasons. If you have specific student performance or research information to share, this will add power to your answer.

If you were teaching the second grade, how would you prepare your room for the first day of school?

This is a class management question. An important objective is to underscore a desire to create an *invitational atmosphere* in your classroom. You intend to capitalize on the initial enthusiasm of students when they first return to school. There are numerous ways to decorate and organize a room, and I am certain you have great ideas to share on the topic. Below are just a few first day issues to consider as you design your own approach.

FIRST DAY OF SCHOOL CLASSROOM CONSIDERATIONS
- Student name tags and desk tags
- Welcome bulletin boards
- Posters with classroom guidelines
- Attractive subject area displays
- Textbook and materials arrangements
- Safety concerns
- Daily schedules
- Designated areas for handouts, homework, etc.

One caveat is worth mention. This is a question where most teachers can speak for some length of time. Resist this temptation. You want everyone to know you will make the room warm, inviting and organized. If you have previous experience opening school and have photographs, you might place one or two in your portfolio for later presentation. Be upbeat and enthusiastic. Provide specific examples to punctuate the features you want to include, but take care not to make this a marathon answer.

KEYS TO YOUR RESPONSE:

- Let the committee know of your goal to create an invitational atmosphere as well as a room organized for instruction.
- List six or seven things you will do in the room to reach those goals.
- If you have prepared a room for the opening of school and have pictures, include a few in your interview portfolio.
- Watch your time.

Students at the elementary level are occasionally removed from class for a special subject or other worthwhile concern. How do you handle such "pull-outs" so the student is not left behind in his or her class-work?

"Pull-outs" are an ongoing challenge for many teachers. They create concern for all parties – students, teachers, parents, and administrators. Nonetheless, they are a fact of life, and if this question is asked, you can be certain they are a part of this school. With this question, the committee wants to be assured of two things. First, you are flexible and understand both the value and necessity of pull-out classes. Second, you will take appropriate steps to provide comparable makeup work and assist students who miss your class.

One approach that addresses the problem of pull-outs is to focus your strategy on the idea that every part of your lesson has a concrete, observable learning component. As such, a handout or parallel assignment can often be provided to allow the student to later master necessary objectives and receive full credit. You will also need a procedure to check each student's progress and identify where material may not have been fully understood. Your direct involvement will be needed to monitor those areas.

Be sure you have answered both elements of the question before you conclude your response. It is very easy to simply launch into what you would do to help students make up the work. Your support of the other curriculum areas and a willingness to cooperate with other teachers is an important message and will clearly identify you as a team player.

KEYS TO YOUR RESPONSE:

- Open by telling the committee that you understand the necessity and importance of pull-out programs.
- Outline the way your lessons will center on specific learning goals so compatible assignments or tutorials can be used to address each goal.
- Underscore how the creative use of time can occasionally free you up to directly work with a student who missed a class.
- Describe how you can work with pull-out teachers to minimize the impact of a student's missed class-time.

If you were given freedom to choose, how would you approach the teaching of spelling?

There are many approaches to this important skill, and you can be certain your school has something already in place. The goal of this question is to see how *you* prioritize and approach this issue.

There are two fairly common approaches to the teaching of spelling that you can identify. The first approach is a program that defines an established list of spelling words for students to learn. These words may be part of a published curriculum, taken from a set of commonly misspelled words, or the school may have developed its own spelling list for each grade. In this case, you need to identify ways to teach these words and reinforce their meaningful use. Avoid the archaic "provide the list and test on Friday" format if you can. It

123

is antiquated and been shown ineffective. The consistent use of words in student writing is a more effective way for students to "own" the spelling words they have learned.

The second philosophy or approach is to develop spelling through observation of student writing. In this case practitioners recommend that students and teachers identify words students misspell in their writing and prepare a list of required words for each student. Other methods identify words from student literature selections, self-selected words, or curriculum-specific terms. However the word selection is made, consistent attention over time will raise each student's awareness of the need for accurate spelling. The net result is better student spelling.

In your approach, make the committee aware of your emphasis on word usage as opposed to recitation. Students do not own the word until they can properly use it in their writing. Many teachers will highlight student misspellings in yellow (red is strongly discouraged, so pick some other color) and require students to fix their mistakes before final papers are submitted for a grade. Other methods can be used to identify spelling errors, but a good answer always includes the details of your idea.

KEYS TO YOUR RESPONSE:

- Begin with a discussion of the current philosophies regarding the teaching of spelling.
- Choose a variety of strategies you advocate and explain how they would be employed in your class.
- Emphasize the necessity that students use correct spelling in their writing and explain a few ways you will promote that goal.

What literature do you recommend to third and fourth grade students?

If you hear this question, keep something in mind; the school leadership does not plan to change its curriculum based upon your answer. They only want to establish your familiarity with the good literature and authors available at your intended grade level. This is a fairly common question, and it will be to your advantage to consider an answer before going to the interview.

You might begin your research by reviewing the suggested reading lists available at local libraries and schools. If you can obtain a copy of your school's required or recommended reading list before the interview, you will see books and authors the school currently suggests. That said; do not recite the school's list back to the interviewers. No sense arousing suspicion. Use such information to identify similar but perhaps even better selections. Select authors and books you believe to be first quality. **WARNING:** *Be prepared to tell the interviewers **why** you like a particular author or selection.* I almost always asked that question, and it was surprising how often the candidate was caught off-guard or stumbled for an answer. In some cases, the person merely knew the name or title and had never done much beyond read the book. This mistake can be a costly oversight and may even remove you as a finalist. Do not allow yourself to be caught name-dropping authors or titles.

KEYS TO YOUR RESPONSE:

- Pre-think your answer to this question. It is commonly asked and important.
- If possible, research the district and determine the kinds of reading the school currently endorses.
- Be prepared to cite reasons for your choices of books and authors along with their benefits to children.
- DO NOT NAME BOOKS OR AUTHORS WITH WHICH YOU ARE NOT FULLY CONVERSANT.

Describe how you would teach a lesson on the use of adjectives to a third grade class.

This is another question you can expect to encounter at an interview. Pick a solid lesson you have taught and look at the teacher actions that made the class successful. Keep in mind, the lesson referred to by the question pertains to teaching adjectives. How will you introduce this topic? What activities will you use to teach the necessary information? How will you check for student understanding? What re-teaching strategies will you have? It might be a good idea to have more than one approach to this lesson. Do not forget technology. If you know of websites, writing workshops, or other items, you can work them into your daily plan or learning stations.

You can substitute any curriculum area you like to pre-think an answer to this question. The committee wants to hear what a lesson will look like in your class. How do you determine your objectives? Do you have innovative ways to present information? How do your activities support what you want children to learn? Do

125

you differentiate instruction within your class? Will there be learning stations? Do you use cooperative learning or groups? Will you use technology? How do you check for understanding? What do you do to monitor class/individual progress? This list can go on for some time, but I think you get the idea.

A central area of committee concern in this question is often the activities you plan and the relative ratio of teacher instruction to student involvement. The better candidates will have two or three really innovative and dynamic kinds of activities to use. I suggest you look for some generic plans that describe the activity but are sufficiently flexible to allow numerous topics. This way you can simply substitute whatever subject area is outlined by the question.

ALTERNATE ROUTE CANDIDATE: Even if you have never been in a class or taught a lesson, you can prepare something for this question. Go back to the Chapter Six on Interview Formats where there is an entire section on teaching a "sample lesson." You should choose a topic with which you are familiar and then simply use the model I gave you to create your own teaching episode. The committee is likely to give you a slightly different subject, but at least you will have the general format ready for use. If you carefully prepare and rehearse your lesson, you will be in a position to competently represent yourself on this tough question.

Although it is difficult to fully pre-think an answer to questions like this, if you have a wide range of teaching strategies and activities available you will make an excellent account of yourself. This is a great question on which to shine so let those creative juices flow!

KEYS TO YOUR RESPONSE:

- Know the elements of good teaching and be sure to incorporate several strategies in your response.
- Identify more than one lesson design and describe occasions when each might be used. This variety will win bonus points.
- The question asks about adjectives. Tailor your response accordingly.
- Have a good sample lesson in your portfolio for review.

How would you teach writing to second grade students?

This is an open-ended question and is so complex that entire books have been written on the subject. Recognize that the committee is interested in hearing about your strategies to teach writing. What writing skills will you prioritize and how often will you include writing exercises in your curriculum? What essential skills must a second grade student master?

Before you even begin to think about this answer, do the one thing that only the *very best* candidates will do. Go to the state website and look up the writing standards required for the various grade levels. If you have done a little advance research and have a sound command of state writing requirements, you can nail a question like this and step right in front of the rest of the competition. Begin your answer by providing a few standards and state expectations for students in a few grade levels. From there you can identify your overall goals for student writing based on those expectations.

ALTERNATE ROUTE CANDIDATES: *Take note of this approach.* It is one you can easily adopt, and it will often put you in front of other less prepared competitors. This is an excellent edge and you should take advantage of it!

Continue your answer with a brief description of the writing process. **NOTE:** *Writing Process is a specific strategy and, if you are not aware of its steps, you need to acquaint yourself with those before the interview.* If you are familiar with the writing process, tell the committee how you use this method in your teaching. Talk about the conferencing and editing strategies you employ. Describe the use of writing folders. Explain any efforts you consistently make to integrate other areas of the curriculum into student writing. Provide a description of how and where student writing will be displayed.

Writing rubrics are essential to the editing and assessment process (See Appendix A). If you do not currently have a few rubrics for use in your class, you should get a copy of the holistic scoring rubric from your state. It will be an excellent reference. Most teachers employ a simplified rubric for everyday use. Remember that writing is a developmental skill and grade level considerations need to be taken into account.

This question asks about the second grade, and you should keep your description of the instruction geared to beginning writers. Show the committee you have a measurable, objective means both you and the student can use to assess writing performance and growth.

Writing is a subject that often evokes follow-up questions. As in the other cases, follow-up questions are a sign of interest and another opportunity for you to showcase your depth of understanding. Stay calm and provide concise responses to the new areas the committee wants to explore.

KEYS TO YOUR RESPONSE:

- Give the committee a good overview of what you know of the state writing standards at various grades. Identify 3 or 4 yearly writing goals based on those requirements. **(You too, alternate route candidate!)**
- Provide background information on your knowledge of the writing process.
- Describe specific teaching strategies you intend to employ and describe where writing will be included in your day-to-day instruction.
- Describe any writing rubrics for this grade level and describe how ongoing assessment will be used to determine existing mastery and design future instruction.
- Take time to speak about home communications and tell how parents might be included in the teaching of this important process skill.

> *Describe a difficult classroom management situation you have encountered and what you did to resolve the problem.*

There are two elements of your background the committee is reviewing with this question: (1) your judgment and (2) the diversity of classroom management strategies you employ. Although classroom management questions often refer to behavior, they can also refer to curriculum planning, class organization, or the management of materials. For this question, the majority of candidates will offer a description of a disruptive or defiant student who needed correction. Their solutions tend to outline a traditional isolate, correct, and reinforce strategy that has been given so often it is now redundant. It might be satisfactory, but such answers are predictable and fail to distinguish one's problem solving skill.

As this is an open-ended question and you are free to provide any response you choose, I would suggest you offer a more innovative problem. Choose something that will demonstrate multiple dimensions of your professional ability. For example, have you had an experience with an unmotivated special needs or ADHD student that required you to collaboratively work with a Child Study Team? Did you encounter a highly gifted child who may have been frequently off-task due to boredom? Have you been involved with a "gang related" predicament? Look into your background for a problem that can demonstrate your child-centered approach and how you may have worked with others to resolve a situation. By offering something unique, you will stand out from the group and provide a more memorable response.

ALTERNATE ROUTE CANDIDATE: You will need to substitute the words "might encounter" in place of "have encountered." Again, it is an open field and you are not severely disadvantaged by your lack of classroom experience. I would suggest you either look online for a possible scenario or talk to another teaching professional. A class management question is likely to come up, so it is worth your time and effort to do a little advance planning on an idea. If you can outline a good potential problem with a rational solution, you have done well. A good area for your research might be **bullying**. There is a great deal of information on this and numerous places to find good interventions. Feel free to try one of your own if that topic does not strike your interest, but for goodness' sake, be sure to do *something*.

KEYS TO YOUR RESPONSE:

- Choose an uncommon problem that allows you to showcase more than one dimension of your classroom management skill.
- Demonstrate your ability to employ and work with others on difficult situations.

If you were preparing an agenda for a meeting of the first grade team, what items would you include for discussion?

Principals and interviewers want to examine the kinds of issues you feel need planning by your team and how you will approach the team process. They will want to determine if your management style will fit with other teachers at your prospective grade.

In listening to past answers that have been provided to this question, many candidates simply focused on the contents of the agenda. This is a sound place to begin but does not go far enough. Consider opening on the agenda and listing a few curriculum issues as these are always a worthwhile part of team planning. Within the area of curriculum you can include topics such as writing process skills, team math problems, targeted spelling words, or other issues a grade level team should address. Additional agenda items would include the construction of a calendar of events, newsletters, or home communications. Special events need to be cooperatively planned. Based on your experience or understanding of a particular grade you can add to this list, but you now have a good idea of what needs to be planned.

The committee will *also* be interested to know how you plan to work with other members of your team. This is an invitation to do what other candidates might fail to do; outline plans for your collaboration with the other teachers. Describe how team members will have an opportunity to place their items on the agenda. Will you provide a form or visit people individually? Will you distribute copies of a "tentative agenda" in advance of the meeting? It is important to give ample demonstration of a cooperative approach to the team process. Show the committee how you will make others an integral part of the decision-making that must go on each day. This information will take your answer to a higher level than the average candidate.

KEYS TO YOUR RESPONSE:

- Discuss the need to include your colleagues in forming the agenda and how that will be done.
- Provide a list of the kinds of items that might be included on the agenda.
- Describe your use of a tentative or advance agenda.

What experience have you had with learning centers? Describe one or two you might recommend for a fourth grade class.

You can adjust the grade level indicated in the question to whichever grade you intend to teach as it will not change the nature of the question. The first part of the question is simple and a brief, direct answer will suffice. You have either had experience with learning centers, or you have not. If you have not been directly involved with the concept, you should make that clear and then go on to describe what you have read or know about these centers. Even if you are an **alternate route candidate** with no direct experience whatsoever, the second part of the question provides you an opportunity to recover lost ground.

There are many fine articles on the topic of learning centers, and it is not necessary to cram volumes of information in one answer. When you frame your response, begin with the purposes for which your centers might be designed. For example, your center might be designed to supplement instruction, provide remedial assistance, allow for enrichment activities, or target an area of student interest. Describe what the centers will ask students to do. Will it be an Internet exploration, question-answer program, a packaged software program, or some teacher made activity? Tell the committee specifically what students will learn and how such knowledge is useful. Here is how a simple answer might be phrased.

> *"A great learning center for a fourth grade class deals with the issue of preserving animals that are considered endangered species. <u>An enrichment center</u> could focus on five or six different animals on the endangered species list such as manatees, California condors, polar bears, or some other high interest animal. A student visitor to the center would choose an animal, review its profile card, visit a website, and complete a brief response form. Conservation efforts and clubs can extend the center's work to the real world. The student might even revisit the same station and learn about all six animals if there is sufficient interest and time."*

Before you conclude your example, be sure to identify one or two learning objectives you want the student to master. You do not want to leave the impression this is just a throw-away exercise; there is authentic learning to be gained. You can also highlight any enrichment benefits, how the student work is related to the regular curriculum, and other values you see for students who visit the center. Have fun with this question. It is a great opportunity to showcase innovative ideas.

 ## KEYS TO YOUR RESPONSE:

- Tell the committee of your previous experience or, if you have none, provide your knowledge of this teaching program.
- Give an example of a center you would use and include any learning goals, student activities, and assessments.
- Demonstrate the ability of your learning center to create an authentic, value-added learning experience for students.

 How would you teach fractions to a class of fourth grade students?

Oh dear. Well, you can expect at least one question to explore your instructional ability on math concepts. Mathematics is on every state testing program and annually maps student achievement along with year-to-year progress. Principals are anxious to know a candidate is well founded in his or her content understanding and instructional skill in this important area. In this question, we focus on fractions because it is a concept that so often presents difficulty to children...and sometimes the teachers as well. In analyzing student performance on numerous norm-referenced tests, fractions are frequently listed as a weakness in the group cluster scores. Whatever math concept your question might address, let the committee know you are aware of the test history for students in that particular area of math.

Questions that ask you how you would teach a complicated concept are best attacked through the use of what is called a "**task analysis**" (Appendix B). Your ability to clearly describe this process will be something few other candidates tackle. A task analysis identifies the outcome goal and then the essential sub-skills a student would need to successfully master that concept. Below is an example analysis for dividing fractions.

TASK ANALYSIS

TERMINAL OBJECTIVE: *Students will be able to* <u>*divide fractions*</u> *such as ½ / ¼.*
Essential <u>Subtasks</u> **to master this problem:**
- The student knows how to set up the problem in written form.
- The student knows the multiplication facts.
- The student understands reciprocals and how ¼ becomes 4/1.
- The student knows the procedure of multiplying fractions.

Once you have these subtasks identified, each one becomes a component of your teaching lesson and you can check each for understanding along the way. To add flavor to the lesson design, tell the committee how you will include visual models, guided practice, and designed activities to promote the all-important initial understanding. End with how you plan to use class work and homework to advance proficiency and build retention. It is an exceptional way to teach any difficult concept and will be a homerun on this question!

There may be follow-up questions where the principal will ask how you determine student mastery? What will you do to assist students that may be slow to grasp the concept? How will you extend learning and see that students recognize the use of fractions in their daily lives?

Finally, our answer must stand out from all the others. So if our use of the task analysis has not already accomplished this, we have one more element to add the finishing touch. We conclude by speaking to every principal's concern – student test scores. Describe to the committee that you recognize how important it is that *students* <u>*retain*</u> *this important math skill* on through to the statewide assessment and into future years. Explain that once you have determined mastery of this skill, students will need consistent distributed light practice to maintain their speed and accuracy. Whereas practice would not be a nightly necessity, a problem or two would be routinely provided every week to ten days. When possible, fractions would be included as part of other problems so the concept would not always be seen in isolation. Most candidates will only talk about the initial teaching of this topic. It is rare for them to describe how they will maintain understanding and proficiency. By including this short discussion as the last part of your answer, you will add a memorable element of vital importance to building leaders. These strategies will have the committee's attention and endorsement.

 KEYS TO YOUR RESPONSE:

- Identify one or two of the challenges you see to the teaching of fractions.
- Choose a specific skill involving fractions and describe your task analysis. Specifically identify the sub-learning components you see.
- Illustrate how you would teach one or two of those sub-learning components.
- Identify how you will check for understanding on the terminal goal.
- Propose a system of distributed practices and periodic test questions to maintain student understanding and test preparedness.

 It has been said a teacher has 25 press releases at the end of each school day – one from each student he or she teaches. If true, what would those press releases say about your class?

What do (or will) students really think about you and your class? Keep in mind that parents' perceptions of the school are a direct function of the messages children bring home about your class. If your class is dull, full of routine work, and uninteresting this is what will be described at the nightly dinner table. On the other hand, if your class is full of interesting activities, lively discussions and warmth, this will also be communicated. With your answer, you want to describe an image of your class that will last in the committee members' minds. There are many strategies and teacher dimensions that lead to classrooms kids love. Listed below are some suggestions around which you might organize your own answer.

ALTERNATE ROUTE TEACHER: When you have only limited experience, this is a subject on which you might get stuck. You can always reflect on the great classes where you have been a student and try to identify what made them resonate with you so well. Beyond that, you should try and get a copy of Bob Fried's book, The Passionate Teacher or Doug Lemov's, Teach Like a Champion. Either of these great works will put you on a great track, and they are interesting, easy reads.

CREATING CLASSES STUDENTS LOVE

- **I create a caring, warm, and safe environment**
  Describe how you go about making each student feel special. Tell what you will do to make the child understand you truly care about his or her success in your class – not only academic but personal and social as well. Talk about ways you will build personal connections to each student so they will see you as a trusted mentor and support person. Provide a description of the physical environment that will promote warmth and student identity.

- **I use instructional strategies that promote interest and meaning**
  The committee wants to hear how you will make your instruction exciting for children, so give it to them with clarity and conviction. Talk about some of the novel ways you have presented past lessons or any unique teaching approaches. Describe something you consistently do to add interest and excitement into your daily teaching. Identify ways you link classroom experiences to the world around children. Explain your use of vivid hands-on activities to enhance performance and interest. A key to this question is a clear demonstration that you are a teacher who will use innovative and stimulating strategies in your class. Think about this answer. Even if this specific question is not posed, elements of your pre-thought answer can be included at other times or during your summary at the end of the interview.

As a way to make your answer stand out from others, you might identify a few ways you try to **differentiate lessons** for students with special needs. Students who find the class too easy or well beyond their understanding can become bored and have less than a first-rate experience. The material and daily activities must be arranged in a way that is within everyone's grasp. The short time you spend on this matter will tell the interviewers you consider *all children* in your planning and are willing to take the extra steps required to insure each child's welfare. What a great message! It is one many candidates will miss, so take advantage of the opportunity. Most importantly, deliver this answer with energy and enthusiasm. A candidate who just monotones this response with a few ideas has no chance to convince the committee their classroom will be any different. But if you follow these simple suggestions, it will be *your* answer that will be talked about when the committee meets to make their final selection!

KEYS TO YOUR RESPONSE:

- If you are an **alternate route candidate** and need help, read books by Robert Fried or Doug Lemov. **(Both books are strongly recommended for your preparation.)**
- Describe your personal qualities and the elements of your teaching style that will create a warm, caring, child-centered classroom.
- Underscore the ways in which you will produce meaningful, high-interest lessons that promote student involvement.
- List a variety of ways you will differentiate instructional patterns and expectations to meet the needs of children with varied abilities.

> *How will you help students see the real world connections that relate to the concepts and skills you are teaching?*

This is an extension of the last question, but it often appears as a separate item. Everyone finds more meaning in new learning when he or she sees how the information relates to his or her own world. For that reason, you want the committee to know how you will make this connection come to life in your class. Field trips, outside speakers, real-life simulations, and technology can be powerful tools to link the daily learning experiences to the everyday lives of children. Home projects and cooperative adventures can also add dimension to the teaching. Let your creative thinking flow and give the committee a real insight on how you will add purpose and worthwhile learning as a part of every class.

If you are just finishing student teaching or are engaged in current class work, you may have already designed a sparkling unit that has lots of bells and whistles. Do not be afraid to refer to this and use it if you believe it highlights the connections we want.

ALTERNATE ROUTE CANDIDATE: If you have had only limited or no classroom teaching experience, think back to exciting units or lessons where you were a student and choose a few good examples. The provision of a practical example for each suggested method that connects your lesson to the real world is a commanding way to make your point.

This is an important question, and you should introduce as much enthusiasm into your answer as possible. Although the concrete suggestions you provide in your answer are important, the excitement you generate in your delivery can also help carry the day. As mentioned above, even the best teaching, if it is described in a lackluster manner, will be flat and unlikely to inspire your listeners. Upbeat and enthusiastic deliveries will enliven the listeners, and you will see the positive expressions around the table. Excitement is contagious and will transfer right to the committee.

 KEYS TO YOUR RESPONSE:

- Specify how you will connect the outside world to your daily teaching.
- Tell the committee how you will use authentic learning, real world problems, and high interest activities to provide purpose to every lesson.
- Give a brief description of a purpose driven lesson or unit your students thought (or will think) highly worthwhile.
- BE ENTHUSIASTIC AND UPBEAT IN YOUR DELIVERY.

CONCLUDING THOUGHTS:

The topic areas an elementary teacher will need to address can cover a broad range of subjects and skills. This chapter has provided good examples of questions you may encounter and offered insight on the professional qualities a principal might want to explore. A thought to keep at the forefront of your thinking is this: *the outstanding elementary school teacher is a highly child-centered, instructionally skilled, and motivated individual.* If by the end of this interview, you have been able to convey a clear sense of these qualities to the interview committee, you will be one of those receiving final consideration for the post. Good luck in your search!

THE MIDDLE SCHOOL INTERVIEW

GENERAL ADVICE ON THE
MIDDLE SCHOOL INTERVIEW:

Middle schools have a different setting and mission from elementary or high schools. The student population is comprised of students who are going through puberty, sociologic conflict, and a myriad of other transitional dilemmas related to the move from childhood to adulthood. As a result, every teacher interviewing for a middle school position must be aware of these issues and the means by which he or she can help students through this difficult time. In your interview there will be a variety of questions designed to test your knowledge of student-related issues, unique middle school programs, and instructional strategies appropriate to the age group.

Some states offer certificates for middle level teaching, and their teacher training institutions offer degree programs tailored to the middle school teacher. Colleges and universities in other states, have insufficient course work to offer even a minor in the middle school area. If you seek a middle school teaching position, you will do well to undertake college coursework that focuses on middle school students. If you can obtain a formal degree or certificate, it is even better. If no middle school certificate is offered in your state, check to determine what grade levels your certificate covers.

Regardless of your middle school coursework, you will be able to present a strong candidacy once you have reviewed and mastered the information provided in this chapter. Two of the more important factors will be your enthusiasm to teach at the middle school and the confidence with which you answer a few basic questions. Let's look at questions you might be asked at a middle school interview.

SAMPLE MIDDLE SCHOOL QUESTIONS AND THEIR ANSWERS:

What do you consider the mission of a middle school?

This question can be tricky because there seems to be differences of opinion among schools as to how their specific mission is described. You can help yourself by conducting advance research on your school. If the prospective school has a handbook for parents, it will generally contain a mission statement and information on that school's specific goals for students. Although those statements are not the real answer to this question, they can help identify things the school sees as important.

The following list contains a number of central tenets that contemporary middle schools generally find important. You should use these ideas to help organize your thoughts and prepare persuasive answers to this and other questions you will be asked.

CENTRAL THEMES OF TODAY'S MIDDLE SCHOOLS

- Students must receive a strong foundation of core knowledge.
- Students must be proficient in process skills such as reading, mathematics, writing, and problem solving.
- Students need help to cope with the social and emotional changes that occur during this time of life.
- Middle schools must help cultivate the growth of strong character and ethical values.
- Students must be exposed to a wide variety of learning experiences and content areas.
- Students must see and experience connections between what they are learning in school and the real world around them.

This is not the all-inclusive list of middle schools goals, but rather a selection of points around which there seems to be consensus. There is one other point where most middle school principals agree; **the primary role of the middle school is not to "prepare students for high school."** If a middle school is effective in carrying out its mission, students *will* be prepared for high school, but middle school goals encompass a much wider vision.

As you shape your answer, open with a short discussion of a few of the above themes. Add an illustration supporting points you make to clarify your meaning.

For example:

> *"There are a number of areas a middle school mission might address. One of the first items would be attending to the social and emotional development of adolescents. Advisory programs are a good example of how middle schools attempt to address this goal. Developing teenagers can derive a significant benefit from ongoing mentorship by responsible adults in the school."*

This statement immediately places you on target with a central issue and establishes your awareness of an important middle school program. Before concluding your answer, add a statement that you would need to better understand the characteristics of students in this school before you could offer specific recommendations on classroom programs.

The committee wants to know if you understand what makes a middle school setting unique. Whether you can frame the ultimate mission statement is not as important as your ability to identify central issues with a few specific programs. Do this and you will more than satisfy the committee. **CAUTION:** *This is another question that can elicit a long answer.* For that reason, I suggest you carefully time yourself to avoid rambling. Discussion of two or three recommended items will convince everyone of your middle school knowledge. That is your goal.

KEYS TO YOUR RESPONSE:

- Conduct advance research on your school and review parent or student handbooks for key information.
- Review the central themes listed in this section along with others you find and open with a brief discussion of a few well-supported ideas.
- Link specific practices or programs that relate to each central theme you offer.
- End with a statement of your commitment to work with the total child and not just subject matter.

The literature on middle schools frequently talks about the importance of "character and values" education for students at the middle school level. If you had to choose one over the other, which do you feel is more important – teaching academics or teaching values and character?

139

Oh brother, this is a loaded question! Interestingly, it was one of the first questions asked of me at an interview for a principal's position. This may initially appear to be one of those mousetrap questions where whichever component you choose, you run the risk of being in error. The quandary created by this concern has caused a number of candidates to get tangled in their logic by trying to divine what the committee wanted to hear. Attempting to determine what the committee wants to hear is almost always the wrong approach and likely to lead down a dangerously slippery path. *In all cases and for all questions, it is best to provide your best, <u>most honest</u> response and let the chips fall where they may.* Even if a committee member should disagree, you will be respected for your candor and the courage of your convictions.

How then do we approach *this* question? The important thing to remember is that you are applying to a middle school. You can be certain the issue of character and values is seen as critically important. The reason for such emphasis is an assumption that people make important life decisions based on their system of values and in keeping with their character. During the middle school years, a significant portion of a person's character and values matures. Failure to provide proper priority to these important areas can lead to calamitous results. I once had a candidate take an interesting approach in responding to this question by turning it around and asking the following question of the committee.

> *"You ask an interesting question, but what would we prefer? Would we rather a student who knows the significance of the Stamp Act develop into a sociopath or would we prefer a well valued, interested student who missed the significance of the Stamp Act and had to learn it later?"*

This response was clearly oversimplified, but it made a very effective point and had a number of committee members nodding in agreement.

In your answer it might be best to lead with the importance of values and character with the addition of a strong statement in support of a solid academic program as the other main ingredient in a first class education. No school worth its certification can ignore its central responsibility to provide a sound, visionary academic program; however, a school would be remiss if it provided an academic background without sufficient attention to the issues of developing adolescents.

Unless stated as an either/or question, this approach allows you to have your cake and eat it too. The trick is to emphasize your understanding of the importance of both dimensions. If, as is the case here, the question is posed as an either/or situation, then you must choose the dimension you feel most represents your philosophy. The point can be successfully argued either way. Many principals suggest the values and character side is safer for a middle school interview. It is extremely important that sound values, healthy habits of mind, and honest character are reinforced during the adolescent years. Ideals such as perseverance, work ethic, tolerance, promptness, responsibility, and patriotism are all recognized as worthwhile values for adolescents to cultivate. You can conclude by returning to a statement on the difficulty of the question because both issues are so important.

KEYS TO YOUR RESPONSE:

- Begin with a short discussion of how and why you see each issue as critically important.
- Be sure to emphasize the role values and character play in the decision-making processes of developing adolescents.
- Select the dimension that best fits your philosophy and expand on why it would have central significance in your teaching.
- Conclude by returning to your view that middle school children have both an academic and values-rich education.

> *What important qualities should new teachers have to effectively work on a teaching team?*

In other words, will your personality and teaching style fit the other personalities on our intended team? This is an important issue and can even be a knock out question. The school must hire someone they are confident will be a good fit to the personalities, work styles, and educational philosophies of the other teachers on the team. Even if you convince everyone you are a good instructional practitioner, should someone suspect you will not be a good team member it is unlikely you will get the position.

Below are a few qualities that lead to solid professional relationships and around which a good answer can be given. You should reflect on your own personality, philosophy, and working style and identify how you possess these characteristics.

BUILDING PROFESSIONAL RELATIONSHIPS
- ***Flexibility.*** Can you adjust your thinking to the wide variety of ideas, plans, and positions sure to arise from other team members?
- ***Chemistry.*** This element is concerned with a person's ability to get along with others. Do you have the "people skills" required to make everyone feel at ease in

141

your company? Can opposing ideas be offered and discussed without tension? This is one of the more important dimensions because poor chemistry can undermine your effectiveness in other areas.

- *Perseverance.* When there is a project or team initiative underway, will you have the endurance to see the project through to its full conclusion?

- *Problem solving.* Teams need someone with good, fresh thinking who can formulate multiple solutions to problems and help decide on a sound course of action.

- *Listening and communication.* These skills are listed together because listening is an important *part of* communication. One must communicate clear and concise thoughts, but he or she must also be a good listener when the ideas of others are presented.

- *Reliability.* If you are supposed to be at a team duty or meeting, will you be there on time and ready? If you have something to do, will it be well done? The team needs to feel confident they can depend on you.

There are other qualities, and you can add a few of your own. Choose three or four of your better qualities from this list and provide a discussion of how they apply to you. Where possible, a personal anecdote or story can add color to your response. If you have had experience working on a team, talk about the positive elements of that work. If you can tie your experiences to any dimensions on the list, you will improve the validity of your statement.

End with a more general discussion of your commitment to the team effort. Your dedication and energy can make a good team even better and you will give 110% to achieving that goal. If you can convince the committee members you are someone who works well with others and everyone will be happy to have you on their team, you have answered the question well.

ALTERNATE ROUTE CANDIDATE: It is unlikely that you will have much if any experience working with a school team or other teaching groups. However, you have almost certainly had work or classroom experiences where you were a part of a team. Those work just fine to highlight your human relations skills. Describe any achievements of teams on which you served. Such success will underscore your ability to effectively work toward a common goal.

KEYS TO YOUR RESPONSE:

- Begin by mentioning four or five of the personal qualities required for good team participation.
- Choose qualities where you are strongest and provide a short discussion of each. If you can describe a practical example, do so.
- End with a statement about your commitment to the success of the team and the diligence you will use to make that success a reality.

What do you see as critical issues a good team of teachers must consider during their common planning period?

The principal wants to determine what you know about how teams and the team planning process are related. Many schools have specific planning formats for team meetings, and you might ask if such is the case at this school.

COMMON THINGS A GOOD TEAM MUST PLAN
- Curriculum placement for academic units
- Interdisciplinary concerns or integrated teaching
- Field trips and related outside experiences
- Advisory activities
- Homework
- Class test schedules
- State-test preparation
- Monthly calendars
- Parent communications
- Student related problems
- Social events

Begin with an overview of as many of these items as you can remember. If you know of other items from previous experience, include some of those as well. There is no minimum or maximum number of items required, but you must watch your time. The best answer will concisely identify a few items and then briefly describe the issues that might be discussed. For example, if you list interdisciplinary integration, then identify activities you would place on your calendar. Discuss how "guiding questions" would be developed for a major teaching unit. (Be aware that the term "guiding questions" has

143

a specific meaning. If you are unsure of its definition, either choose something else or look at work from Heidi Hayes Jacobs, Columbia University for more information.) Provide sufficient detail to show that you think things through, but do not go on so long that you begin to hear light snoring from the gallery.

End with a statement that you understand how the team is responsible for the educational program for its students. The committee will ask follow-up questions on any areas they consider important. Try to relax – if you have reviewed our discussion of this question, you will give an excellent answer.

KEYS TO YOUR RESPONSE:

- Start by providing a list of items to which the team should attend to in the planning process.
- Select a few items from your initial list and add an in-depth discussion of how the planning should take place.
- Provide examples of your work on teams in the past.
- End with a general statement on the necessity of good planning and the team's responsibility to plan the entire program for students in its charge.

How familiar are you with interdisciplinary units and how would you plan to include these learning experiences in your class?

Integrated instruction or interdisciplinary units have become more common in the pedagogy of middle schools over recent years. The concept refers to units of study where two or more disciplines are combined, and the concepts learned in one discipline are similar enough to enhance those taught in the others. For example, the English class might study, To Kill a Mockingbird while students learn the rules of evidence and argument in their Social Studies class. The concepts of evidence and argument are then employed to analyze the legal case presented in the novel. Students apply what they learn in Social Studies to Language Arts and both disciplines receive benefit.However, the question asks that you also discuss how you would *plan* interdisciplinary teaching in your class. You can select a few from the list offered here.

PLANNING CONSIDERATIONS FOR INTERDISCIPLINARY UNITS
- Describe how you will use the team-planning period to develop curriculum maps or teaching calendars.
- Identify where time frames might be adjusted to facilitate integrated teaching.
- Develop "guiding questions" and group activities that will direct student learning and assessment.
- Describe how assessment will take place and what quality control procedures will monitor the unit.

These planning steps constitute a good answer for you to offer. As the better candidate, explain how you might incorporate important concepts from other subjects into your own *daily* teaching. This response might sound something like the following:

> *"The large interdisciplinary units are excellent, and I am eager to see what my team and I can plan in that area. I should add, however, that I intend to integrate other subjects into my daily teaching on a regular basis. For example, when I am teaching students about conservation, I can ask them to research some of the literature and history of this movement to reinforce the real-world purpose of our study. This involves both social studies and literature, and students can see how different subjects work hand in hand."*

If you can provide an example such as this, it will be well received and move your answer ahead of others. If you think about it, I am sure there are things you can envision to integrate different subjects in your teaching. Add those strategies to the others and move toward the top of the class.

NOTE: *If you have a well-planned interdisciplinary unit already completed from previous coursework or school experience, includes a one-page summary in your interview portfolio.*

<u>KEYS TO YOUR RESPONSE:</u>

- Open your answer with a description of what you know on the subject of integrated or interdisciplinary instruction.
- Provide an example of a unit you have already taught.
- Describe the planning that is necessary to create a new unit.

- End by demonstrating how you independently integrate instruction in your class on a more regular basis.
- DO NOT FORGET TO ADD A SAMPLE TO YOUR INTERVIEW PORTFOLIO IF YOU HAVE ONE.

What role, if any, would parents have regarding the education of their student in your class? What would you do to produce and nourish productive parent involvement?

Experience and research suggests that as children move through the grades, parent participation in the school tends to decline. Middle school is traditionally a time when such involvement begins to diminish. Parents stay relatively close to their child's school experience through about sixth grade, but in grades seven and eight parent participation wanes. Some parental detachment is understandable because adolescents begin to seek more independence. That said; too little parent involvement is not good. This question requires you to identify ways you plan to increase parent communication and involvement. Here are a few ideas to consider for your answer.

TEACHER ACTIONS LEADING TO INCREASED PARENT INVOLVEMENT

- ***Class letters*** are mailed at the beginning of units to provide information on upcoming lessons and what parents can expect at home.
- ***Phone calls*** are made to alert parents to positive class behavior or results. Parents like to receive "good news" phone calls. These can take under a minute, but their effect is most encouraging.
- ***Email*** is now widely used and in many schools comprises the bulk of communication with the home. Newsletters, announcements, and class information can be efficiently sent to every home using this resource!
- ***Homework hotlines and school websites*** are used to keep everyone informed of assignments, school news, and calendars. Your prospective school is likely to have their own website.
- ***Parents are invited to special class presentations or luncheons*** that the students organize. If students are to make presentations of their projects to the class, parents can be invited for the day.
- ***Special evening programs***. Cooperative programs that involve both parents and students such as "Math Counts" or "Science Night" can be organized. One teacher had the parents come in for a <u>Chef's Training</u> class that the *students taught!* The stomach is a wonderful tool for winning friends – just ask me.

- **Student letters to parents**. The *students* write a short letter about the exciting things they are doing in class and mail it home. Since e-mail is now easily available, this can be another avenue.
- **Great Work Postcards**. The teacher keeps a pack of post cards handy, and when a student contributes something special or completes exemplary work, the card is filled out and mailed. The students can address two or three cards that you keep. This reduces clerical problems.

You can see how this might work. Show the committee you have some ideas and ingenuity of your own to increase parent involvement. Let the committee know that you recognize the role of the parent in promoting the success of the student in your class. Tell them you plan an active role for the home to promote their student's success. You need parents to stay abreast of homework, communicate on important family issues, serve as a class parent, or even chaperone events. You want parents to keep education a family priority. Such goals are easy to recite, but you need workable strategies to promote these relationships. A well-constructed plan will move you ahead of other candidates who only "talk the talk."

This is a lot of information to consider, but the following is how an answer might be phrased. Use this sample to shape an answer of your own when you are faced with a question on this topic.

> *"I realize these things are sometimes easier said than done; however, I do have some strategies in mind to promote parent involvement. First, I want to establish a pattern of positive communications to put the parent at ease with our contacts. For that reason, I call each parent at least once a quarter with a positive report regarding his or her child. Second, I plan to have a few special classroom events where students will do presentations and parents will be invited to attend. In addition, I intend to involve myself in the PTO and work with parents where they see me in a different role.*

As with many of the suggested answers, a short, succinct listing of two or three clear points can be used to good effect. Your answer might employ different involvement strategies and you should only include those where you are familiar enough to provide a full description. Everyone must see that you are attentive to the teacher's role in this effort. Leave the committee with the understanding you will take specific steps to help every parent be a part of their son's or daughter's education.

KEYS TO YOUR RESPONSE:

- Begin with your recognition of the trend for parent involvement to decrease as students get older.
- List the kinds of activities you and your team might collectively take to maintain parent support and participation.
- Identify ways you will establish a positive pattern of communication with each home.
- Conclude with a restatement of your understanding of the important contributions parents can make in the success of their student.

Research has indicated that many disaffected students were "turned off" to education during their middle school years. What will you do to prevent this from happening in your class?

Should you uncover the definitive answer to this question, please e-mail me immediately so we can co-author a book and make a great deal of money. The complexity of the issue notwithstanding, this question is one that principals like to ask.

H. L. Mencken once wisely said, *"To every complex problem, there are a host of simple solutions – all of which are wrong,"* and so it is with this question. Nonetheless, it is on the table, and we must deal with it by presenting ways to keep our class interesting and as motivating as possible.

Through the work of Hunter, Sapphire, Gardner, Lemov and others, numerous strategies have been identified that increase student interest, participation, and purposeful learning. This question presents an opportunity for us to stand on the shoulders of these giants in education and use their ideas to describe how we will create the kind of classes students want to see.

KEY INTERVIEW STRATEGY: *Consider ways to make your point with precision as opposed to volume.* Good answers are made better when you speak in specific terms. To accomplish this, phrase an answer that contains three or four central ideas around which specific activities are designed. It might sound like the following:

"I realize middle schools have a special responsibility to maintain student involvement. In my view, some of the things most responsible for student detachment from their

education include: (1) a sense that school has nothing worthwhile for them, (2) dull and boring classes, and (3) a continuing series of negative experiences or failure in past classes."

This approach breaks the question into three very important, manageable pieces. Address each piece along with a strategy to deal with the identified problem. *An exhaustive number of strategies for each issue is not warranted or desired.* One or two will convince everyone you are on the right track.

"First, I want to address the boring, uninspired lessons about which students continuously complain. I can overcome such complaints by breaking each lesson into several different parts and include two or three hands-on activities to keep students moving and involved. This variety of teaching platforms will promote interest and student involvement. Beyond that, novelty, humor, and well-crafted instructional episodes will be used to focus their minds on the joy of learning.

Use what you know from past experiences, methods courses, workshops, or inspirational teachers from your personal history. Bring out your best thinking and spice the answer with specific teaching examples whenever possible. **TIP:** *If you have a portfolio to show, come back to answers like this and use one of your unit designs to place an exclamation point to the end of the presentation.*

Many applicants will focus all their attention on the instructional side of this issue. They miss the all-important affective dimension of this problem. We can do better. Place the interview committee on notice that, in your opinion, **students do not become disaffected *only* because of uninspired teaching.** Very often, there is also a history of school failures, a lack of school involvement, a sense of isolation, and a perception that teachers do not care that alienates students from school. Be prepared to talk about the importance of these affective concerns and identify concrete teacher actions you intend to undertake to minimize such negative experiences in your class. For example:

"We all know how consistent patterns of failing grades can de-motivate students and shut down their enthusiasm to learn. My goal is to consistently promote legitimate success for every student. The focus cannot only be on grades, for it is also necessary to build each student's self-confidence. Nothing breeds success like success, and I intend to use a regular pattern of successful class experiences as a springboard to higher motivation."

You may select a different dimension from your philosophy, but these few sentences will leave the committee with a good feeling about your insight. In any middle school interview, you are well served by that result!

KEYS TO YOUR RESPONSE:

- Begin the response by defining a few central *causes* of disaffected youth in school.
- Provide two or three solid *strategies* you will use in your classes to minimize the probability those causes will present themselves.
- Close your answer by describing specific ways you intend to *address the affective issues* that underlie disaffected behavior.

Bullying is a very common problem in middle schools. To students who are on the receiving end of abuse, it is educationally debilitating. What role do teachers play in minimizing this behavior in students?

This problem has reached epidemic proportion. Schools are highly focused on the issue, and a question in this area can be expected. Open your answer with the following: **RULE #1:** *The role of the teacher is central to the solution of this problem.* The teacher must take the initiative to prevent and defuse unkindness in the classroom. *Bullies are present in every school and rely on the failure of adults to intervene.* Explain how you will exercise a policy of zero-tolerance to unkind behavior. You will put a stop to put-downs, insults, or other cruel remarks. Courtesy and supportive behavior will be modeled, required, and expected from everyone. Tell the principal you intend to be at your door between classes to watch hallway activity (a favorite place for bullies to harass others) and put a fast stop to any questionable behavior.

Go on to talk about the values and character issues you would like to address during homeroom, advisory or activity periods. Most middle schools have time when teachers and teams can work on social issues. Discuss how your team can teach students the important values of tolerance, kindness, and mutual support. There are many commonly accepted values to address, and you can be sure the committee will be interested in hearing about those that interest you. A proactive approach to prevention as opposed to just a reactive response will work well in this answer.

Close with a statement about your concern for the disastrous consequences that can arise when harassment and bullying are left un-addressed. Newspapers have chronicled a number of such incidents over the last years. A common element in students who bully and prey on others is their ability to avoid adult interference. Illustrate your knowledge of this fact and provide assurance this will not be the case in your class.

KEYS TO YOUR RESPONSE:

- Begin with a statement of your awareness regarding the issues driving the problem and tell how the teacher must play a key role in their prevention.
- List specific steps you plan to take in your class to promote an atmosphere of respect and safety.
- State your recognition of harassment as a central element in many school tragedies. Add your intent to reduce this problem in your class.
- Provide assurance that you will be anxious to assist in any school-wide or team efforts to reduce student harassment or unkindness.

Describe how your grading practices can be adapted to make adjustments for students with special needs.

Look at what this question asks and what it does not ask. It asks about your grading policy for "special needs students." It does not ask you to describe your entire grading policy. The committee wants to determine your flexibility regarding special needs students and what grading strategies you intend to employ.

First, assure everyone you recognize how multiple factors should be considered before settling on an assessment strategy for a special-needs student. You need to speak with the case manager about the student's IEP, specific goals, and assessment practices that may have been used in the past. You want to develop a strategy in cooperation with the case manager so it can be a mutual effort.

From this point you can catalog specific evaluation strategies such as authentic tasks, conferences, drawings, small group projects, open-notebook questions, or other options that allow the student to demonstrate his or her proficiency. Suggest that in some cases a student goal may be fulfilled by his or her mere participation.

The important message to convey is how grading will be completed with expertise and compassion. Each student will be viewed individually and progress will be measured in a realistic manner.

KEYS TO YOUR RESPONSE:

- *Focus* your answer on flexible, wide ranging grading practices for special needs students.
- Outline how you and the case manager will determine when and where modifications to grade practice are in the interest of the student.
- List a variety of grade strategies you employ and how you design an assessment plan in collaboration with the student's case manager.
- End with a commitment to view each student as an individual and utilize a compassionate and realistic approach to determine his or her grade.

CONCLUDING THOUGHTS:

This chapter has a great deal of information. It is impractical to attempt full recall. Once you have read the information, go back to the **KEYS TO YOUR RESPONSE** segments and revisit those ideas. If you are unclear of specific points, you can reexamine the more complete discussion in the text. If you have a computer, you may wish to select a variety of questions and enter them with the main elements of your answer. These can be printed out later and provide a study sheet or individual note cards.

Middle schools are exciting places with high-energy students and innovative programs. When you interview, understand the committee is looking for a person who is committed to the middle school and the young adolescent student. If your heart is really at the high school or elementary school, you should focus your attention on interviewing for those jobs. Some candidates apply for middle school positions because they need a job and a middle school teaching position was listed in the newspaper. Since their certificate covers the middle school, an application was sent. For those who follow this strategy, there is **BAD NEWS:** *A person's true feelings and lack of commitment to middle school education will always come across during an interview, and one is not likely to do well if that happens.* On the other hand, if middle school is just what you want, make sure the committee is aware of this preference. Enthusiasm coupled with a few good answers can make all the difference. So, you now have the skills – *Get that Interview and Get Hired!*

THE HIGH SCHOOL INTERVIEW

10

GENERAL ADVICE ON THE HIGH SCHOOL INTERVIEW:

This chapter provides questions commonly found in interviews for a high school or 7-12 position. Please note that the issues or qualities addressed by these questions are not necessarily exclusive to the high school but are ordinarily of slightly higher interest to committees at a secondary level. The items included have come from several sources. Many are the questions I used over years of leading district and high school interview teams, while others are from principals around the country. In selecting the questions, only those frequently asked or likely to be part of an actual interview are included. A few more difficult questions will help you prepare for those longer, more in-depth interviews.

When interviewing for positions at the secondary level, you should recognize the relative isolation of such teachers. High school teachers are organized into departments of specific subject areas where teaching teams are rarely used, and interdisciplinary planning is uncommon. When teachers do work together, it is generally an informal arrangement between colleagues rather than a regularly scheduled event. The relevance of such isolation is your need to identify how you will reach out and establish communication with other professionals. School officials will take note of your spirit of team involvement.

High school interviewers will have a higher interest in identifying your subject matter competence and instructional skills, and you are likely to encounter fewer child-centered questions than in an elementary or middle school interview. This statement should not be construed to mean that high schools are *disinterested* in student-centered teaching. The elementary and middle school chapters contained many extremely compelling answers describing a student centered teaching stance, and you will certainly find these ideas useful. Simply realize that high school questions more naturally tend to focus on content and instruction.

SAMPLE HIGH SCHOOL QUESTIONS AND THEIR ANSWERS:

Seniors who have already been accepted by colleges often believe it is no longer necessary to put forth their best efforts. What steps would you take to prevent this let down?

This is a common problem in high schools, and the wise candidate is ready for questions on *motivation.* A brush up on variables that affect the area of motivation and a complete discussion of this is in an earlier chapter. An excellent approach to questions on high school motivation is to identify a few specific strategies and activities to promote active student engagement.

Consider opening with a description of the differences between extrinsic rewards such as college acceptance or GPA and intrinsic rewards such as personal interest or the satisfaction of success. This introduction sets up an opportunity for you to catalog specific steps to raise student awareness of how process skills learned in your class will transfer to success in both college and later life.

Place the committee on notice that you see the problem presented by the question as an outgrowth of weak motivation rather than student complacency. By recasting the question in this way, you will have seized control of a more manageable response strategy.

KEY INTERVIEW STRATEGY: *In cases where an answer offers a variety of good steps you can take, identify the best ideas and deliver them in concise statements one after the other.*

Below are a number of variables that can positively affect student motivation in older students. Choose two or three that fit your teaching stance and construct a compact, hard-hitting plan of action. The best deliveries identify the strategy, give a brief discussion of its importance, and then provide a practical example – one, two, three, and move on. We will look at how this might sound in a moment, but below are a few good ways to motivate high school students.

METHODS TO INCREASE MOTIVATION

- Use attention grabbing lesson designs such as discovery, surprise, or novelty.
- Connect important lesson components to real-life or worthwhile skills.
- Establish a classroom climate of patience, support, and individual care.
- Provide meaningful (the student values it) rewards for successful performance.
- Allow for frequent opportunities to recognize students for success.
- Increase accountability by requiring frequent progress checks and student performance.
- Allow for student choice on the kinds of assignments, study topics, or assessment requirements.
- Increase the quantity of innovative and enjoyable activities.

Research has shown all of the above strategies promote student interest and engagement. You must simply identify a few around which to build a sharp, high impact response. Remember; use the above outlined three step delivery. Look at this sample.

"To keep students involved toward the end of the year, I like to motivate them through the use of choice. This is a strong motivator because seniors seem to like the idea they are directing their lives and have control. I accomplish this in two ways. First, as a group we look through the last units of the book and select the ones that seem most profitable to study and prepare for college. Second, I supply a number of ways students can study the information and a few activities from which they can choose. Through having control, students are required to act in a "college-like" way and assume more personal responsibility. That's the goal!"

Did you see it? One, two, three, and move on. Look at the answer again and identify the recommended three-step tactic. Its strength comes from its laser-like focus on the issue presented by the question. Keep in mind the committee asked about "college bound" students. Extra effort was taken to relate the answer directly to that group.

Think through the outlined suggestions and you will find these suggested actions are complimentary and can be manipulated to work together. Conclude by noting how no single strategy works in every case or with every student. But, as you come to know your students more fully, you will be in a better position to select those practices most likely to match their personality and needs.

KEYS TO YOUR RESPONSE:

- Note the differences between extrinsic and intrinsic rewards. Then describe how you will increase student awareness of how such skills transfer to college work.
- Review a variety of motivation strategies and select two or three you feel offer the most impact. Use our 1-2-3 delivery strategy.
- End with a statement of your need to know the students and select variables that fit the characteristics of those individuals.

If we examined your student grade distribution in your last school, what would we find?

Here is a question on grades and be careful with your answer. Grades are a serious business in high school because they affect such things as GPA, college admittance, sports eligibility, and access to elite groups such as the honor society. With this question, many an interviewee assumes the real question being asked is "how many failing grades were given in his or her classes?" **AVOID THE TRAP!** *Do not focus your answer on the low end of the grade spectrum. Balance your response so that you address <u>both</u> ends of the grade curve.* Of course, the committee will be concerned if you tell them there was a ten or fifteen percent failure rate. In fact, such an answer might even knock you out of the race. But grades affect a variety of things and strong student performance is a central expectation of principals. **The more astute candidate will focus on the <u>upper end</u> of the grade scale and speak to how students not only pass, but also prosper in his or her class.**

The answer to this question need not be long. In fact, precision will help maximize the power of your response. There is nothing like an extended philosophy speech on academic rigor to put the committee into its own state of rigor mortis. Long-winded philosophy speeches are generally considered the private domain of superintendents on the opening days of school. You need only demonstrate concern for student success and a commitment to a strong academic program.

A good place to start any answer on grade distribution is to draw a distinction between the common, bell curve model of grading and the approach you will take in your class. Hans Andersen, Professor of Education at Indiana University, has made a particular point of describing how the bell curve is an inappropriate model for education (Andersen, 1970). When the goal is student mastery, there is an expectation that students *will* learn what we teach. In successful teaching, a grade distribution curve will have a sharp skew to the right because of the high success rate. Look how you might phrase this concept:

"In education we have for many years accepted the bell shaped curve as the norm for grade distributions. In my class, the traditional normal curve is not appropriate. First, a perfect bell shaped distribution often describes the results of random activity. My teaching and student success is certainly not a random activity. Second, I intend to take the necessary steps to insure that the majority of my students are learning enough to be at the B or A end of the grade spectrum. Moreover, I am unhappy if <u>anyone</u> attains only a D or F level of proficiency! Those numbers I diligently try to keep at zero!"

In these half dozen or so sentences, you have answered the central issue posed in the question. The principal sees a teacher with a sound philosophy and commitment to student achievement. But we are not quite done.

Now move to the second phase of this answer and provide *practical measures* to meet this goal. Good teachers take numerous steps to promote successful learning. Select a few from your background or training and provide one or two anecdotes that show how you have maintained high student performance in the past. That statement can sound like this:

"Each quarter I included an outside assignment that was directly linked to material we had learned in class. The projects were divided into two levels of difficulty, and students could choose one that met their needs. Students knew exactly what was expected and how to achieve an "A." I supplied rubrics, anchor papers, and models to demonstrate precisely what I wanted. As projects went forward, I held conferences and provided specific feedback to help each student remain on track. The conferences also let me know who needed more help. By using this approach, I have consistently been able to help students attain a legitimate high level of success and still maintain a high level of academic rigor."

The compact nature of this response is what we want. The statement provides five separate student success builders in one short statement. And did you notice the last sentence? "Maintain a high level of academic rigor." That is a very important item. Anyone can insure better success by "dumbing down" the content. You have now put the principal on notice that you intend the opposite; increase the academic rigor! It is an **excellent** point to make.

Think about what you have already done or intend to do. Identify strategies you see as the most successful or promising. What have you really done to help students succeed? Some possibilities include before or after-school help sessions, peer tutoring, outside credit, retakes on work that was below a B, alternative assessment strategies, take home quizzes, or the inclusion of other grade boosters. Any of these can be woven into a response for this section.

Close your answer by returning to the underlying concern of the question, student grade-success. Provide assurance that you will do everything possible to ensure that students will meet high standards of performance and you look forward to their success. This puts the final touch on a good answer.

ALTERNATE ROUTE CANDIDATE: Just because this question says, "In your last school," do not think you are off the hook. No such luck. The committee will just rephrase the question and ask what kind of grade distribution would you "expect" to have and what would be your goal. The response you offer will take on the same characteristics as have been provided. You will simply change things to the future tense. BUT, take my word for this. If you offer the answer given here, you will be every bit as impressive as any other candidate they interview!

KEYS TO YOUR RESPONSE:

- Begin by describing how the normal bell shaped curve will look different in your class because of the high success rate of students.
- Offer one or two descriptions of things you do to ensure student mastery and grade performance.
- End with a statement of commitment to student success in a rigorous curriculum.

If you are the person we hire for this position, tell us about how you plan to get a fast start. Perhaps you could walk us through your first 30 days of school and what you would do.

This is a question I have often asked candidates, and it has always surprised me how little forethought some have given this subject. Principals and department chairpersons want a teacher who will hit the ground running. You will need to demonstrate how you are someone who has a definitive fast-start plan. To do this, you will need to have prepared your short-term plan of action before you ever arrive at the interview. Those who begin to think about this only after the question is asked rarely do well. You will do better.

If you have done some research on your school, you may already know some of the things that took place over the last year. If there are programs, teaching strategies, or curriculum initiatives you know to be ongoing, then by all means include one or two in your own approach. For example, if you know the school places a high value on authentic assessment, then describe how you want to kick off your first unit with authentic assessments and have students demonstrate important concept mastery. Such connections are very effective.

As you approach the body of your answer, I suggest you break the response into separate sections with two or three action steps for each section. In these next paragraphs, I will offer some ideas to consider; however, the actual answer must be a reflection of your own teaching stance and the things you feel would be most important. This segmented approach will allow you to deliver the overall answer in a clear, compelling way.

THE FOUR PLANNING AREAS

Curriculum is a great place to begin your discussion. Let the committee know that the established school curriculum will be the primary document to inform all of your decisions. You can describe any special opening events you might plan, speakers, projects, or high interest activities. Will you work with others prior to the first day of school to integrate your curriculum or produce guided questions? Will you have any special presentations to capitalize on initial interest? Will you need special technology or a SmartBoard in your room? It will be important to let the principal see that you intend to start student involvement on day one and continue with a well-constructed series of lessons. Try to find an innovative and engaging student activity or project to include.

Room arrangement and organization for the opening of school is critical. Describe what desk arrangements you prefer. Describe your bulletin board use. Will there be displays? What materials will you need? How will you organize student materials? You want the committee to have a mental picture of a room that is highly inviting and organized for instruction. It reeks of the idea that, "this is a place where great learning occurs!"

Student connections and relations is an area often omitted by lesser candidates, but establishing solid student relations from day one pays big dividends…and the committee knows this! Spend a little time to explain how you want to learn more than the name of each student. Describe how you expect to identify student interests and what they do when they are not in school. Speak to your intention to model and require courtesy and respect between all parties in the class. If you speak to how positive student-teacher relations assist the atmosphere and motivation to learn, you will have taken a step that few other candidates will consider. Jon Saphier, in his book, The Effective Teacher has an entire section on this topic (Saphier, 2009).

School service and commitment is an area almost every candidate I ever interviewed left out! Yet, this is an outstanding opportunity for you to demonstrate how you are a better fit for this post than any of the other candidates. Take a few minutes and identify specifically where you see yourself in the overall school picture. This is the perfect place to talk about how you would like to be part of the school club programs, enrichment opportunities, tutoring, or coaching. If you can help with the school newspaper or yearbook, bring that up now. You want to end your answer with this piece because it is the one area that is likely to set your answer apart from the other candidates.

Now take a look at a way to structure this response.

*"It is interesting that you ask this question. It is one that I have given a great deal of thought to in recent months. The way I have broken this out is to lay out my plans in a few different areas and perhaps I can do that with you now. **First,** I want to have great unit plan ready to go that will include a lot of activities and special plans that will capitalize on the enthusiasm young people usually have when they first come back. Those ideas would likely include............(briefly list a few special items). **Second,** so that everything runs effectively, I have considered doing some special things to the room arrangement as well. They would include............(two or three items). The **Third** concern will be to establish a great classroom atmosphere and cultivate productive connections with all of my students. The things I believe will help achieve this goal include............(identify in quick succession your ideas on this). Finally, I just want to briefly tell you that I plan to be an integral part of the entire school and not just my own class. I would be very interested in....................(identify your own ideas). Together, I believe all of these ideas will interact to maximize my chance of a great start and begin my career as the kind of involved, professional, and passionate teacher I know these students need to have in the front of their room."*

By organizing your answer around a few important themes, you will make it easy for the committee members to follow your line of thinking. As you can see, the power in this answer will come as a result of your ability to quickly and professionally tick off a set of ideas one after the other. That said; it is one of those answers you need to have considered and prepared in advance. You are unlikely to pull all these ideas together on the spot.

Finally, in giving your answer, be sure to demonstrate enthusiasm about this first month. Your energy is contagious, and you can show how much you anticipate the new school year by injecting some passion into your answer. It will be seen by the interviewers, and you will have done well!

ALTERNATE ROUTE TEACHER: If there is ever a question that will allow you to demonstrate your "capacity" to fill this position and be an outstanding fit for their school, this is it! Do your homework and prepare a strong answer ahead of time. Put it on an index card and review it until you have the ideas firmly in your mind. Even if this precise question is not asked, you might find another good place in which to put at least some of the answer highlights. Remember; every time you can do something along this line, you have demonstrated your ability to handle the duties and excel in their classroom.

KEYS TO YOUR RESPONSE:

- Note that the established Course of Study or Curriculum Guide will govern all of your curriculum plans.
- If you have identified initiatives or school programs in advance, look for ways to link your plans to one or two.
- Break your answer into the four separate categories: Curriculum, Organization, Student Relations, and School Service.
- Identify three or four things *you* plan to do under each category.
- Be upbeat and enthusiastic in delivering your answer. Use your smile and passion to convey a positive approach to the challenges of that first all-important month.

> *Let us suppose you have a student who has been frequently off-task throughout the year, rarely prepared, and often treats others with disrespect. Today, when you ask the class to work in small groups, this student leaves his seat and seems to be disturbing another group. When you ask him to please return to his own table and begin the assignment, he blows up and says, "If you ever assigned anything worthwhile, maybe I would work. You just want to get on my case, and I'm sick of it. My group doesn't want me and can do it without me!!" What will you do?*

This is an example of what is known as a "behavioral question." Behavioral interview questions have become more and more popular over the years because they present real situations and make the candidate describe what he or she will do. They test a candidate's ability to deal with difficult circumstances and provide excellent insight into their teaching stance and problem-solving ability. There are now interviews where *all* the questions are based on actual situations. As a high school applicant, you should be prepared for one or two questions in this format.

Here, the committee wants to know what you are going to do when "the shouting" starts in your class – and at some point it always does. A good start to your answer is to emphatically state that you *will not* engage the student in a power struggle or high-tension dialogue. This opening may sound similar to the following:

> *"Before giving my response on what I <u>will</u> do, perhaps I should tell you what I <u>will not</u> do. These kinds of confrontations sometimes arise, and we all wish they wouldn't. I have an entire class that will be watching and I am not going to add any energy to this argument by trying to publicly debate or further antagonize the student. My first actions will be to remove energy and diminish the obvious anger."*

There is a very important phrase in the wording of this question:*"... frequently off task throughout the year."* Do not let this phrase pass without answer. Principals hope no teacher would allow the situation described in this question to go on **all year**. You certainly would not and you should make that clear. You would have been working with this student on his off-task behavior, consulting with the home, and involving other building professionals long before the situation reached this level.

However, confronted with this explosive predicament, the committee wants to know what you will do *now.* Unless you are planning for a short interview and early lunch, sending him to the principal's office is not an option. A first step you might offer would be to separate this young man from the group while you provide the remainder of the class a "do now" assignment or some other relevant independent work. You must limit your first discussion with the student because you still have a class to teach, but the **first order of business** must be to *restore order* and *defuse the situation.* Let the committee know you will approach this volatile confrontation with a calm and deliberate voice. Since working with his study group was one of the student's problems, you should offer a few thoughts as to what might effect a better situation. Changing the student's location, using a learning center or briefly working together with the entire group to get the student re-started can do this. Let the committee see how you will act as a problem solver. You will need additional time later for a longer discussion to address the courtesy and respect matter, but for now you need to bring down the anger and disruptive behavior.

Later in the day, when there is more time, you might involve the parents, a counselor, or a social worker. Note to the committee that there are actually two issues which need your attention and work: (1) the relevance of the assignment and its perceived lack of value and (2) his feelings of alienation from the group. Whether this student felt the assignment was interesting should not be an issue for negotiation. Students do not get to choose whether they will work based on their level of interest. Certainly, you can review the kinds of work required and look for ways to add interest, but that is not the issue with this student. The immediate issue is acceptable class behavior and mutual respect. Stay focused on those points.

With regard to the student's feelings of alienation from the group, you can interview the other students and obtain valuable insights. Use this information along with the services of other professionals to deal with the human-relations problem that appears to exist. Given this question's information, the student's group alienation may be a long-term issue in need of more direct intervention. Immediate steps you might consider include changing the members of his group, changing the location of the group, or increasing the amount of supervision you provide.

This question allows you to display your ability to manage student behavior in a difficult circumstance. The committee wants to know you will not lose your composure, and you have the insight required to handle real problems. It is a great opportunity for you to shine, so make the most of it.

KEYS TO YOUR RESPONSE:

- Begin by focusing your initial effort on defusing the situation and avoiding a power struggle.
- Make sure the principal knows you would not have let this situation get so far out of hand before you took proactive action.
- Identify your strategies to restore order and stabilize the situation.
- Discuss your intention to involve others in creating an appropriate long-term solution.
- Close with your approach to improving the class environment that contributed to the outburst.

One of your female students tells you that boys have been making fun of her and, in low tones so that you could only partly hear, made suggestive comments. They are also writing obscene remarks on the desks and perhaps even sending off color text messages. She is not exactly sure which boys, but it is coming from the back. What are you going to do?

In our most professional voice, we might just call this one a real doozey! It is another of those popular situational questions to explore how you will handle a potentially explosive situation. With sexual harassment suits at an all-time high and getting higher, school districts are increasingly concerned with teachers and how they handle such problems. Take care in giving your response as this is another case where a wrong step can damage your candidacy.

KEY INTERVIEW STRATEGY: *With any behavioral question, take at least a few seconds to diagnose one or two important underlying issues and then design a strategy to address each one.*

In this scenario we have a complaint of sexual harassment from a female student. Let the principal know you will take action immediately. Indicate your intention to *first review board policies* or school guidelines for any required actions. There are likely to be board policies and they may be very general, nonetheless, you must first follow any practice the school district has in place.

KEY INTERVIEW STRATEGY: *Situational questions are best answered with a set of decisive and concise descriptions of your steps.*

District policies will provide specific initial direction, but you should also take a few steps of your own. Principals will be impressed if you can offer concrete actions you plan to take. For example, look at the following:

> *"After I review existing policies I would implement a three step plan of action. **First,** I will assure the young lady that I take her comments very seriously and will get this behavior stopped. This means I must investigate the young girl's statements as completely as possible that day. Further action will depend on what I find and if I can identify any parties who may be involved. **Second,** I will place any identified parties to this behavior on notice that their actions will not be accepted, and I must discuss appropriate consequences with the principal. **Third**, I will document the incident with my findings, place any actions taken on file, and notify the principal so he or she is aware of the incident."*

You may feel inclined to offer a different set of actions better suited to your teacher stance, but you can see the phrasing for a sound approach. Many teachers will step in and move the young student's seat to a place where it can be more closely observed. This might not solve the graffiti or side comments, but it does show you want to use actions and not lip-service.

Be advised that this particular answer lends itself to an important follow-up question; what will you do if you are unable to identify specific individuals in your investigation? This circumstance will require you to take additional steps. You will need to provide a clear and firm restatement to your classes regarding your stand on the harassment of others. Second, you will need consistent vigilance and watch this situation closely over the coming weeks. In fact added vigilance will be required in either event.

It is essential that you let the committee know of your intention to make the principal aware and keep him or her fully informed. Tell everyone that you are willing to participate in any additional steps regarding home notification. In my experience, I like teachers to call the parents, let them know of the complaint, and assure them that action is being taken. **BEFORE** a teacher makes <u>any</u> home contact on a matter like this, he or she <u>must</u> speak with the principal and allow him or her to offer advice. You can also speak with the nurse or school social worker to set up at least one session of counseling.

The committee needs assurance that you understand the gravity of sexual harassment complaints and will act in a way that protects the student, the school, and the teacher. A good answer to this question will secure confidence that you are a person of good judgment. Judgment is an important teacher quality and it is not one often taught in college.

 ## KEYS TO YOUR RESPONSE:

- Establish your understanding of the gravity of such allegations and your intention to take action.
- Review any board or school policies to identify required action.
- Tell the principal exactly what steps you will take immediately to protect all parties.
- Assure the principal of your willingness to participate in follow-up activities with both the home and any recommended counseling services.

CONCLUDING THOUGHTS:

During the chapter introduction, it was suggested that high school teachers should expect more questions on content area expertise. Yet, this chapter contained no questions that directly quizzed subject competence. You will find these questions in the coming chapters that relate to specific subject areas. You should carefully read and consider these chapters, they are important to your preparation.

High school positions carry unique burdens because the age group is older and more socially advanced than elementary and middle school students. Generally, high school students are not as easily motivated as the younger students and require a higher level of sophistication in teaching material. On the other hand, good teaching is good teaching – at any level. If you can offer a sound command of the principles of learning, content area knowledge, and good classroom management, you will be an excellent candidate. The trick is to make the committee understand that *you have* these skills. Armed with the information in this and the following chapters, you will be more than ready to do just that, so take charge and let them know who you are!

LANGUAGE ARTS QUESTIONS

GENERAL ADVICE ON INTERVIEWS
FOR LANGUARE ARTS POSTITIONS:

At the secondary level, Language Arts classes have significant importance to principals and interviewers for two important reasons. First, such courses deal with communication and literacy skills essential to successful living. Second, the content of subjects in this area strongly transfers to both the SAT and the State Proficiency Test. Student performance on these tests is frequently used as a measure of how well schools serve their community. They are also a prominent part of the school's state report card and publicly reported in the newspaper. Interviewees can count on a thorough set of questions to explore their philosophies and practices if they plan to teach in this discipline. Test preparation is another important concern and questions in this area ought to be expected.

Because every student must take English, regardless of their past performance or aptitude, you need to think about how you will demonstrate your ability to teach students at all ability levels. It is not uncommon for student skills in reading or writing to range from three years below to two years above grade level. In many schools, significant numbers perform below grade level. Your capacity to diagnose and deal with both skill deficiencies and enrichment teaching will establish you as someone who can teach a wide range of abilities. It is important that you convince the committee or your ability to educate students at all levels.

A fundamental theme to consistently express throughout your answers is that of literacy development. Emphasize the aspects of your teaching that deepen and strengthen student ability to interpret the world and communicate in an intelligent, competent manner. Literacy is an essential process skill in any well-formulated educational program. Beyond this, it is a skill that will materially influence a student's prospects for successful living.

SAMPLE LANGUAGE ARTS QUESTIONS AND THEIR ANSWERS:

What do you know about our state standards in Language Arts and how would you ensure that your students reach these standards?

With the rise of the NCLB regulations, every state was charged to establish written standards and grade level benchmarks in all core discipline areas. School leaders are rightfully focused on making sure every student in their school demonstrates the required proficiency and meets the standards mandated by the state. General goals might include proficiency in written communication, critical reading, speaking, and listening. One of the academic standards for English 1 in the state of South Carolina provides the following:

> *Students produce essays that are coherent, well-organized, and demonstrate a command of Standard American English. Using the writing process, students compose various types of writing: narrative, persuasive, expository, technical, reflective, and analytical.*

This standard represents one that is repeated in almost every state and is an excellent example of one you can use to begin your answer to this question. By paraphrasing this one sentence, you will have addressed several core goals of any literacy program.

If possible, get a copy of whatever state document is in place for your state. If you are not sure where to find them, go online and log onto <u>www.taskstream.com</u> (Appendix C). Once there, go to the "Standards Wizard." This site does have a fee. Every state is listed and there is a mountain of pertinent information. Familiarize yourself with each requirement and any specific performance indicators defined for student mastery. For example, New Jersey has five separate standards with a set of specific proficiency indicators for each standard. To support teachers, there is an accompanying *Frameworks* document that outlines suggested teaching strategies and assessment plans. Many states have similar support materials. If you plan to teach language arts, it is important you be aware of the requirements students must meet – *particularly as they are part of a state assessment test!*

KEY INTERVIEW STRATEGY: *To answer any question on standards a three-step formula will serve you well.* **First,** *give a broad overview of your knowledge of the standards' requirements.* **Second,** *choose one standard and outline specific teaching strategies that will promote initial student understanding.* **Third,** *describe ways to deepen initial student proficiency and maintain his or her retention through a regimen of distributed practice.*

The question specifically asks about your approach to mastery teaching – *"how would you insure your students reach these standards?"* Be sure to respond to this matter carefully. The basics of mastery teaching include the highlights of what you will do to make your initial instruction a high quality experience. Once you have established a sound degree of original learning, you must outline how you will diagnose to what extent students have mastered your content. Finally, you will speak to ways you can deal with students who are below the mastery level. Tell the committee the only way to "insure" competence is through ongoing diagnosis, instruction, and reinforcement. There is no shortcut. **NOTE:** *Chapter12 on Mathematics will have additional information on the elements of mastery teaching, and you should review that information as well.*

KEYS TO YOUR RESPONSE:

- Give an overview of your knowledge on the standards for your state.
- Choose one standard and outline a concise set of steps to teach and reinforce the related proficiencies.
- Show the committee your approach to mastery teaching through the use of consistent assessment/diagnosis/remediation strategies.

> *What strategies do you use to identify and deal with students who are reading significantly below grade level?*

The question has two main parts. The first part is concerned with your *identification* of students who may have pronounced reading difficulties. The second part asks about your ideas on how to deal with students who are below grade level. Your answer might focus on the use of classroom diagnostics to identify individual reading levels. Of course there is an even more accurate approach that takes even less time; ***check the most recent standardized test results!*** Tell the committee how you would review the portion of the *School Report* that provides standardized reading results by student. This is a standard report and available in most schools. Ask the principal or interviewer if they make copies of these reports available to teachers. With this report, you can see in a matter of minutes exactly who among your students is reading below grade level *and why.* You can always add your class observations to the evaluation process, but standardized results will quickly and accurately point you in the right direction.

KEY INTERVIEW STRATEGY: *The use of standardized test score analysis can be employed in any question where a diagnosis of student ability is required.*

The second component of the question is directed toward how you plan to work with below-level readers when you design instruction. Here you must identify teacher actions to directly address the various ability levels in your class. If you reviewed the Test Report, you already know exactly in which area(s) students fell short. Use this information to explain how you will differentiate your expectations for reading responses, homework, questions, and class assignments. Discuss how you might use cooperative learning, literature circles, or other student learning arrangements to minimize student limitations. Focus your committee on the promise such ideas offer for enriched student understanding. Your phrasing for this portion of the response might sound like the following:

> *"I never let students struggle from behind with no assistance from me. From my analysis of the State Report, I will know the clusters areas in need of improvement. I intend to design both group and individual instruction based on these findings. Unfortunately, I am only one person, and there may be a number of students who need support. To address this I expect to include a variety of support opportunities to help everyone stay abreast of the instruction. Some of the strategies I employ include: . . . ."*

From this introduction, go on to describe a teaching plan that sustains the learning process of slower students. Such strategies as choice in literature selection, independent conferencing, special small-group breakout sessions, and computer-assisted instruction are all good examples of how you can support below level readers. A concise, direct answer will be appreciated because it provides the committee members only the information they need to hear.

To this point you have focused on more general methodologies. A strong conclusion will add specific ways to directly work with *individual* students and improve each one's reading ability. This differs from full-class remediation in that it outlines a plan for each student's personal improvement in his or her reading skills. You can now link your opening statements on the importance of test analysis and how you will use the *Individual Student Report.* The *Individual Report* gives you the student's weakest and strongest skill clusters.

The insight you gain from the test analysis regarding a student's specific skill deficiencies allows you to provide targeted support in the *precise* areas where data suggests he or she is struggling. The information can also be used to arrange supplemental instruction for small groups composed of those who share a common deficiency. This well-directed review of how you use test data to improve student performance will place you above most candidates.

KEYS TO YOUR RESPONSE:

- Tell the committee how you will use standardized test data to make initial diagnostic evaluations of your students.
- Describe a variety of in-class support strategies for students who may be struggling with the work.
- Identify a strategic plan to improve every student's personal reading ability.

> *Speech is a fundamental element of good communication. What will you do to enhance the ability of students to formally and informally speak?*

This is a process skill about which much is said but little is "taught" in many of today's schools. You can find many classes where students are asked to give oral reports or make presentations to the class. Those experiences fall well short of the mark required by this question. State standards in English universally contain public speaking requirements. This means they must be <u>taught</u>. To teach students how to informally and formally speak, a teacher must provide instruction on all the essential sub-skills. It is fair to ask the committee if a specific public speaking curriculum is already in place. Expect answers to range from sketchy overviews through very specific curricula and performance expectations. For purposes of our discussion, we will assume the committee gives you very little beyond their recognition that public speaking is a tested skill that needs your attention.

As with the earlier question on literacy, if you have a general idea of the state requirement, then by all means lead with that! Here are some high school requirements from the State of Arizona. If you had an interview in Phoenix, you could frame your entire answer around just one of these requirements.

- LS-P1 *Deliver a polished speech that is organized and well suited to the audience and that uses resource materials to clarify and defend positions.*

- **LS-P2** *Deliver an impromptu speech that is organized, addresses a particular subject, and is tailored to the audience.*
- **LS-P3** *Deliver oral interpretations of literary or original works.*

If you do not know the specific state standard for the question asked, then begin with three or four solid objectives that underlie what you see as essential proficiencies to master this skill. In this case, you might feel students need to learn how to speak before an audience. Or perhaps they should have instruction to help them master the art of argument and debate. As part of the informal speaking requirements, students must also learn to speak extemporaneously (see LS-P2 above). There are other forms of speaking as well, and you can choose those you feel most important. A few concrete ideas as to how you will teach students to speak in a variety of settings might sound like the following:

> *"To approach public speaking, I like to break the teaching into a few component parts that will target specific requirements in the state standards. The areas I see as important include a student's ability to address an audience, present sound arguments in a debate, and speak extemporaneously. Let me go on and talk about some things I can do to teach students about these important elements of public speaking."*

In your response, try to limit the discussion to two or three items as more can make your answer too long. The committee simply wants to establish your general level of understanding and hear a few methods you might employ.

Once you outline the content to be taught, illustrate specific ways you plan to teach those concepts. Depending on time, you might even give a fast overview of a sample lesson and include a regimen of distributed practice to maintain proficiency. Since you already mentioned argument and debate, explain how you might teach the basic elements of debate in a short series of lessons. Address the issue of practice by underscoring your use of debate and point-counterpoint discussions throughout the year. Note that because speech is so essential to daily communication, you will have opportunities to continuously reinforce these skills.

One last suggestion that will help vault you over other candidates is the use of assessment rubrics.

KEY INTERVIEW STRATEGY: *When you are working with a frequently used process skill, suggest the use a rubric to help students conduct peer and self-assessment.*

A good rubric will identify those critical elements required for skill mastery plus observable performance levels (Appendix A). Many publishers have included examples in their teacher editions of textbooks. There are entire books devoted to the subject of assessment and rubrics are often included. It is an important tool and has a variety of uses. Closing your answer with an overview of how these will be used to insure readiness for the State Proficiency Exam is a winner!

KEYS TO YOUR RESPONSE:

- Open with any understanding you have of state requirements.
- Describe sub-skill areas critical to the mastery of public speaking.
- Outline a teaching plan to help students master that one or two important skills.
- Catalog a variety of speaking requirements and opportunities you will use throughout the year so students will deepen their proficiency.
- Explain how you use rubrics to help students understand critical public speaking elements and conduct self or peer assessment.
- Underscore your use of rubrics to insure student readiness for the State Exam.

> *Writing is a complex process skill that every educated person must master. What is your approach to the teaching of writing?*

The central issues posed by this high school question are very similar to those we examined for the elementary school. Student mastery of this skill is constantly measured and used as an indicator of a school's quality. This is true in all fifty states, and you can be somewhat confident you will hear a question on your ability to teach writing. When answering this question, you can sometimes assume certain skill levels to be already in place. Unless you are interviewing in a very low performing school district, you should not start with writing fundamentals; performance expectations for high school students are more advanced. If you will be expected to teach remedial classes, ask for more information about the entry-level skills you will encounter.

First, let's examine a writing proficiency from the State of Indiana. Indiana has 10 separate writing requirements, and each one has several indicators of proficiency students are expected to meet. Following is just one of those standards:

9-10.W.2 *Write informative/explanatory texts to examine and convey complex ideas, concepts, and information clearly and accurately through the effective selection, organization, and analysis of content.*

Wow! There is a lot going on here, wouldn't you agree? And this is just one of the ten standards. Obviously, your answer could not cover all ten items even if you actually knew them. The good news is that it does not have to. The committee's interest is only that writing will be addressed in your class in an ongoing, effective way. But, knowing one of these standards will give you a great place to begin your answer.

In the event you do not know any specific standards, you can simply begin with how you intend to extend student writing proficiency past simple basics and add power to individual writing style. Cite the need for a powerful vocabulary, strategies to develop rich textual composition, and the use of writing tactics such as alliteration, simile, metaphor, and so forth. Books on power writing offer numerous suggestions; and, as writing will almost definitely be somewhere on the interview sheet, I recommend them to your attention. Catalog the variety of writing purposes you will include in your teaching. Some essential purposes might include job applications, business letters, memoranda, research reports, college application essays, letters to the editor, or other writing students must master. Tailor your response to grade level expectations, but show your ability to introduce rigor and stretch to writing exercises.

Prospective high school teachers should speak about research writing in their answer. Many discipline areas require students to conduct research and write papers anywhere from a few to fifteen or twenty pages in length. The required skills to write scientific research will differ from those required for a literary analysis. Because you cannot feasibly address every kind of writing, it is best keep to your approach generic. Describe ways you will teach students to identify and use data sources, construct convincing arguments, synthesize ideas, and develop logical lines of thought. There are also technical aspects of research such as footnotes, tables of contents, references cited, and style. Be prepared to review the various research styles such as APA or Chicago. Explain how you will work with content area teachers to maximize the benefit of student writing techniques so they can be extended across a wide variety of subject disciplines.

As with other process skills, rubrics can be an extremely effective way to help students understand a project's essential elements and conduct self or peer assessment. You need only highlight a few rubric criteria with concrete examples of benchmarks to define exemplary performance. A nice addition will describe how "anchor papers" or models can be employed to provide exemplars for the students.

An important concluding discussion will outline the use of writing portfolios to maintain an ongoing record of student growth and performance. List the kinds of writing a good portfolio will contain, outline how students will identify papers to include, and suggest a frequency for portfolio reviews. *Do not forget electronic portfolios. This is a perfect place to use that information because many schools now require students to maintain one!* Although almost everyone is now familiar with *e-Portfolios*, it is surprising how few candidates spend any time talking about them when interviewed. Perhaps that will be the case in this school and why shouldn't *you* be the one with the most articulate discussion in this group?

As you can see, there is a lot to cover with this answer. Therefore your response might take a little longer than other answers. As long as you are not repeating yourself or wandering, you will maintain the attention of the committee. A more complete response will leave an excellent impression on the minds of the committee, so organize your thinking and go for it.

KEYS TO YOUR RESPONSE:

- Focus your answer on the more advanced writing skills unless you are otherwise directed.
- Highlight skills essential to power writing and provide an example of how you would teach one of these skills.
- Catalog the variety of writing purposes to which you will teach.
- Talk about how research or project papers will be used to add sophistication to student writing. Extend this discussion to include writing in other subject areas.
- Describe where and how writing rubrics, anchor papers, and support information will help students self-edit and improve their writing skills.
- Close with a discussion of writing and e-portfolios and their use in your class.

Our curriculum requires students to read and interpret good literature. If you were asked to choose a book for a 10th grade class in American Literature, which one would you select and why? How would you design the instruction for studying this work?

If you are an English teacher, you can expect a question on book selection at almost any grade level. The question has universal appeal because of its ability to provide insight into a candidate's knowledge of literature and how this knowledge transfers to his or her instructional approach. The question draws out what an English candidate views as important, identifies their familiarity with authors, and provides information regarding teaching methodologies.

First, understand there is no specific reading selection that represents the "right" answer. There is a wide variety of works and authors from which to choose, and you should decide on something from your own repertoire. Have a few ideas in mind before you arrive at the interview and pre-think how you will address the kinds of issues posed in this question.

Once your selection is made, speak directly to the characteristics of the author and his or her work that make it a superior teaching example for tenth grade students. Remember too, a book's popularity or interest is an insufficient reason to select it as a core reading. Be sure your choice represents a superior example of this literary genre or demonstrates a style of writing that is unique or noteworthy. Add ideas on how your selection will provide a vehicle for smooth transition to the writing process; the more versatile a selection, the stronger your answer will be. Feel free to add information about what makes this author a noteworthy model for students to study. If you choose a well-known author, he or she needs less explanation than someone who is less well recognized.

The final element of your answer must take your book selection and craft a solid teaching design. This must be done by you and specific advice cannot be offered. When you describe your teaching approach, you should underscore a set of high-interest activities that will require students to analyze and appreciate the literature piece you selected. Showcase strategies such as small group book talks, written reflections, webbing, analysis designs, evaluation responses, journals, debates, discussion techniques, and so forth. It is important to convince the committee you can select good literature and use an innovative, unique manner to capture its essence.

 ### <u>KEYS TO YOUR RESPONSE:</u>

- Select a book with which you are familiar that offers a variety of literary elements.
- Describe how your author is a significant writer and what he or she offers to students who study his or her works.
- Provide a concise outline of the teaching design and how students will analyze this work.

Is preparation for the Scholastic Aptitude Test (SAT) something that should concern teachers of language arts? If so, what specific steps would you take to prepare students for this test?

The first element of this question is the easiest – *of course* SAT preparation is a legitimate interest of language arts teachers. If your interviewers did not think it was important, then why is this question even on the interview? In fact, if you hear this question, you know the SAT is, for some reason, a fairly large issue. In truth, SAT scores are a matter of concern for all academic area teachers. As the verbal section of the SAT is in part a direct reflection of skills learned in your class, an added burden might rest on your shoulders. This responsibility is a logical place to begin your response, but first make one key distinction; *the SAT is <u>not</u> the curriculum.* You will therefore need to identify logical places where you intend to teach those skills necessary to maximize student readiness.

An example might be how you teach students the various types of analogy bridges and their identifying characteristics. You can cover grammar and usage tactics. Critical analysis of various reading selections is important. There are many areas appropriate for direct instruction, and you should provide one or two good examples.

Describe any process skills related to SAT competence that can be addressed as ongoing objectives. Examples might be critical thinking and analysis. List a few ideas on where opportunities for divergent thinking skills will be enhanced. As the SAT includes a wide variety of literature genre, cite how your curriculum will acquaint students with such diversity. It is important to display your commitment to a long-term strategy for student readiness.

One word of caution concerns the numerous SAT readiness programs on the market. There are computer programs, preparation manuals, and stand-alone courses that purport to help students prepare for the SAT. These materials provide good examples and strategies you might want to include in your instruction. For example, a good computer program would make an excellent learning center in the back of your room. **SUGGESTION:** *I would not suggest you propose packaged SAT programs as stand-alone units of study.* The committee will be more impressed with your personal long-term approach than quick-hit solutions.

<u>KEYS TO YOUR RESPONSE:</u>

- Yes, of course SAT preparation is an important concern. However, you should make the distinction that the SAT cannot dictate the entire curriculum.

- Identify specific areas of your curriculum where drawing a connection to the SAT would make sense.
- Describe one or two long-term process skills taught in your class that measurably add to a student's SAT readiness.
- Explain where use of learning centers or stand-alone curricula can extend instruction and reinforce specific skill areas.

If we allow you to attend any workshop you like in your field, what would you choose to attend and why?

The key phrase in this question is, "in your field." School principals are interested to know where you would focus future professional development activities. The specific workshop you choose is not as important as your explanation of why that area was chosen. For example, if you tell the committee you want to attend a workshop on writing strategies, you should be able to explain what you intend to gain and where you will use these new strategies. If you are applying to a school in Florida, workshops on teaching to the Florida Content Standards might be a safe choice. Actually, you can use this response for any state as long as you know the correct terminology.

Highlight a strong commitment to professional growth and personal development. The enthusiasm of your answer will be strongly noted by the committee. Principals want professionals who will constantly seek opportunities to improve their teaching skills. Use this question to demonstrate your intention to be a life-long learner.

KEYS TO YOUR RESPONSE:

- Choose an area of your interest and explain what knowledge you will gain as well as how that knowledge will be translated into classroom actions.
- Make a strong statement of commitment to personal development and the concept of continuing education for teachers.

Experts have identified a skill called "active listening." What does this term mean to you and how would you teach this skill to your students?

This can be a difficult question to answer when it comes out of left field at an interview. However, as listening has become a more recognized essential skill in communication, it is worth mentioning. A point you will want to make is that "active listening" is more than just attentiveness. It refers to a person's ability to recognize the meaning behind words and then make interpretations based on what they hear. At the secondary level, an active listener is able to do such things as identify various speaking styles and purposes, determine speaker credibility, evaluate media messages, and deal with a variety of presentation purposes. The "active listener" is able to *interpret and respond* to what he or she has heard.

With this broader definition of "active listening," you might want to choose one of the above-mentioned skills and propose a compatible lesson. Should you choose to do this, it is important that you identify specific teaching strategies that will check for student understanding. Because listening is largely a covert action, it is more difficult to assess – but it can be done. Look at the following example to see how such a diagnosis might be phrased.

> *"I need to know when students understand the concept of credibility. This requires strong active listening from the student. To insure that students have this knowledge, I like to use an activity that students will find both interesting and highly worthwhile. After listening to three commercials, I have the students identify which speaker was the most credible and what techniques he or she used to convey his or her message most effectively."*

This activity requires students to "demonstrate" their listening and evaluative skills. It gives the teacher a clear reflection of what the student has both heard and learned about the analysis process.

KEY INTERVIEW STRATEGY: *When you are describing an instructional segment or something you need students to learn, it is vitally important to also provide the committee your diagnostic strategy.*

If you fail to establish the means by which you will evaluate student concept mastery, you will have missed the opportunity to establish a key element of your teaching skill.

As you develop this response, consider the many places where listening is an important part of daily student activity. Suggest one or two places along with a good lesson design to reinforce a listening skill. It might sound something like the following.

"A regular part of my class is the inclusion of oral presentations by students. When a lesson contains an oral presentation component, we go over the importance of listening and develop a rubric for students to use when they provide feedback to the presenter. This rubric, along with the specific information students must provide a presenter, promotes a good pattern of active listening."

As you can see, this information tells the committee you are a candidate who recognizes precise ways the skill of active listening can be taught as an integrated part of the curriculum. It will also show how you understand the principle of active participation and its ability to secure on-task behavior in students. There are many places where listening is important, and you should choose those that fit your teaching style. The specific area is not as important as the explanation of how it will be taught and measured.

 ### KEYS TO YOUR RESPONSE:

- Begin your answer with a concise definition of the term "active listening."
- List several of the sub-skills contained in active listening, then choose one and describe how you will know students are using this skill.
- Choose an instructional design you commonly employ and show how you can incorporate the development of listening skills inside that plan.

 The consumption of good fiction is an important component of reading literacy, but there are other literary genres. What advanced reading tactics and skills would you teach to students reading fiction and other literary genres?

As pointed out earlier in this chapter, high school students must master higher levels of literacy competence. Here your answer must address one of the more advanced reading skills. To meet this need, you might address how you will teach students the techniques writers use to manipulate the reader's emotions or frame of mind.

"It is important that students in my class understand some of the more advanced skills required to critically examine a piece of fiction. An area I like to explore with my classes is the devices an author uses to manipulate the reader's emotional state."

Your answer will be stronger if you provide a specific author and title. You should add ideas on how you would help students identify the devices that a particular author uses to manipulate emotion so the committee will see how you provide depth to your instruction. There are other areas to consider as well. For example, you might address how students will study the relationships between literature and literary criticism. What are the characteristics of key literary movements? Think about the more advanced ways literacy skills have been developed in your classes.

Note that the question asked about "other literary genres." This is an important element of a complete response, and you will now be ready for it. List three or four different genres your class will address and why each is important. The beginning of your answer will sound something like the following.

"It is critical that students study a variety of good literature. For example, students should experience poetry, yet poetry normally evokes little enthusiasm. I like to begin the instruction of poetry by having students read such classic works by Shakespeare and Keats. From this foundation we move to more contemporary poets such as Frost and Sandburg. We then look at poetry in musical lyrics. Lyrics by Johnny Mercer are terrific examples of poetry. Finally students look at artists of their own choosing and analyze their poetic elements."

As you can see, this outlines a design to teach an important genre. It is not necessary to present every bell and whistle for the unit. The committee will be pleased if you identify a few literary forms and a meaningful way to teach them.

When you are ready to conclude your answer, consider ending with a question. You can insure your answer will hit the right target when you ask the committee if there is a specific genre they were interested in hearing you discuss.

"Before I conclude my answer, is there a specific area of literature you wanted me to discuss that I missed? If so, let me know which one and I will be happy to give my thoughts on that as well."

This ending can be used at any time when you may feel the committee still has questions, or you are not sure your answer was quite spot on. The only caveat is to use it only once or twice. More than that will become redundant and sound too rehearsed.

KEYS TO YOUR RESPONSE:

- Begin with a few advanced literary elements you intend to teach.
- Provide one or two examples of key analytic skills and describe how they might be taught.
- List a variety of genres you feel are important. Identify one genre to expand and demonstrate your teaching approach.
- If you are not certain you included all the points in which the committee had interest, end with a question that allows for further exploration.

CONCLUDING THOUGHTS:

Language Arts is a cornerstone discipline in every school; therefore, there are important interview goals for you to achieve. Be sure the committee knows you have an in-depth understanding of the required writing skills for high school students. You should convey an ability to organize innovative lessons. The committee should see you as an educator who is flexible and dynamic. It is suggested you read this section through a few times and familiarize yourself with the issues we discussed.

For all questions, your answers must reflect your own experience and teaching style. Be proactive and organize your thinking on the pertinent issues before you attend the interview. The exact questions a committee is likely to ask will be different than those in this chapter. However, many of the central issues described in this chapter will be present. If you know how to approach those key issues, you will be ready! Good luck!

MATHEMATICS QUESTIONS

GENERAL ADVICE ON INTERVIEWS
FOR MATHEMATICS POSITIONS:

The good news for prospective math teachers is that this is one of the more difficult positions for many school districts to fill. There are far fewer certified mathematics teachers than elementary education or secondary social studies teachers. Well qualified math candidates are more likely to receive interview invitations than their counterparts in more populated fields of study. Still, good districts will attract a formidable field of applicants, and you need to be ready.

Mathematics is another discipline that is always a part of the state testing program. Results are federally reported and made part of every school's public record. The public and media use these reports as barometers of school and student effectiveness. In addition to the state test requirements, mathematics teachers who have college preparatory courses must also consider the Scholastic Aptitude Test (SAT) and the ACT. No matter how the course assignments are to be structured, mathematics candidates can count on a very thorough set of questions to uncover their philosophy and strategy for student test preparation.

An added area of special interest to principals and supervisors will be the candidate's ability to work with students who have difficulty with math. Even if you teach Algebra, Geometry, or Calculus you can expect to encounter students who struggle just to keep up while others breeze effortlessly through the material. Interview committees will explore your plan to work with these diverse populations.

A fundamental interview goal is to establish your credentials as a strong practitioner with an array of instructional strategies that meet the needs of all students. Let the committee know you recognize how important it is to reach *every* student and maintain his or her competence into and through the spring achievement tests. Now examine the general mathematics themes and interview questions that may be asked.

SAMPLE MATHEMATICS QUESTIONS AND THEIR ANSWERS:

What do you know about our state's requirements in 8th grade Mathematics, and how would you ensure your students meet these requirements?

For all states there are student competencies in mathematics children must master. Where a state administers a competency test on those requirements, an applicant can almost count on hearing this question. Look for your state standards and initiatives in the area of mathematics and identify how the state determines student achievement. If you are not sure where to find them, go online, log onto www.taskstream.com and visit the "Standards Wizard." (Appendix C) Every state is listed, and there is a wealth of information. The principal and committee will assume you are aware of these requirements and ask questions that deal with this knowledge. Such questions are often asked early in the interview, and they are important. To prepare, you should get a complete copy of the K-12 Core Standards or whatever documents are in place for your state.

In Kentucky for example, the state high school standards can be found in, *College and Career Readiness Standards in Mathematics.* The requirements are organized by mathematical themes such as equations, co-ordinates, functions, and other more advanced topics in mathematics. A good approach would be to log onto one of the many websites that have multiple teacher resources and browse the options for teaching to the Kentucky requirements. As of this writing, http://kentuckymathematics.org/resources/standards. asp would be one resource that meets this need. Every state will have its own guides, and these are readily available through an inquiry on almost any search engine. These are excellent resources; and, if you can review a copy before your interview, you should make an effort to become an expert on at least one proficiency area. This advance study will prove useful on your interview day by helping identify a variety of specific examples and practical lesson applications.

Look at the question the committee posed in this case. There are two significant parts. (1) What do you know about the standards, and (2) how will you insure student mastery?

KEY INTERVIEW STRATEGY: *When organizing a response that has multiple parts, go from the general to the specific.*

In this instance, begin with a brief overview of your general knowledge on state mathematics standards and how they might apply to the grade level(s) you will teach. Add a specific example of at least one standard and its required competencies. Once the standard and its proficiencies are explained, move quickly and provide an illustration of how you might teach that proficiency in your class. Here is a simple example of how this approach sounds.

> *"One of the standards requires students to solve real-world problems. As problem solving is an essential process skill in math, I have students engage in a variety of real world problems throughout every chapter. For example, a required problem-solving skill involves the ability to use measurements. As an activity, I could require every student pretend he or she is a parcel post worker who must determine the least amount of wrapping that can be used on an oddly shaped package. This is an authentic task that requires both math reasoning and measurement skills."*

Let us review the approach once more. Identify the standard, specify the required proficiencies, and give a practical example. It is crisp and effective. Before you conclude this response, provide a description of the observable and measurable indicators you will use to determine student mastery on the competency you chose. In this case we used an "authentic task." This is a specific process described by a number of educators including Kay Burke (Burke, 2009). If you plan to use this term, be certain you know its meaning and application.

NOTE: *The question uses the phrase, "all students."* That is an important element and can be easily lost on a less astute candidate. The complete answer needs to discuss plans to help slower students reach a mastery level. Here is phrasing to help you formulate your own approach.

> *"In my experience, not all students master the concepts of measurement right away. This is especially true for the metric measurements. To help those students, I would create two learning centers in my room with computers and CAI (Computer Assisted Instruction) programs on measurement. I give diagnostic quizzes all along the instructional path, and students who need a little more time or information can either use the learning centers or get 1-on-1 assistance. To provide the 1-on-1 assistance, I might use faster*

students who have already mastered the concept as tutors. Student tutors would receive extra credit when their teaching bears fruit. As soon as their student demonstrates mastery on the proficiency quiz, the tutor receives bonus points on his or her grade. Through the use of these two strategies, I have found (or expect) student achievement can reach 100%."

To close this question, cite your concern that students maintain their knowledge into *and through* the spring test season. Some candidates only worry about insuring initial student mastery. This should not be good enough for you. Make a point of telling the committee you want this learning to be *owned* by the students. Using whichever math concept you spoke to in your answer, illustrate a program of distributed practice on those newly mastered skills to help keep the learning fresh and proficient into the future.

KEYS TO YOUR RESPONSE:

- Be sure you have done your homework and fully understand the standards required by your state.
- Open with an overview of your knowledge of state standards.
- Select one standard and outline its importance along with a teaching strategy. Be sure to include a way to assess student mastery.
- Discuss your plan to provide for those who display difficulty with the concept so all students can attain mastery.
- Close with a discussion of how you will use distributed practice and periodic refreshers to maintain student mastery into and through the spring test.

Mathematics is a subject where, if a student gets left behind and does not understand early concepts, it is difficult to catch up later. How do you monitor such things, and what adjustments do you make when you see this happening?

When you hear the terms "monitor and adjust" in the same sentence, it is safe to assume the interviewer is familiar with the work of Madeline Hunter. Although this work goes all the way back to the 1970 and 80's, much of Hunter's work remains embedded in the educational lexicon of today. If you are familiar with the Madeline Hunter instructional model, you can include Hunter terminology in your answer and feel safe that it will be similar to the district's instructional philosophies. If you have not had Madeline Hunter training, do not be concerned, you can still provide a great answer.

Because of the hierarchical nature of mathematics, there is a higher need to insure students are mastering content at each step of the process. In this question, you are asked how you "diagnose" student learning and what instructional adaptations you employ as a result of that diagnosis. There are many ways to determine what students have learned and understand. You have probably studied a number of them in your methods classes or at least seen them in use where you have been a student. Use your background and the information here to outline a comprehensive plan that checks understanding at "critical learning points" and then makes teaching adjustments based on that feedback. This process is known as "diagnostic teaching," and I recommend you use that exact term. It is unlikely the committee will hear it from anyone else, and you know how we like that!

The first thing you need with any new teaching is a strong task analysis to identify the "critical learning points" (Appendix B). Once you have the essential sub-tasks, you can organize a student progress check for each one. If students demonstrate competence on these, you have a concrete indicator that you can move forward. This is an excellent way to "monitor" the process of learning, and very few will describe it.

> *"When I check understanding, it is extremely important to know <u>when </u>and <u>what</u> to check! I want to closely monitor those "critical learning points" where, if students are not on board, there is a high likelihood that they might indeed get left behind. To identify those points, I do a task analysis that will show me which sub-tasks must be thoroughly mastered before students can ultimately meet the final objective. I build in checks for understanding at each sub-task point and do not move forward until I am confident in the results. I can quickly check by using such things as good diagnostic questions, soliciting choral responses, or conducting a simple desk activity I can observe as I circulate through the room. This routine tells me about both individual and group mastery."*

The segment of this answer that is likely to catch the attention of the interview team is your focused check on the "critical sub-tasks". Be sure to emphasize this in your discussion. The second point of emphasis should be the variety of simple strategies to conduct that assessment. You use questions, choral responses, and observable performance. You can add to this diagnostic feedback through such data collection methods as homework, journal writing, board work, and recitation. Cooperative assignments yield valuable information but can also provide opportunities for students who may still be a little fuzzy

187

to catch up. I need to admit that I was one of those students who was almost *always*.......
uhhhhh.........a little "fuzzy" when it came to math. Yet, here I am, so somehow I
got through.

Now you must address the second part of the question by detailing how you will alter
the teaching based on your diagnostic findings. When one adjusts teaching based on
the feedback from a check for understanding, there are essentially only four actions to
consider, and you should just tick them off one at a time.

POSSIBLE TEACHER ACTIONS BASED ON LEARNING DIAGNOSIS
- If all of the students demonstrate satisfactory understanding, I can **continue the lesson as planned**.
- If the class exhibits minor misunderstandings, I may need to **clarify or reinforce weak understanding**.
- If the class has serious gaps or misunderstanding, I will need to **re-teach using a different instructional strategy**.
- If there are such serious misunderstandings that the entire lesson must go back to the planning board, I will just have to **abandon ship, go back to my task analysis, and think anew about how to teach the concept**.

This set of teacher actions is straight from Madeline Hunter, and it has served teachers
well for many years (Hunter, 2004). Use it.

An excellent conclusion to this answer describes how you will proceed when general
class understanding is satisfactory, but just one or two students might still be struggling to
master the content. This occurs fairly often, and you can move ahead of other candidates if
you address this common problem in your answer. Believe me, there are excellent teacher
actions you can take when only a few students are below proficiency. Here is a response
to consider that addresses such a concern.

"If there are just a few students who do not understand, I will move the remainder of the class to guided and independent practice to build their proficiency. I can then form a small group of students for special instruction or added guided practice. If the class is not yet ready to work independently, I might employ a few <u>Look Again</u> *handouts that contain detailed explanations for students to take home. The "Check Now" questions at the end of the chapter will let me see how these students are doing. If after a few of these steps a student is still confused, I can utilize student tutors or off-class special help sessions to provide even more direct instruction."*

188

There are many ideas you might have other than those presented here, and you should include those as you see fit. But, do conclude with how you will assist the struggling student as this is at the heart of what the committee was trying to get at in its question.

KEYS TO YOUR RESPONSE:

- Open on a strong practice and describe your "diagnostic teaching" approach. Describe how you will determine the lesson's "critical learning points" and conduct a check for understanding at each one.
- Add a few specific examples of the techniques you will use to check for individual and group understanding.
- Identify the four teacher actions you use to respond to diagnostic feedback and the learning threshold required to trigger each action.
- Close with your strategy for those times when you have only one or two struggling students and the class is ready to move forward.

Mathematics is a subject area some students fear. They may have had negative past experiences, a poor academic history, or perhaps just a poor self-image regarding their ability. What will you do to raise their comfort level and lead them to become more confident learners?

Educational leaders want teachers who are able to create classrooms and lessons that lead to consistent student participation and positive learning experiences for all. This question comes to the heart of how you will connect with your students and bring vitality to the teaching/learning process. Within this question are the larger themes of motivation and student perceptions. It wants to know how you will foster confident learners with healthy self-esteem. This is a complex issue, and there are entire books devoted to the subject. *Your* answer, however, need only focus on what you can realistically accomplish in a daily 45-minute period – insufficient time to warrant a review of the entire book.

The committee's question can be approached more easily if it is rephrased to ask, "What will take place in your class to raise student comfort and confidence levels?" To that end, begin by detailing how you will organize instruction and class management so students will feel safe and successful. Students can become anxious if the material is beyond their ability to understand and/or if there is a tense atmosphere in the room. In order to design

189

lessons at the right level of difficulty with well-organized teaching approaches, you can again use a **task analysis**. You can begin new chapters or concepts with some preliminary assessment of student readiness *before* you begin the real teaching. This diagnostic step will keep you from launching a teaching lesson when too many students demonstrate a lack of readiness.

You should also address the issue of student anxiety. The presence of remedial materials, student tutors, differentiated homework, and/or re-takes on important tests or assignments can materially lessen student anxiety. Describe how you will employ a wide variety of student assessment strategies to reduce grade tension. Reflect back on things you have done to support students or perhaps even things that might have helped you. Once you have gathered a set of successful ideas to fit your own teaching stance, you are ready to answer this part of the question.

The second component of this question is how you will produce "more confident learners." Use the "success for all students" message contained in the first part of your answer to set the table for this part of the response. Students often lack confidence when they have experienced multiple years of failure or frustration. Conversely, their confidence increases when the number of successful learning experiences rises.

In mathematics, you can increase the probability of success when you increase the frequency and variety of assessment opportunities. It also helps when you reduce the amount of material to be mastered for any one assessment. If students do not demonstrate mastery on the quizzes or short tests, you can always add opportunities for students to identify their mistake(s) and retake only the portions where they were unsuccessful. Explain how your goal is to provide every possible means for students to demonstrate genuine mastery of the material and receive *full* credit for their effort. Note to the committee how you will reward additional effort and avoid any grade reduction simply because it took a bit longer. There are some who claim the added opportunities and time for selected students is unfair to others who were successful on the first attempt. I respectfully disagree. The goal is the learning, not the time. The real unfairness is treating all students alike when there are such obvious differences in background and ability.

Self-esteem problems can increase when individuals do not learn as fast as the other students. The wise teacher can render this a moot issue by providing the necessary support for *all* students to master key concepts. Give serious thought to this form of mastery teaching and tell the committee how you plan to employ its principles. Whatever path you decide, be sure the interview team knows that you believe consistent, legitimate *success* is the *only* real avenue to increased self-esteem and math confidence.

KEYS TO YOUR RESPONSE:

- Start your discussion by stating your understanding of the problem.
- Identify ways you will organize the curriculum and manage instruction so as to teach at the right levels of difficulty for students.
- Highlight a variety of means by which you will provide strong support to every student.
- Catalog the ways you will build successful mathematics experiences for each student.

> *One of the most common complaints a teacher hears from students is, "Math class is boring!" What will you do to change this perception and make your class an interesting, exciting place to learn?*

Be assured that mathematics has not cornered the market on the problem of student boredom. You can insert the name of any discipline and the statement remains accurate. It is unlikely you can make every minute of every class "interesting and exciting" to every student; however, there *are* things you can do to extend the vigor and vitality of mathematics lessons. Everyone has experienced the math teacher who begins each class with a review of the homework, has students go to the board with their solutions, discusses errors, spends five or ten minutes on new material, and gives the next assignment. Good heavens, we *must* do better than that!

This question asks for specifics on how you will provide innovative instructional lessons and novel approaches to teaching. It opens the door to many possibilities, but you can simplify the approach by framing your answer around *motivation*.

> *"Keeping my class from becoming boring or routine requires daily attention. As I think about this problem, it seems there are several areas where what I do as a teacher can influence how students will view my class. These might include: (1) a strong and clearly defined purpose for each lesson that students must learn, (2) the use of innovative teaching strategies wherever possible, (3) the use of technology to bring dimension to the class, and (4) the building of strong relationships between me and my students."*

You may have different views on the topic, but it is important to identify three or four central themes around which you will develop a complete answer. The above are just some ideas to help move your creative mind in the right direction. Look at these items in isolation to see how they can be presented and explained. Whichever items you decide for yourself, you will need to give the rationale behind each choice.

The **purpose of learning** is a logical place to begin helping students gain enthusiasm for the new concepts. Let the principal know that when students are unaware of the value of your lesson, "being bored" is a natural extension of that ignorance. Therefore, you see the connection of your lesson to the real world of students as essential. The more worthwhile the lesson, the higher the probability will be for student engagement. Tell the committee you see "engagement" as one of the strongest antidotes to student boredom. Other things you can use to fight boredom will include outside-speakers, field experiences, career connections, and personal anecdotes that describe a concept's specific use. Make a point that one of your main goals will be to keep fresh and novel elements in your class so that it does not become routine and dull.

The next portion of your answer will pyramid right off this last point. You will use strong **lesson designs and innovation**. Look over your lesson plans. Describe how you will include several different formats along with solid learning activities. Active student involvement is essential during every class. By the way, one student at the board while the others are supposedly critiquing the answer _does not_ qualify as active involvement. I've had that teacher and my IQ declined five points in his class! Changing class routines will help maintain what Jon Saphier calls "learning momentum" (Saphier, 2009). Select a few of your favorite lesson designs that incorporate high student involvement and have them ready to share with the committee. A brief anecdote to amplify your answer can be a compelling punctuation to this portion of your answer. It is vitally important that you include one or two high impact teaching strategies at some point in your answer. Here is a novel approach to the practice of checking for student understanding.

> _"One class strategy I might employ from time to time will be the use of dry-erase boards during the discussion. I will ask questions and have students respond on their boards. When they are ready, I will say 'up boards' and look at the responses they have written. Students are likely to find this somewhat novel, and we can have a lot of fun with it. For me, however, the value will be its effective use in quickly finding out who knows what."_

How about the use of technology to add high interest and innovation to your class? Do you know of virtual or online learning opportunities for students who demonstrate advanced ability or interest? If you can provide the names of good Internet resources, this significantly increases the strength of your answer. Even if the school might not have computers in your class, include this information in your answer.

You may wish to add an overview of your room arrangement. Will there be current and interactive bulletin boards? Will there be learning centers that target a variety of purposes? Will there be displays of student project work, career information, or other interesting topics? The feeling tone in your class can have a strong influence on interest, motivation, and student learning. Bland classrooms can significantly contribute to the boredom of students.

Madeline Hunter lists a phenomenon called "with-it-ness" as one of the intangibles that can make a class an exciting place for both students and teachers (Hunter, 2004). Success in cultivating sound connections to the world around students can only arise from your consistent attention to the many interactions you have with students over time. Teachers <u>must</u> make it a point to reach out to every student, every day. Discuss the importance you place in keeping your classroom and student relations fresh with great ideas and relevant learning opportunities. Others will leave this out, and that omission provides you an opportunity to say something special.

In conclusion, look back at your teaching as well as the good teaching you experienced while you were a student. What made the classes you have taken more memorable? Include elements of your background and experience that you believe will make your class into one that students see as memorable and worthwhile.

KEYS TO YOUR RESPONSE:

- Form your answer around three or four dimensions of motivation that will define your teaching stance.
- Cite the dimensions individually and give examples of how you will address each one in your class.
- End with a discussion of the importance of human relations in creating classes where students feel respected and valued.

Our curriculum and current standards require that students be able to use mathematical tools such as calculators. Explain how you use and teach students about calculators and other mathematical tools to increase their ability to think and solve problems.

There is more than one part to this question, and you should clarify what they are. (1) Explain how you teach students to use calculators or other mathematical tools, and (2) describe how this increases their ability to think mathematically and solve problems. These explanations are quite straightforward, and you need not spend an exorbitant amount of time on the answer.

Begin with an explanation of where and how you allow students to use calculators. Exponents, roots, long lists of calculations, trigonometry, calculus derivatives, graphing equations, and other high level functions all need explanation. You should tell the committee how you approach the teaching of at least one of these advanced functions because, unless the classes you plan to teach are primarily remedial math, instruction in four-function calculations will fail to impress a high school committee. If you have an anecdote about an innovative lesson where calculators were used, share it with the committee. Most principals and supervisors like to know about your actual work with students. The only caveat is to watch your time. Stories have a tendency to run long unless you make an effort to be brief. A good rule of thumb is to limit less complicated answers to two or three minutes.

The question also asks you to describe how you would "increase their ability to think and solve problems." This goes beyond just using the tools. To frame your answer, consider employing Bloom's Taxonomy to describe how you can use calculators to extend student thinking through the analysis, synthesis, and evaluation levels of complexity (Krathwohl, Airasian and Cruikshank, 2000). If you have designed projects or class activities that promote high order thinking, provide a brief description. Do not forget the question asked about problem solving and application. If you have an authentic task or problem-solving activity, this is a perfect place to insert that information. As we have repeatedly said, the specificity of examples adds power to your answer.

 KEYS TO YOUR RESPONSE:

- Identify the parts of this question so that they can be approached separately.
- Provide details about how you would teach advanced calculator functions and provide at least one example.
- Use Bloom's Taxonomy to discuss how calculators or other tools can be used to extend student thinking through the higher levels of thinking.
- If you have an authentic task or problem that requires calculators, describe that to the committee.

> *What will you do to help students master the content and process skills that will be necessary to perform well on the SAT or ACT?*

WARNING: *Questions on test preparation can be a deal-breaker.* If you are applying to a high expectation district, SAT results are an important concern. Principals need to feel confident you are aware of this and can provide the kind of instruction that will lead to strong test performance. The irony in this question is a good answer will not carry the day, but a poor answer can badly damage your viability.

If Algebra or advanced math classes are in your projected schedule, this question or a close relative can be expected. If you are not familiar with the requirements of the SAT math section, learn all you can about the central skills and test formats students must master. Most bookstores have test-preparation manuals and a brush up might be in order. The information contained in these sources should provide a reliable entry to your answer.

There are many things a teacher can do to help students ready themselves for the SAT or ACT. Describe some of the test's formats and how you will mirror those designs in class activities or homework. Explain how you will employ mastery lesson designs to teach some of the more frequently tested concepts. You might consider the use of an SAT or ACT preparation program as a learning center in your room. You can have an "SAT Question of the Week." The idea is to consistently provide learning opportunities that cultivate and reinforce strong mathematics skills. This coupled with distributed practice and sample test formats will sharpen student proficiency and deepen their test management awareness.

An important point to make is that whatever SAT/ACT preparation is done, it will be a part of the regular curriculum and not discrete units of study. Principals do not want the core curriculum supplanted by a "teach to the test" agenda. There are numerous ways to help prepare students for these tests, and you only need to choose a few that demonstrate your approach to the question's key concerns.

KEYS TO YOUR RESPONSE:

- Begin your answer with an overview of what you deem to be critical areas students must understand.
- Identify a variety of classroom strategies you will employ to teach and sharpen those skills you identified as essential to student success on the SAT or ACT.

- Catalog outside enrichment experiences that will be available throughout the year.
- Let the committee know that test preparation will be a part of the class and not a stand-alone unit of study.

What interdisciplinary connections do you see for mathematics to the other content areas?

Teaching math across the curriculum or integrated instructional patterns have become more prevalent over the years. The literature has increasingly recognized how concepts in one discipline can enhance student understanding and skill in other subject areas. The synergy created from teaching interrelated, complementary skills and knowledge is an important relationship every learner can appreciate.

If you have had experience or coursework in how to design interdisciplinary units, this is a place to describe that experience. High school teachers have limited cross-discipline planning time, and you will need to reflect on occasions when you may have worked with members of different departments or independently to create connections to other subject areas.

There is no need to worry if you have not previously been part of this type of planning. You can talk about how you would use and reinforce concepts from other subject areas in your mathematics class (Jacobs, 2010). A few ideas on how math can be used by other disciplines include: (1) the use of logic and mathematics in making legal arguments, (2) mathematical reasoning in the science of genetics or forensic medicine, or (3) the use of mathematics in the world of advertising. You can describe how mathematics is a part of music composition, military battle plans, art, or any of a thousand other connections. Present four or five innovative ideas on where other disciplines could enhance the teaching of math concepts in your class. As long as you demonstrate a few novel and innovative connections, you have answered this question well.

KEYS TO YOUR RESPONSE:

- Provide a short overview of what you know about integrated instruction and why you see it as important to the students in your class.
- Give examples of cross-connections you can make in your teaching. A good anecdote will work well.
- Describe any ways you would work with other departments or teachers to develop interdisciplinary connections.

CONCLUDING THOUGHTS:

When applying for a mathematics position, understand that the committee is looking for a candidate who possesses a strong understanding of the discipline, uses innovative classroom instructional strategies, and has an ability to engage students at all levels. Deliver your answers with feeling and energy because enthusiasm is contagious. In this chapter's discussion, sample questions identified a number of places where you need to pre-think an answer and fashion your best thinking. It is insufficient to merely "think" through possible answers. Write the key points of your response down on an index card or piece of paper. You may think of a great example, but if you do not have it in writing, you are likely to later forget an important detail. Prepare ahead by reviewing the response keys at the end of each sample question, and you will be ready to establish a strong candidacy. Deliver those good answers and step right to the front of the candidate line!

"A teacher affects eternity; he can never tell where his influence stops."

— Henry B. Adams, **1907**

SCIENCE QUESTIONS

GENERAL ADVICE ON INTERVIEWS FOR SCIENCE POSITIONS:

Science education is another position where some schools find it more difficult to find qualified staff. This is especially true in the physical sciences such as Chemistry and Physics. In one state, there were reportedly only two physics education graduates over an entire year. Yet that same state had posted over fifty vacancies. However, unless you hold a certificate for that subject area, you will find things to be quite competitive, especially in the biological and general science categories.

Because the field of science teaching has so many sub-disciplines such as general science, earth science, biology, chemistry, physical science, physics, and specialty areas, this chapter cannot possibly provide an in-depth analysis for each subject area. You should, however, expect to hear questions related to the specific content for which you are applying, and you will need to be up to speed on the most modern curriculum ideas and teaching methods for that subject. Specific content questions are especially likely to be asked if a supervisor or department head is part of the interview team. This chapter will provide more general examples across a variety of areas to provide insight as to how the more generic science questions are likely to be framed. Each question is designed to illuminate the knowledge necessary for a basic theme, general teaching practice, or specific skill set required to teach science.

ALTERNATE ROUTE CANDIDATE: In this chapter you will find a wide variety of relatively common questions asked of a science candidate. The answers provided can easily be adapted to someone with limited or no classroom teaching experience. You will see these adaptations as you go through the information. The largest challenge for you will be the use of practical examples. Since you have not taught, you will not be able to cite specific use of the strategies or ideas we present in our sample answers. Still, you have had some pedagogic training and have undoubtedly been in classrooms for a large part of your life. You can certainly draw upon those resources to formulate a classroom practice you might *intend* to use. The addition of these examples is important to the development of that "capacity to meet the expectations of the position" we have said is so essential. For that reason, you must pre-think these examples and render them to writing. As you prepare for your interview day, you will use these to sharpen your mind and make focused preparations. With this kind of preparation, you will be more than ready to shine and compete with the very best candidates in the interview pool.

SAMPLE SCIENCE QUESTIONS AND THEIR ANSWERS:

Some science pedagogy speaks to the necessity of "constructivist learning." Tell the committee what this means to you and how your classroom will build on this important learning theory.

Gulp! I have asked this question dozens of times and simply watched the uneasiness it has caused and the changes to a candidate's body language. Sad. But, the good news is that this question is much easier than it sounds, and by the time we are done, you will be absolutely on fire with good ideas should anyone try to ask you something similar.

With this in mind, the first thing that needs your attention is the term "constructivist learning." It is interesting to listen to candidates describe what they believe this kind of learning involves because you get such an array of answers. The simple answer is of course rooted in the works of people like Piaget. Constructivism is a theory about how the brain learns in human beings. It contends that humans construct their own understanding and new knowledge through their experiences and the way they impact on ideas or information they already possess. As such, the individual mind that must create its own meaningful connections if new material is to be understood and maintained.

One of the most important works in the last ten years on this kind of brain research was done by David Sousa in his book, <u>How the Brain Learns</u> (Sousa, 2005). In this book, Sousa makes it clear how ideas are moved to long-term memory. He describes how students must mentally work with the various new concept pieces and construct a context for them. Once this is complete, the new learning can move off of the short-term "work-table" and into long-term storage. This requirement makes a case for direct student engagement as opposed to the more passive approach inherent in the all too prevalent "lecture" method of teaching. This is an excellent work, and if you can articulately speak to its ideas and relevance in your interview, you will be a light year ahead of almost every other candidate.

With these understandings of what constructivist learning is, the question moves to the kinds of experiences that lead to a well-disciplined constructivist learning environment: the kind of environment you intend to describe in your answer. A very nice work that sheds light on this question is, <u>In Search of Understanding: The Case for Constructivist Classrooms, 2nd edition</u>, by Jacqueline and Martin Brooks.

If you are an **alternate route teacher** or someone with limited classroom teaching opportunities, then your experiences with this kind of lesson has likely been as a student. Either way, you will recognize the important elements of good constructivist learning environments in the modern science classroom.

Now let's look at how you can address the second part of this question which deals with how your class will promote a "constructivist" environment. As with all answers, you need to describe the teaching that fits your individual stance and lesson style. But, we do need to accurately and fully outline some high impact ideas that can paint a vivid picture in the minds of the interview committee. Below are some classroom ideas that will provide the kind of active classroom this question demands.

PROMOTING ACTIVE CLASSROOMS

- With every concept and new learning, there will be hands-on activities that require students to work with the ideas and their applications.
- Small groups and investigation teams will be formulated that require students to do individual research and go deeper into the meaning of classroom ideas.
- Authentic learning tasks will be required to demonstrate mastery of important concepts.
- Laboratory investigations will move from the old-school cookbook approach to the more contemporary experiences where students will be required to analyze and draw conclusions.
- Technology applications will be a part of the class so that students can do online research and find new applications for what they have learned in class.
- Individual projects and real-world applications will play a role in requiring students to conduct synthesis level thinking.
- Outside experiences and work in "the real-world" will require students to apply their classroom learning to the everyday problems in their own environments.

There are many other classroom tested ideas you could include, and this list is by no means all-inclusive. But, you can see that in all cases, students are required to work with ideas and "do" science, not just hear or see its concepts. The answer you provide will be a reflection of your own teaching style, but it might sound something like the following:

> "To provide the class environment you ask about in your question, my classroom will be a place where students come to be _engaged in science_ and not _just hear about science_. That is accomplished through a very wide array of regular classroom activities which include some of the following strategies. (1) I consistently include a mixture of hands-on activities and formal laboratories to extend the concepts we are studying through practical applications. (2) My laboratory experiences are regular and require application as well as proper procedure and analysis. (3) Through the use of small, highly challenged investigation teams, students are required to take new ideas and research them for deeper meaning. (4) I use authentic assessment tasks to be sure students know how a concept or application is used and not just memorized. There are many other things, some of which I gained through the book, _In Search of Understanding: The Case for Constructivist Classrooms, 2nd edition_, by Brooks. The bottom line is that I want a class that has vitality and active learning experiences taking place every day; and, based on your question, I believe that is your desire as well."

Let me tell you; if you give something like that answer, you will knock the committee members off their chairs! It is tight, hard-hitting, and has provided exactly the kind of information that paints a picture for every member to see. And, did you notice how we quietly name-dropped the title of a great book and author? I know: sneaky. But, if there is something that will set your answer above everyone else's, it is the fact that you are basing your response on well researched and proven ideas in the literature.

We will add one more ingredient to our answer that will cement our place at the top of the candidate list. We will add a specific example of just how one of these classroom experiences will actually look! Use something from your own repertoire, but here is one example that was used in an Earth Science class in Tennessee (actually _my_ class).

> "For example, students might study a unit on rocks and minerals. As we explore this unit students will engage in several hands on activities. One such activity might have students study how to name and classify rocks by identifying their unique physical characteristics such as hardness and acid sensitivity. Students will then work through a WebQuest to see how rocks and minerals can be used to reveal geologic history. Once

students have internalized classification procedures, they move on to a full laboratory experience that will require them to go outside and identify local rocks or minerals. The culminating activity will have students work in small research teams to put together a representative rock collection they can use to tell a Power Point story about the geologic history of East Tennessee. When students are finished with this unit, they will own every concept and idea we set out to teach. Best of all, they will have a lot of fun doing it and remember the experience!"

When you add your own teaching lesson, it will derive strength from two sources. First, it will clearly show you know how to put the ideas of your opening statement to work in the class. They were not just words, they were an action plan. Second, what you describe in the example will be clearly seen as engaging, fun, and highly worthwhile learning. It is precisely the kind of experience they would like to have for their own children! You have no idea how often that kind of feeling can extend itself into a job offer.

 KEYS TO YOUR RESPONSE:

- Begin with a <u>concise</u> definition of the constructivist movement, the key contributors, and the way those ideas will influence your teaching. Use the names of well-known writers.
- Select a variety of classroom strategies and activities and catalog them one after the other with a brief explanation as to their relevance.
- Pyramid off your initial list by providing a dynamic example that incorporates two or three of the features you previously mentioned. The more "fun" and interesting you make this example, the more the committee will see your class as the kind they want in their school!
- End by equating what you have described with the original question, and let the committee know that *this* is the kind of classroom they want in their science department.

 Science can be a difficult discipline for special needs students. How can you adapt your class so these young people can enjoy a sound science experience?

Science is a subject where special education students are often included as a part of the regular class. This is particularly true in general and earth science, but it can occur in the so-called college prep courses as well. You need a specific plan for modifications you might use with included students.

The chapter dealing with general questions contained ideas on how to teach mainstreamed special education students. However, that discussion did not speak about the unique problems related to science teaching. Open with a short affirmation of your enthusiasm to teach special needs students and a commitment to make these students a full part of your class. It is important that the committee see you are not reluctant to work with special education students.

As said time and again throughout this book, the controlling resource when designing instruction for special education students is the student's IEP. As you work to incorporate the features of this plan into your classroom teaching, you should speak directly to the student's case manager or learning consultant. He or she has helped develop the goals and modifications and can be of great assistance in your work with the student. A sound answer to this question must begin with how you will put the IEP and Learning Consultant (LC) to work in your planning.

Unique issues for the science teacher include how you will adapt science investigations and laboratory experiments to maximize the involvement of special students. Be sure to cite any additional safety practices you might recommend and how they will be monitored. Demonstrate how the learning requirements can be structured so they are within the intellectual reach of every student. Because science can sometimes address concepts or activities that exceed the IEP limitations, you will need to describe how you can work with the case manager to develop parallel but relevant work for the student. This might include a special learning station, Internet activity, or other hands-on experience.

The question specifically asks about which class modifications you will consider. Beyond what was previously discussed, you should mention adaptations such as special grouping arrangements, modified laboratory report requirements, special assessment features, alternate textbook or reading materials, added opportunities for art or other more kinesthetic experiences, or special one-on-one mentoring with other classmates. Your goal is to let the committee know you are a person who recognizes the value of a science experience for special needs students.

There is one last point you should make to the committee before you conclude your answer. Assure everyone that you will take deliberate steps to create a science experience that is both successful and stress-free. Describe how you will work out an individual grading plan with the case manager that will be sufficiently varied to allow students to demonstrate their understanding through multiple avenues. Notify everyone that you will adjust and not eliminate curriculum. It is essential the committee understand you will maintain consistent content expectations and educational experiences for everyone.

KEYS TO YOUR RESPONSE:

- Open with a short affirmation of your enthusiasm to work with special needs students.
- State your intentions to work with the case manager and collaboratively develop a sound program of study that is in compliance with each student's IEP.
- Catalog specific classroom modifications in laboratory procedures and science content knowledge that will promote student success.
- Specifically state that you intend to *adjust* curriculum expectations and not *eliminate* them.
- End with a commitment to make the class as stress free as possible but still maintain a curriculum similar to that of the other students.

> *When you assign students a science project, what are its design elements and how do you determine successful student performance?*

The committee obviously thinks projects are worthwhile or this question would not have been asked. Begin the discussion with your views on the importance of independent research and the elements of a good science project. Describe a project assignment you have made or might make in the future and tell about how you might put such a design in place if you are selected for this position. In your answer, be sure to address the committee's central question regarding the critical "design elements." Consider how students will choose their topics, the level of required experimentation, the research format, the report's length, and any specific writing requirements. Will oral or visual presentations be required? Will there be interdisciplinary connections to other areas such as English or Math? If you address a variety of these considerations, you will have your answer moving in the right direction.

Regarding the determination of project grades, you might employ some of the options included in the previous example such as rubrics, presentations, or displays. Tell the committee about the handouts and guides you intend to provide. Identify which elements of the project are graded and outline their assessment plan.

DON'T FORGET: *If you have a great class project you have used or seen in the past, include a one-page overview of that project in your interview portfolio! This, along with work samples or pictures of students at work, will add two exclamation points to your candidacy.*

KEYS TO YOUR RESPONSE:

- Begin with a discussion about why science projects are an important part of your teaching.
- Identify a project you have assigned students and categorize its critical elements and desired learning outcomes.
- Discuss how you will grade the assignment. Be sure to define any rubrics you will use.

Students often ask why they have to learn something or why what they are studying is important. How do you answer those questions?

How many times have we heard the phrase, "Why do we have to learn this stuff, anyway?" This is another way of saying, "I don't see any purpose to what we are doing." A science lesson's purpose can be lost unless the teacher establishes a clear connection between the content and the student's world. Principals want to know prospective teachers understand this obligation, and they can create lessons that communicate a clear, worthwhile purpose to what must be taught.

Begin your answer with a statement that establishes your intention to provide a consistent rationale for the units and concepts defined in the curriculum. Make it clear that you intend to link instruction as closely as possible to the real world of students. By providing meaningful class experiences, you hope to decrease the frequency with which this question is asked.

> *"When I hear this question from students, I immediately know they have failed to see the purpose of the lesson. In my classes we will spend time to establish the purpose of each study area, before we begin the teaching. In my daily teaching, I will need to make the lesson components as meaningful as possible. There are specific ways I can do this. Let me outline a few now."*

At this point, the use of a specific example or story will be sufficient to give the committee what it requires. Think about any previous classes you have taught or seen and identify a lesson where a purpose was provided that resonated with you or your students. Specific ways teachers can establish purpose and meaning include the use of outside speakers, videos, career connections, field trips, Internet sites, models, authentic problems, or service-learning experiences. There are others and you should choose those that best fit your style of teaching.

An effective way to establish a purposeful learning experience is through the use of something called "meaning." Meaning is defined as the level to which students see the material as related to them. The literature contains numerous articles that identify classroom methods to help students derive meaning from a lesson (Hunter, 2004).

HUNTER'S VARIABLES THAT LEAD TO INCREASED MEANING
- The new learning has **high interest examples** the student understands.
- The lesson has **novel or vivid activities** to capture interest.
- The lesson helps students **solve a problem** they see as important.
- There is a **structure and organization** the students find easy to follow and understand.
- The new information is **closely related to something students already understand**. (You must help make such connections.)
- There is a relationship between what is taught and its **application to the real world** of students.

When giving your answer, you do not need to tick off the entire list of variables. In fact it might be best to confine your approach to just a couple of the variables that most closely target lesson purpose. Power comes from providing that crisp list of examples to illustrate how you intend to promote a worthwhile purpose to your teaching.

"One way I like to create meaning in the lesson is to show students that what they are learning in the current lesson is related to something they already know. For example, when I teach students about inertia in a Physical Science class, I can explain that we all know what happens when a large object strikes a large immoveable mass. But, as we all know, once we get that large object moving in one direction, it is sometimes hard to stop. Consider the Titanic. She was cruising along and all of a sudden there is an iceberg dead ahead! In this case, wouldn't we all agree that her "inertia" is what killed her? If we are to learn anything from this tragic event, we must know what factors contributed to Titanic's inertia and why this was such a problem. In fact we also need to know why inertia might even be a problem for you!"

207

This is a great example of creating meaning because it combines several variables. It relates the concept of inertia to something with which students are familiar. It has a high degree of interest and pictorial vividness. It poses a problem that students might be interested in solving. It involves them in hands-on activities. WOW. The committee should like an example like this!

Close with your recognition of the fact that no single strategy can fit all students. Individuals have unique perspectives and interests. For that reason, you intend to establish a strong purpose and use as many variables of meaning possible. Trust me on this; if you include the key elements of the response outlined above, you will have nailed this question to everyone's satisfaction.

KEYS TO YOUR RESPONSE:

- Begin by defining the real problem – the lack of perceived purpose.
- Catalog the ways you will establish clear links between what is taught and the student's world.
- Cite the ways you will enhance "meaning" in your teaching.
- Conclude by noting that a variety of methods are required to establish purposeful teaching.

Safety is always a concern for laboratory science. How do you keep this important matter a priority for students?

This is a straightforward question and science candidates can usually count on a safety question. Liability concerns need to be addressed at the interview stage of any teacher search. A complex answer is not required. The principal and committee just want to know you will take standard precautions and make good judgments to insure everyone's safety.

Let the committee know you will consistently assess any safety features in your lab to insure they are fully operational and ready for use. You will post and teach clear safety instructions. Specific investigations may require additional safety procedures, and those will be taught as needed. You will model good safety practices yourself. You might also administer a safety test or quiz to be sure your students know and understand the rules before they begin work. Talk about how you will deal with students who violate safety standards. If you address these areas, the committee will be well satisfied by your answer.

KEYS TO YOUR RESPONSE:

- Do not overcomplicate the question when a simple answer will do.
- Talk about the various pieces of safety equipment you will want in your laboratory and their importance.
- Underscore a few general safety concerns and announce your intention to teach safety measures, not merely recite the rules.
- Conclude with a strong statement that good safety will be consistently modeled in the room, and students will be expected to follow acceptable procedures.

Tell us how you determine that a student understood the science concepts you taught and did not merely memorize content for the test.

I include this question because it raises an important issue called "understanding." The nature of "understanding" has its basis in explanations originally provided by Benjamin Bloom back in 1955 (Anderson, David R, et al., 2000). Many candidates will answer this question by using the Bloom definitions. He is an excellent source, and his definition serves the purpose. However, we can do better – a lot better!

The last 25 years have brought significant advancement to our appreciation of how students come to understand. For our discussion, we will use an expanded description of this term as outlined in the book, <u>Understanding by Design</u> (Wiggins and McTighe, 1998). They describe six interrelated variables that make up mature understanding. Even if this precise question is not posed, these ideas can be used in many ways, and it will be well worth the time spent to internalize this expanded description of the term "understanding."

WIGGINS AND MCTIGHE'S VARIABLES OF UNDERSTANDING

1. **EXPLANATION:** Apt explanations of theories that provide knowledgeable accounts of events, actions, and ideas.
2. **INTERPRETATION:** Narratives and translations that provide meaning.
3. **APPLICATION:** The ability to use knowledge effectively in a new situation and diverse context.
4. **PERSPECTIVE:** Critical and insightful points of view.
5. **EMPATHY:** The ability to get inside another person's feelings and worldview.

209

6. ***SELF-KNOWLEDGE:*** The wisdom to know one's ignorance and how one's patterns of thought and action inform as well as prejudice understanding.

Fashion your answer around a description of teaching practices that foster the development of these abilities in students. An excellent approach is to describe a designed activity that promotes one or more of these variables. You might suggest the use of discussion techniques, independent study projects or "think tank" activities that can lead to better student understanding. Your goal is to provide a lesson strategy that will produce the kinds of behavior Wiggins and McTighe list as indicators of student understanding.

> *"Guiding students to truly understand the material is critical to good teaching. Memorization only brings information to short-term memory and will usually not last longer than the day of the test. Two of the ways I know students "understand" is when they can apply the knowledge to a new situation or if they can provide different or unique insights that use the information."*

Here we included two of our definitions to exemplify ways we can identify student understanding. This, however, is not quite enough. We must also take the answer to the next step and supply a practical example. This may be difficult to do on the spur of the moment, and I suggest you take the extra time to pre-think a response.

> *"I can draw an example of this from when I would teach taxonomy in the Biology class. After I conduct my lesson on the ways we classify living things, I show students a few examples of dichotomous keys, and we work together to identify a few sample organisms. From this point, I might give students a variety of new items to classify and they have to use one of our keys to make their decision. If they can do this – I will know they understand the concept of taxonomy. To extend and reinforce this initial learning, I could ask students to go out in the field, collect a few samples of their own, and then use the key to classify them. Once they have done all this, they have shown the required insight, application and understanding I required. Even more, they will <u>own these skills</u> well into the future."*

You possess many strategies of your own, and the best approach is to choose those with which you feel most comfortable. Be assured, if you employ this broader definition of understanding and clearly show how you employ it in your teaching, your answer will be a winner!

210

KEYS TO YOUR RESPONSE:

- Study the broader definition of the term "understand" as provided by Wiggins and McTighe.
- Choose two or three of the variables and discuss them.
- Provide at least one practical example from a lesson you have taught.
- **ALTERNATE ROUTE TEACHER:** Pre-think a classroom example you can use by either selecting something from your classroom experiences or researching an online resource.

> *Science "literacy" is a topic that has received a great deal of recent attention. What will students do in your class to enhance this skill?*

Literacy involves both the reading of science and the ability of students to communicate their knowledge and understanding of science. In today's schools literacy across the curriculum is a major concern because all states have identified literacy standards in the core academic areas.

The only way to increase science literacy is to have students engage in both the reading and writing of science. Your response can begin with a quick outline of various writing opportunities you might include in your course. These can consist of such things as journals, lab reports, projects, research papers, book reviews, or reflection pieces where students have to communicate their understandings of science. Talk about how you will engage students in the reading of science and list any required reading that might be part of your class. Indicate how you will provide ongoing opportunities for students to express scientific viewpoints or information. Student expression of scientific ideas is a very important element of literacy.

> *"I think it is important for every student to be a consumer of good scientific literature and be able to express his or her ideas in a coherent way. In our genetics unit, the entire class will read 24 pages of the book, The Double Helix, by James Watson. We will discuss this reading in class and write a reflection piece on the real world of scientists. Some students will present their ideas to the class for discussion."*

Literacy activities can and should be a part of every unit. It does not have to be an "extra" concern. With thoughtful development of class activities, it can be an integral part of the normal teaching process.

KEYS TO YOUR RESPONSE:

- Identify where you will incorporate writing and scientific literacy in your regular teaching.
- Give an example of an outside reading that will extend student experience into the literature of science.
- Identify how you will use and teach this reading selection in your class.

CONCLUDING THOUGHTS:

Prospective science teachers should understand that the most important part of selling themselves to the committee rests in their ability to produce classes that will be exciting places for students to learn. These classes must be full of interesting activities, discussions, experimentation, and dynamic interaction.

Interviews for science teachers will focus on several key areas such as content knowledge, laboratory investigations, assessment practice, safety, instructional practice, and planning. Additional relevant questions to a science interview are identified in other chapters, and I urge you to read those as well. Read the questions provided by this chapter a few times and prepare your best thinking on the topic areas we have identified.

You will notice that the names of significant educators and books are sprinkled throughout this book. Where possible, mention such individuals and references by name. When you are able to quote the ideas and works of well-known educators, a message is conveyed that you are someone who knows the important philosophies and educational leaders of our profession. This perception can only help your candidacy. Once the principal realizes you have great answers to his or her questions and a commitment to children, you become a player! You are ready, so attack this interview with enthusiasm. *Now go get hired for that great science position!*

SOCIAL STUDIES QUESTIONS

GENERAL ADVICE ON INTERVIEWS
FOR SOCIAL STUDIES POSITIONS:

You may be seeking a middle or high school position in the social studies area. The teaching demographics for this discipline show a much larger number of candidates particularly at the high school level. Whereas, it would be better were the applicant pool not quite so large, you can be assured that with the information in this book and a little preparation on your part, you will be one of the most formidable candidates on any school's interview list. That, you can take to the bank, so let's begin!

In general, middle school curricula are primarily devoted to World and U. S. History, but high school positions have a considerably wider array of courses such as European History, Government, African-American History, Economics, Sociology, or Psychology. As we did with the other discipline areas, this chapter will provide advice to prepare you for general interview questions in the Social Studies area. These will explore both your general content knowledge and teaching methods with regard to social studies instruction. Narrow questions in particular subject disciplines are not included because of their limited scope of relevance for all readers.

Candidates for a social studies position must be prepared to demonstrate how they will relate the key elements of a school's curriculum to the contemporary world. Because History is often a required course for all students, class management, your ability to teach heterogeneous groups, and human relations are areas the committee is likely to explore. History often has classes composed of a variety of ability groups, and the demand for sound management is a common concern.

As you prepare for the interview, spend time to identify a few innovative lesson ideas from your past teaching or course preparation. The area of social studies is one that can be interesting, exciting, and highly relevant to the students. It can also be painfully boring and uninspired. There is perhaps nothing worse than sitting through an hour or two of a root canal by a teacher who barely moves the needle on the life functions machine. The difference is not in the content but in the teacher's skill, and you must provide clear evidence you are the inspirational teacher the school needs.

ALTERNATE ROUTE TEACHER: The good news is that the only disadvantage you will have on these questions is the lack of direct classroom experience. For that reason, you will not be able to speak about what you "have done" and will instead have to focus on what you "will do." However, the good news is that you have been out in the world. You know first-hand the issues in today's society and have that pragmatic, hands-on background that can only be gained through direct experience. This will provide insights and realistic information that can easily make the classes you teach come alive with real-world connections. Do not be reluctant to point to this advantage from time to time because it is the one place where you might actually be able to outshine someone who only has teaching experience or has just graduated. Your background has a richer color and depth, so use it!

Review the sample questions included in this chapter and consider how your background and skills fit the suggested response. As you think about the information offered by each question, you will need to reflect on your background and experience before you finalize an answer.

SAMPLE SOCIAL STUDIES QUESTIONS AND THEIR ANSWERS:

Describe the opening activities and lessons you might use if you were beginning a 6th grade unit on the Civil War.

The purpose of this question is to determine how you use the important first days of a unit to initiate activities that will lay the essential foundations for study. The teaching topic in this question is not especially important as any long-term study area works equally well. What is important is the way you will present an interesting, enthusiastic introduction that can lead to a productive learning experience. The critical first days of a unit must set the stage and motivate students to engage in active learning. You want to establish a framework on which to construct the key ideas you will explore as the unit moves forward.

When answering this question, you will need to start by outlining a strong hands-on activity that capitalizes on initial student enthusiasm and hooks them into the topic. Whatever the topic might be, think about ways to make the opening few classes novel and memorable. As this question deals with the Civil War, you want an opening that includes a high level of student involvement in an enjoyable activity. There are so many outstanding websites on this topic that you are sure to find an entertaining piece if you do not have one of your own. One such Internet source ties into the PBS series by Ken Burns. It is at http://www.pbs.org/civilwar/classroom/activities. html. In the meantime, below is an example of how you can open your answer on this question.

> *"I believe that the opening days of a new unit are critical. I want to capture student interest and get them involved as quickly as possible. For a Civil War unit, I might begin by asking everyone if they have ever studied this topic before. Of course most everyone will say yes. Great, because I want to divide them into four teams and hold a "Jeopardy like" contest with the buzzer set I have. The questions will come directly from the topics we are studying. There will be prizes for the top two teams so as to make the competition a little keener. Once we finish the contest, some of the questions can be placed on the board, so we can discuss how to study them. This will get us off in the right direction and set the stage for our coming lessons."*

In your answer, go on to identify how you will provide students meaningful reasons to study the Civil War. Underscore any exciting special events you plan such as speakers, artifacts, video clips, or other high-interest items. Since the question centers on the Civil War, you might describe class activities that help students identify the unique aspects of this war. This may be done through role-playing or skits, scenario analysis, or public debates. Such activities help students empathize and mentally connect to the important issues that fueled the conflict. Add your own ideas to those offered here, but a good answer will demonstrate imagination and innovative lesson designs.

KEY INTERVIEW STRATEGY: *Whenever possible, make the ending of your response as powerful and memorable as possible. The last thing a committee hears should be something worth remembering.*

An excellent addition to this answer is a description of how a visual organizer can be used to help students focus on important concepts and ideas. The "advance organizers" are simply study guides that might have images or Power Point slides on the left side of the page and some blank lines on the right. Students can follow your lesson and actively work at the same time. Your description of a system to organize the unit might sound something like the following.

> *"Before we actually begin the instruction, I like to provide the students with an "advance organizer" of what they must learn and any important tasks they must accomplish during the unit. To achieve this goal, I take six to ten central themes or objectives, write them in student language, and arrange them in a sequence everyone can follow. I write everything on the overhead projector, and students follow along on a compatible handout as we progress through the unit. As important information or ideas unfold, I refer students to their organizer. The central ideas are also posted around the room, and we refer to them as the unit unfolds. This guide helps keep everyone on track."*

Your personal approach might be different, and the above is only a suggestion. The important message to convey is that students will clearly know your expectations and the important elements of the unit. The use of **advance organizers** allows everyone to coordinate their thinking and approach to the unit of study. It is an extremely powerful tool and one that most candidates will not identify. That is why your answer will be remembered!

KEYS TO YOUR RESPONSE:

- Start your answer with a brief discussion on how you will establish initial student enthusiasm.
- Outline your strategy to introduce course goals, objectives, and purpose.
- Select a few key ideas or concepts you will teach about the Civil War and describe an innovative way to teach each.
- Identify the key elements of the unit and how you will provide an **advance organizer** that alerts students to what they must learn.

> *One of the better-known statements regarding history is, "Those who cannot remember the past are condemned to repeat it." What would you do in your class to illustrate this maxim and help students internalize its meaning?*

This is an interesting question because it allows you an opportunity to demonstrate how you will tie the student's knowledge of history to contemporary policy making. According to the author of this question, it was designed to assess three things: (1) the candidate's general history knowledge, (2) his or her ability to craft an on-going objective that would continue through the full semester, and (3) his or her ability to use current events as a regular part of the classroom.

When you address this question, describe how you would open the unit with an anticipatory set that asks students to analyze an incident in which history has influenced current policy. This can be done with an example where a famous figure blundered because he or she ignored a historical precedent. For example, military leaders often study the lives of great generals and battles of the past. It has been suggested that Germany's failure to recognize the significance of Napoleon's failed Russian Campaign contributed to the undoing of their entire eastern campaign during WWII. Perhaps if the logistic nightmare of a harsh Russian winter had been considered, this front would not have been opened and the entire course of the war altered. An anticipatory set that uses this information might be structured as follows.

> *"I would ask students to consider this question. What happened to the German army when they tried to invade Russia during WWII? List some of the major obstacles that confronted them."*

Advise the committee that you expect the brutal winter conditions of Russia to be among the answers students would provide. From this point, you can set the stage for the coming lesson.

> *"Yes, the winter was a huge factor. Now, does anyone remember what happened to the army of Napoleon when he tried to invade Russia? Would it have helped had Germany taken heed of the history of that campaign? How might that reflection have affected military policy? In the coming days we are going to look at a variety of occasions where history could have influenced an important decision. More importantly, we are going to look at what is going on in the news today and identify historical precedents that might be useful in crafting contemporary policy."*

With this beginning, you can discuss how you would make the relevance of history to today's world an ongoing theme in your teaching. There were numerous times throughout history when this maxim was significant. As such important past events are reached in the curriculum, historical connections to later events can be drawn and reinforced. If you have examples or your own, be sure to add one or two and strengthen your point.

Take the last few moments of your answer to cite where history may be influencing current policy-making. World leaders often use their knowledge of history to craft treaties and agreements with other nations and individuals. Be sure to explain how students will be required to analyze where current world events are being influenced by historical events. An extremely poignant example is the terrorist attack on the World Trade Center. Were there historical pointers the United States missed? How was this attack similar or different than terrorist attacks in the past? How did Desert Storm influence the decisions of the second invasion of Iraq? You can be confident that if you offer an overview of the ideas presented in this discussion, you will be one step further than most other candidates!

KEYS TO YOUR RESPONSE:

- Begin by describing a teaching set that uses an important historical event that connects to today's world. Explain how this will establish the foundation to teach the concept described by the question.
- Underscore your intention to make this concept an ongoing theme that runs through the curriculum over the entire year.
- End by citing an example of current day policy making that you would use to drive home the importance of this concept to students.

A criticism made of current high school graduates is they do not have a fundamental understanding of democratic citizenship and the operation of our government. If you were to teach a 9th grade social studies class, how would you fashion a unit of study to minimize this perceived learning gap?

Whether the lack of citizenship on the part of young people is a real or perceived problem is not the issue. The mere presence of the question provides license for you to assume the committee feels it is a concern in need of attention. Although the ninth grade history program can vary widely from school to school, the question allows you to assume citizenship is a legitimate part of this school's curriculum and, as such, a logical place to include a unit on this topic.

Entire books have been written on civics, and you obviously do not have time to address the matter to that level of detail. Include only a few critical points in your answer and deliver a brisk, concise response. Because the essential concepts of participatory citizens are an important part of every community, you have an opportunity to use your creativity. Be sure you do not just outline the information students will be taught. Add some activities, outside experiences, and other more innovative lesson design features.

Open with a few civic concepts you feel are essential for students to understand such as the Constitution, the rights and responsibilities of good citizenship, democratic participation, and government organization. Be sure to indicate your intention to teach a lesson or two about the organization and function of the students' local government.

Once this discussion is complete, illustrate the activities and interest-building experiences you intend to provide for students. For example, talk about how the Internet and other technology could be used to extend learning. Most local and county governments have a website and students can learn a great deal from just a few visits. If field experiences are available, take advantage of those. Propose guest lectures, enrichment topics, research projects, on-line courses, video or DVD programs. Link what you are teaching to the real world issues surrounding students today. You might consider an outside project that involves student attendance at a town council or planning board meeting. These high impact experiences lead directly to participation in the democratic process and drives directly to the heart of the question.

The key to this answer will be your description of meaningful lessons that include hands-on activities to show students how and where their democratic participation is necessary.

RESEARCH TIP: *If you are not sure you have a great lesson on <u>any</u> topic, go online and look for great resources. The small amount of research you do can pay big dividends during your interview.*

You want to help students enjoy this unit as it may establish positive transfer to future action. By creating this more comprehensive vision, you will rise above the usual dry recitation of just what students need to know.

KEYS TO YOUR RESPONSE:

- · All units begin with a core of knowledge the students must understand. Open with a discussion of a few core requirements.
- · Describe a wide variety of hands-on excursions into the ways students can participate in their government.
- · End with a short explanation of why you believe the strong activity centered approach will lead to positive transfer of good citizenship habits.

CONCLUDING THOUGHTS:

As you consider the response suggestions provided in this chapter, make every effort to draw upon your daily experiences and personal teaching philosophy. The committee wants to hear how you will bring history to life in the classroom. A key to your success will be the enthusiasm you provide to each response you give. Many good answers lose their impact because they are delivered with no energy or intensity. Be creative, demonstrate your skill and make a statement. Good answers delivered with passion almost always carry the day.

SPECIAL AREA INTERVIEWS

15

GENERAL ADVICE ON INTERVIEWS
FOR SPECIAL AREA POSITIONS:

There is a wide variety of teaching positions that come under the heading of "special areas." Some of the more common are in the fields of instrumental music, vocal music, fine arts, drama, art, technology, physical education, or business. This chapter will primarily address the more common questions that might be asked of any applicant. Where appropriate, we will provide some specific direction to particular areas where a unique situation might exist.

As a related arts teacher, it is important you enter the interview with a clear picture of just what your classes will add to the overall quality of the educational program. You will be asked questions pertaining to your teaching style, curriculum goals, philosophy, performance standards, grading practices, and how you intend to make classes worthwhile to your students.

Everyone is well aware many special area programs have been either eliminated or sharply cut as a result of tightening budgets. You may be asked to articulate a case for the value of your specific field of study, and you should be ready to do so. Be assured the class has value and school officials see the program as worthwhile or it would not be a posted position.

ALTERNATE ROUTE TEACHER: If you are coming into this area with a background of employment experience, be sure to consider just how those experiences will add to your ability to make your lessons bristle with relevancy and interest. Whether you are a musician, artist, business person, radio or television employee, or some other professional, you have a unique background and an array of anecdotal stories to liven your discussions. You know what the real world applications and expectations are. You may have community connections that could lead to internships or on-site partnerships. Look carefully at your background and be ready to make the case regarding just how much added dimension you can bring to the position. Related arts classes are often some of the best places to hire a good strong teacher with your background. Be sure and let the committee know why you are just that person.

As for all interviews, the best prepared candidate will arrive at the interview with a sharp game plan and confidence he or she will be the best candidate. In this chapter, we will work together and give you that advantage!

SAMPLE SPECIAL AREA QUESTIONS AND THEIR ANSWERS:

Can you explain to us how you will go about making your course of study an integral part of the school curriculum and not simply a stand-alone offering outside a student's overall program?

Dr. Robert Andrews, who has extensive experience as a K-12 administrator, suggests this was a question he asked of all prospective special area teachers. Andrews believes that the related arts teacher must articulate his or her offerings with the other disciplines. How you will do this lies at the heart of this question.

There are two courses of action around which to begin your response. First, outline specific articulation steps you plan to take. If you have an opportunity to preview a few courses of study in advance, look for topics where your curriculum is a match. If you are not able to do this, then just speak generically on how you will address integration with other classes.

The second portion of this answer concerns your intention to work with other staff on curriculum matters. Explain how you intend to work on school-wide curriculum committees, strategic planning efforts, and budget committees to make your classes relevant and cost effective. Perhaps your area could become an addition to an enrichment program for students. All of these ideas speak to the wider involvement of you and your specific program.

The final suggestion is to offer a practical example of how you have, or would approach this issue. Choose a specific subject and show what you would do. Here is a short example of how it might sound.

"By way of example, one of my curriculum topics is "musical genre." I chose to work with Swing Music to integrate our studies with other curriculum strands. I met with the grade level social studies, language arts, and PE teacher to see where we might find a match. As a result, we developed a short thematic unit around Swing Music that included the jaded history of swing as a counter-culture in the late 1930's, an analysis of the movie "Swing Kids," and a short dance unit in the PE class. We also had the principal approve an assembly where we brought a Swing Band to the school and had a demonstration. This is the kind of integration I would want to bring to this position if I am chosen for the job."

Do you see how easy this can be, now? Simply choose something from your curriculum that might be a good thematic unit. I know, I know…perhaps you have not done a unit like this and hardly know where to start. In your case, go online and look up "thematic units." There are many examples, and you can find the one that fits you. But, provide an example such as this and the committee will see you as a very strong candidate.

KEYS TO YOUR RESPONSE:

- Set out the initial framework of your answer in terms of integrating your curriculum to other subject areas. Underscore your desire to incorporate a collegial approach to the planning process.
- Identify how your program might become part of an enrichment or extended educational opportunity.
- Make clear your intention to serve on school-wide committees and initiatives to make your course one that is up to date with best practices, a solid addition to the overall program, and cost effective.
- Give a practical example!

Budgets are always an issue and we only want to include courses of study that have significant value to our students. Why should your area of study be one of those we include?

This question is likely to be on your interview in one form or another, and if you do not have a good answer for this one, we may as well pack up our briefcase and look for a good restaurant for lunch. This is something I am certain you have thought about and will have very little difficulty in answering. Still, you should think about how you can sharpen your response in a way where it will not sound like every other candidate the committee will see.

In most cases, other applicants will simply provide a response that speaks to such things as how the class provides a life-long skill, enhances a student's ability to lead a quality life, or has relevance to essential skills for everyday living. Just wonderful; all excellent points to make and you should also include these ideas. Obviously you have to tailor the answer to your own area, but you already know enough qualities to effectively make your case. No matter what you choose to say, this portion of your answer cannot be provided in a matter-of-fact, ho-hum style. If you cannot bring energy and passion to your response, how can the committee sense you are someone who can inspire students to enthusiastically engage in your program? Whereas we don't want to gush all over the conference table, we do want some positive body language, a smile or two, and an upbeat tone in our voice.

This is a good beginning, but now let's look at something others may fail to address; an omission that will allow you to set yourself apart. Think carefully about your teaching area, then do some research. Find out what is taking place in the school, what initiatives are underway, what accomplishments have been lauded, and what success stories match your program. Draw attention to the elements of your class that will most compliment the mission and direction of the school. In short, *match your plans to their plans!* If you can effectively make these connections, you will move your name to the top of the preferred candidates list.

KEYS TO YOUR RESPONSE:

- Open your answer with the specific benefits that your course will have on the overall quality of life and special skills to be offered.
- Research the school program and history to match your answer to what the school has identified as important.
- Deliver your answer with energy and enthusiasm!

Subject areas such as yours often include students who have a variety of special needs. These students might have such concerns as ADD/ADHD, perceptual impairments, or even severe physical limitations. What will you do to safely make these students a regular part of your class?

The public schools of today are experiencing an ever growing population of special education and 504 plan students. In almost all cases, you can expect the vast majority of such students to be a part of your classroom. Before you go to your interview, you need a good answer to the question because this or something very similar to it has a high likelihood of being asked.

You need not approach each learning disability separately. Instead, lay out a specific philosophy and a few general modifications you will have in place to meet every student's specific needs. Make clear your intention to make your class one that will have worthwhile things to do and learn for everyone, but care will be taken to put things at the right levels of difficulty. If there are potential safety issues, describe how you will address those and still provide comparable requirements.

Keep in mind there will likely be IEP's or 504 plans in place. Explain how these documents will guide the modifications you will include and where the case manager will be included in your decision making.

Finally, speak to your intention and ability to make all students feel like they are valued members of the class. Describe a few steps you will take on behalf of special needs students to develop sound interpersonal relations and a supportive feeling tone. Often, such students can become easily marginalized in mainstream settings. Let the committee know that you are aware of this problem and will not let this be the case in any class you teach. Make this element of your answer the last one that you provide because, at the heart of this question, is the concern that these students will be in a quality environment with a teacher who cares. That teacher would be you!

Physical Education Teachers: You will have a number of special issues to address in this question. The first is individual accommodations for all students with special needs. Some students will have physical limitations while others might be overly impulsive or even have oppositional behavior problems. When you have 25 and 30 students in a gym, special needs students can present unique safety issues. You will need to offer clear structures and procedures to minimize these concerns. As mentioned above, talk about how you will seek guidance from the case manager and make accommodations that comply with the IEP's. Former teachers can be an excellent resource and provide insight as to what might have worked in the past. It is important that you make understood that you do not see yourself as the only professional who will work towards making your class a productive and safe environment.

 ## KEYS TO YOUR RESPONSE:

- Describe your class as one where every student will find worthwhile things to study.

- Outline specific steps that will be taken to insure the tasks and subject matter will be at the right level of difficulty.
- Point to how the subject matter and course content is often exactly the kind of class special needs students find most enjoyable and within their abilities.
- Let the committee know you will use the IEP's and case manager in order to guide your decisions on modifications and grading.
- Conclude with a strong statement to explain how you will make each student feel like a valuable member of the class and develop strong student relationships.

Grades in special area subjects can often be a difficult issue. Because your subject matter is frequently tied to personal performances and natural ability, the issue of "fairness" is often raised. How do you approach evaluating student progress and grades?

If there is anything a principal learns over the years, it is just how personal the issue of grading is to teachers. For that reason, I will not try to dictate specific ways to answer this question. Instead, we will confine ourselves to a few general concerns and a few red-flags to avoid.

The question provides a main concern of the committee; *fairness*. If you are a teacher in a performance area such as PE, music, or art then you know how some of your students can excel with very little effort. Others seem to be far less talented and will likely produce results of more limited quality. The interviewer wants to know how you plan to make it possible for such students to still receive the more exemplary grades of A or B. What criteria will you use to measure student performance and student growth? How will you make your practice fair to students of all abilities? How you do this is up to you, but all of these issues will need to be addressed when you explain grading policies.

These are a few red-flag issues to avoid. The first is to stay away from anything that sounds like a "one-size fits all" practice. I have heard prospective teachers describe such things as "minimum standards" in a way where there was no room for any realistic modification. Such rigid standards were often couched in the language of "fairness to the other students." Before you fall into this trap, recognize that principals and department heads almost all agree that if there is one thing patently *unfair*, it is an inflexible set of expectations that mousetrap less capable students. Principals who hear such answers assume at some point this will be a problem that arrives in their office. So just be aware, principals *detest* it when they arrive at school and a set of parents is already waiting in the office to complain about the grading practices in *your* class. This is sure to delay the morning coffee ritual and put him or her in a *very* foul mood regarding *your* performance. You will not want your answer to even hint that you might present such a problem.

A second red-flag concerns how "student participation" might play a role in your grading process. This is not to say that student participation *should not* be included, but rather that you need to behaviorally define what that means and how it looks in practice. Too often, "student participation" has come to mean such things as you simply behave in class, raise your hand, sit quietly in your group, or follow the rules. Such criteria can be overly subjective and essentially unexplainable in concrete terms. If student participation will have a significant role in your grading plan, then design a rubric or some other device that will show the committee you have specific *behavioral indicators* to separate exemplary from marginal performance.

Physical Education Advice: Because PE might have a larger class size than the typical classroom, there is an added burden to outline a more comprehensive plan on how you will observe and evaluate individual performance. Units that involve competitive sports and a team approach can be especially difficult to quantify; however, you can expect that someone on the committee might ask you to define how you grade such activities. For example, how much is skill and expertise counted in relation to effort and participation? How will such things as "dressing out for class" and getting into squads affect student grades? If a student has a medical reason for not participating, how will that be handled and made part of student evaluations? These and other questions are likely to be asked, and you will need a well-constructed response.

Music and Performing Arts Advice: These are areas where evening performances and rehearsal schedules can often impact a student's grade. In addition, many students who are not especially talented will be in your class. You can expect to be asked how an absence from a rehearsal or performance will impact a student's overall grade. Will students with lead roles such as first chair in the orchestra or an acting lead in the play receive more credit than lesser roles? This can often be justified because of the additional work and responsibility, but think through the rationale that will guide your policy. In all cases, as long as you have a reasonable criteria and objective basis on which grade decisions are based, you will find the committee receptive to your plan.

KEYS TO YOUR RESPONSE:

- Describe the specific system you use to grade students so that students of varying abilities will be able to achieve even the highest grade.
- Outline how performance expectations will be accommodated to meet the needs of students who have only modest talent or initial skill.
- Avoid the red-flag areas and keep your practice from becoming too inflexible or subjective.

Parents are critical to a student's education and represent an important concern for teachers. What will you do to establish quality communication and relations with the parents of your students?

An ongoing concern of school administrators is that parents will tend to pay more attention to student performance as they relate to core area subjects and less attention to the elective and special area programs. This is often in evidence at such times as Back to School Night where elective program teachers see far fewer parents. Yet, we would all agree that your class *should be* just as important as any other. To improve on this involvement pattern, it will be important for you to cultivate a sound system of communication and dialog with parents.

Because so much of your work has a student performance element, you will have an added opportunity for public interaction. There are annual music concerts, art shows, plays, fashion shows, sporting events, and other occasions for public presentations. Tell the interview team about where and how you intend to keep parents involved regarding their students and these events. Newsletters, emails, and websites are resources you should use to promote parent involvement. Are there times when parents can be invited into the school for daytime exhibitions? Will you make phone calls or reach out to parents in other ways? The principal of the school needs to be certain the teacher he or she will hire is someone who will actively involve the parent community. Think about ways you will accomplish this goal and be ready to nail this answer.

Music and Performing Arts: If you will direct the band, color guard, school play, or other performing group, you might have something similar to a Band Parent or Performing Arts organization. You will need to be able to describe how you will work with these organizations and what you might do to promote a good relationship. Parents might be involved behind the scenes in such things as costuming, set decoration, ticket sales, snack bars, and the other necessary work needing to be done. Think about how you will manage and promote their involvement in these activities. Take the opportunity to explore ways your program can promote solid community relations. For example, you may be able to be involved with town parades, fairs, performances in the park, or other public events. You could do outreach in assisted living facilities, local churches, or other public service entities. Do not miss the opportunity to describe how your program intends to reach out to the community and place the students in the best possible public light.

Physical Education Advice: Because your area is often closely related to the sports programs, you have an opportunity to explain how you can assist with a wide range of outside activities. You might have a sports booster club where you can maximize parent involvement. There may be opportunities to coordinate school programs with local recreation programs. For example, can you conduct free or low-cost coaching programs? Can you help with basic first aid classes for parents? Perhaps you can organize or assist with a summer or sports camp opportunity for the town. As with music, be aggressive in presenting yourself as a candidate who has good ideas and an active desire to involve yourself in the community. Parent relations have a great deal to do with your visibility and involvement beyond just the school day.

CONCLUDING THOUGHTS:

As a teacher in one of the related arts areas, your responsibilities might well extend beyond the end of the school day. You will have special challenges to meet the needs of a wide range of student abilities and interests. Often, your work will serve to promote public relations between the school and community. Most of all, you have the opportunity to be a very special person in the lives of students. For many young people, it is the teachers in elective and special courses that become the highlight of their academic life. As their teacher you can forge a relationship and bond that will extend well beyond the walls of your classroom or gymnasium. It is important the interview committee sees that you are someone who can build these great relations with students. You need to present a clear picture as to how your program will be an enjoyable and exciting place for students to learn. Do these things and you may be just the teacher this school is seeking!

"The scientific mind does not so much provide the right answers as ask the right questions."

—Claude Levi-Strauss, **1964**

SPECIAL EDUCATION INTERVIEWS

GENERAL ADVICE ON INTERVIEWS
FOR SPECIAL EDUCATION POSITIONS:

Over recent years, more and more jobs have become available in special education. Federal and state legislation dealing with the handicapped as well as rising public pressure for services have resulted in significant changes to the way schools manage special needs students. There are now more special education employment categories and job opportunities for prospective teachers. In addition, working conditions for special education teachers have changed dramatically. These changes have placed increased demand on teachers to stay current in both their knowledge of the law and specific state requirements that impact their teaching.

Institutions for professional training and the workplace have responded to the demand for special education professionals by introducing more courses, additional fields of study, added certification categories, and improved staff development programs. Today, the requirements for teaching in the field of special education have become very demanding. Even the traditional mainstream teacher needs to know how to work with special students. If you are applying for a position in the field of special education, interviewers will test your instructional skills, understanding of the law, and ability to work with a variety of learning disabilities.

ALTERNATE ROUTE TEACHERS: The field of special education is one of the few areas where the alternate route does not work well. There are too many laws, specific skills, and technical requirements that need to be mastered before a person is ready to enter this teaching field. With that said, we desperately need caring, understanding professionals to work with children who have special needs. If this is a field in which you would truly like to work, then you should look at your state requirements for certification. Often there are accelerated programs or MAT programs that are anxious to have professionals from other fields. Look into these and find one to fit your schedule and get started. No matter what your age or personal situation, if this is what you truly want to do, then this is the time to move and just do it*!*

I will share a little conversation I had some years ago regarding my pursuit of a doctoral degree. One of my friends who had just received her Ed. D. asked what I was planning to do about my own doctorate. I responded with the usual, "Oh, I don't know. It's another 3 years past where I am, I wouldn't even get the thing until I'm in my 40's (don't laugh, I then thought that was OLD!)." She laughed at me and said, "How old will you be in three years if you *don't* go get the degree?" Hmmm. Moral of this story…? Never let the fact that something might take a little longer than you like deter you from acting on what you want to do. Now get going and I will see you at the interview!

TEACHER OF STUDENTS WITH DISABILITIES (TOSD):

The TOSD has become an extremely important role in public education. Students in today's schools are far different from those of the past. In addition, the knowledge base in the field of special education has advanced to a far more sophisticated level. Our ability to diagnose learning problems has risen such that student disabilities are identified earlier and more often than before. Some claim we now over-identify children, but the fact remains that this increase has created a tremendous need for special education teachers.

The combination of increased student numbers and a rapidly rising number of school litigation cases has led to a shortage of certificated special education teachers. Well-qualified, motivated special education teachers are highly sought by school districts across the country. *This is the good news!!* But, the good news notwithstanding, you will still have to do well at the interview to prevail. As with all good positions, *other excellent candidates are likely to compete for the job you want.* In that regard, you must approach the interview process in a way that prepares you for the competition. Do your homework and construct a comprehensive interview strategy. These next pages will show you how.

SAMPLE SPECIAL EDUCATION QUESTIONS AND THEIR ANSWERS:

The confidentiality laws are an important part of your work with special education students. If you are co-teaching a class, what information would you want to share with other teachers and what kinds of information should remain confidential?

The area of confidentiality has become an important concern for school administrators because growing legislation and increasing lawsuits regarding student privacy represent a significant school liability. As a TOSD, you will be privy to a great deal of sensitive information. It is essential that the interview committee know you will use good judgment when you disseminate student information to other parties. As you consider your answer, you want to begin by speaking to a "need to know" requirement attendant to all confidential information. Talk about the difference that exists between teachers who have a student in their class and other staff members who have no consistent contact with the student. When there is a teacher who works with a child on a regular basis, then you as a TOSD have a responsibility to convey any IEP information that affects his or her work with that student. In addition, if there is an anecdotal record pertinent to the student's past school performance, this information can also be shared. Let the committee know that something conveyed in confidence will remain confidential unless it represents a possible danger to the student or others. Educational concerns such as student reading levels, test profiles, and class performance are important details that can greatly assist a professional. Let the committee know you understand how teachers rely on you to provide this kind of relevant information.

Before you conclude your answer, underscore your understanding of the need for care and sensitivity about when and *where* confidential discussions or activities should take place. Even when it is appropriate to convey confidential information, it must be done in a place that is private enough to insure that other parties will not overhear the conversation. In a school building, this can be tricky. If you convince the committee you are aware of this matter, you will demonstrate your depth of judgment.

KEYS TO YOUR RESPONSE:

- Recognize the importance of student confidentiality.
- Use the "need to know" criteria to guide your selection of those to whom you will share confidential information.

233

- Conclude with your understanding of the need for caution about when and where confidential material is shared.

How will your assessment program for included students be structured and what steps will you take to promote student success?

Because the term "included student" is present in this question, you can conclude two things. First, assume that you are in a co-teaching classroom with a regular education teacher. Second, there is a likely assumption that the students in your care are expected to receive a comparable education to the other mainstreamed students. It is likely you have already established a system by which you determine student progress and grades, so as you approach this answer, you will simply need to articulate what those judgments entail.

Here are a few things you should consider when framing your answer. I am certain you are well aware that the basis for determining the progress of any special education student is his or her IEP. Of course, the committee will want to hear you say it again, so humor them and go through all that. However, we need to take it to a much better platform than just a general IEP discussion. You should focus the attention on the *specific evidence of progress* you will use in making those evaluations of progress. The identification of four or five observable, measureable indicators will be the cornerstone of your assessment. Speak directly to how performance on activities, work products, and pre-post assessments will determine just how much progress is being made. You need this committee to see you as a *clinical* practitioner and not just someone who can "talk a good game." You have no idea how many candidates just spout one general theory after another and never really address "how" they will base the grade decision.

Remember the second issue I pointed to earlier, this committee has an expectation that everyone in the class will need to have a comparable experience. You need to make a special note that every Special Education (SE) pupil's progress will be measured against the performance objectives of the class. Tell them you will work with your co-teacher to make the expectations fair, but there is no reason to exclude a requirement for any class objective unless it is unreasonable or contrary to elements of the IEP. Let the committee know of your plans to work with the co-teacher to make any necessary modifications, but that every student's final grade will be based on his or her observable accomplishments.

This question asks how you will promote student success. This means the committee wants to know how your grading practice will promote student performance. You have dealt with this before and just need to package your ideas in a concise way. As with every good answer, stick to the concrete, observable things you will do and cut down on the flowery rhetoric. Leave those answers to the kind of candidate who loves the sound of his or her own voice. We will describe our methods of providing the students positive performance feedback, clear indication of their progress and what they are doing well, personal support in places they need help, rewards for excellent effort, and a continuing "can do" atmosphere. Talk about the way you will involve the support class to re-teach or reinforce learning.

A second element to your answer, one that only a very few candidates will hit, involves what you will do to motivate students who are not performing up to expectation. I used to call these students my "reluctant clients." We have all had them, and they think their only cause in life is to place us into an insane asylum as quickly as they can. They will be unsuccessful (usually). Talk about the ways you will use consistent monitoring to insure their engagement. You will add scheduled performances and benchmarks that will raise their level of accountability and concern. You will break larger assignments into smaller assignments that seem less daunting. You can add meaningful rewards for success. These reluctant clients need your continuing attention and, when legitimate, your recognition and praise!

The sense of meaningful success is one of the most powerful agents of motivation we know. Talk about how you will build on each student's success to promote continued effort and learning.

KEY INTERVIEW STRATEGY: *A powerful way to enhance your answer is the use of a personal anecdote that describes how you successfully worked with a particular student in the past.*

Such success stories live on in the minds of the committee well after the interview has closed. If you can show the committee that you recognize the positive influence of success and specific ways student grading can be used to promote performance, you have answered this section well.

KEYS TO YOUR RESPONSE:

- Identify the primary basis of grade determination as fulfillment of the student's IEP.
- Identify the *specific, measureable* progress indicators you will use in evaluating students.

- For common class objectives, describe how you will work with your colleague to establish clear performance expectations to make up the remainder of a student's grade.
- Outline how you will establish an individual assessment program as opposed to the "one standard for all" grade practice.
- Talk about you will motivate students and work with the "reluctant clients."
- INCLUDE A SPECIFIC ANECDOTE OR EXAMPLE OF YOUR WORK!

Special education students often see themselves as second-class students, less worthy than their regular education classmates. What can you as the teacher do to minimize such self-esteem problems?

Put the interview committee on notice that you see this is an ongoing problem in every school and a concern for every caring educator. The committee wants to insure your sensitivity to the issue and hear about actions you will take to reduce such student anxiety. Direct their attention to what you now do on a daily basis to maintain student dignity and self-worth. For example, explain how during class discussions you include *all* students and treat them as valuable participants. Underscore reinforcement strategies you will use to promote high student participation. Catalog a few ways to recognize good work or effort. The simple truth is that nothing can change a student's feeling of self worth but success. That is your goal.

For the Teacher of Students with Disabilities, the level of difficulty represented by the daily work is an ongoing issue because students with vastly disparate IEP requirements are present in the same room. Take time to let the principal know how enthusiasm for learning can decline if expectations are too high or so low there is no legitimate challenge. If you know how to do a task analysis (see Appendix B), give insight as to how this will help you design instructional activities that fit each person's unique level of readiness. This portion of your answer must leave the committee with a clear understanding that you are a teacher who will design daily work at the right level of difficulty for every student.

Delineate how a lack of confidence and self-worth often come from a long-standing history of failure and poor school grades. Let the committee know how you intend to reverse that trend if it has been a problem in the past. Build patterns of success by guiding and supporting student work until it reaches an acceptable level.

End with a description of how you will involve parents and other professionals to reinforce student feelings of self-worth. The chances for negative opinions to flourish in a student's mind are diminished when all of the adults work together and promote self-confidence. Your answer should reflect your own ideas and dimensions, but it is important that the committee recognize your awareness of what underlies poor self-image and your enthusiasm in trying to maximize feelings of self-worth in your students.

KEYS TO YOUR RESPONSE:

- Describe ways you plan to maintain student dignity, provide equal treatment, and recognize individual accomplishment.
- Explain the process you will use to set worthy expectations and establish achievement goals students can attain.
- Articulate how you will establish a pattern of success by insisting that unsatisfactory work be corrected and resubmitted until passing grades are earned.
- Underscore your intention to communicate with the case manager, other professionals, and home to enlist their support in making each student's experience in your class positive.

> *If you are the teacher for a support class with eight students, what steps will you take to assist those students in the completion of work for their regular education classes? How will you work with the regular education teachers on each student's behalf?*

As a Teacher of Students with Disabilities, you may be asked to teach a "support class" for a small group of students. In such classes, your role is to work with the student and keep him or her abreast of all work. You will also work with the mainstream teacher to cooperatively create the most effective teaching situation for the included students.

With this question the committee is asking what specific actions you will undertake to work with the student during his or her time is in your support class. Some issues to consider when framing your answer include:

CLASSROOM ISSUES FOR SUPPORT TEACHERS

- **What materials from the mainstream class do you need in your room to help assist students in their daily work?** You may want to get copies of all classroom books and materials to keep in your room. It will help if you also have copies of the written curriculum on file. You also want copies of daily handouts or class workbooks. Any instructional aids used in class will assist you in working with the student.

- *How will you stay abreast of what is taking place in the class and each student's performance?* You must describe how you will communicate with classroom teachers and what information you will need regarding daily student work. If the students maintain assignment planners, you will need to check them on a regular basis. Perhaps the teacher can provide copies of overhead transparencies and handouts you can keep in a notebook or file.

- *What responsibility will you place on the student to stay abreast of his or her work in each class?* You should work with each student to promote his or her personal responsibility for the day's assignment. If the mainstream teacher has informed you of what is taking place in class, you will be in a position to monitor student efforts to stay current. Once students know you are keeping track of their daily effort and have high expectations, their accountability is raised, and they are more likely to assume personal responsibility.

In summary, select topics from these classroom issues and describe how they will be accommodated by your communication with classroom teachers. Let your principal know you will consistently monitor student progress and reinforce student efforts. If you address the central issues contained in this discussion and add your own strategies, you can feel confident the question was well answered and you have moved a step closer to a job offer!

KEYS TO YOUR RESPONSE:

- Describe which materials and necessities the mainstream teacher must provide for your support classroom. Include things that put you in a position to <u>know</u> what is taking place in the mainstream class.
- Define the strategies you will use to communicate with the mainstream teacher and stay abreast of student progress.
- Outline specific measures you will take to make the student responsible for his or her own work.

> *Recently, there has been growing numbers of children with Autism Spectrum Disorder. Tell the committee what you know of such students and how you will work them.*

A more current issue facing every teacher is how to work with children on the Autism Spectrum. It is complicated and *not easy!* The committee will expect that you are familiar with the variety of conditions suffered by "children on the spectrum" and the many ways such conditions present themselves. Tick off the three core defining features of: (1) impairment in socialization, (2) impairment in verbal and non-verbal communication, and (3) restrictive repetitive patterns of behavior. You should discuss this information in as much detail as you think is necessary and then give an overview of your planned work with such students. Outline a plan to help teachers in mainstream classrooms to cope with children on the spectrum who might be in their class. This needs to be a sharp answer because, well handled, it is one that can genuinely separate you from the rest of the field.

In the event you are not as up to speed on how to work with children with autism, let me offer a strategy. Like you, I need a quick means to get up to speed and put together a great answer. I would suggest you go by your local major bookstore, such as Barnes and Nobles, and browse their education section. Very often you can find just the book you need right on the shelf. You can get a cup of coffee (latté if you are feeling more upscale that day), sit down at one of their tables, and find a bundle of ideas to include in your answer. You might even want to drop the name of the author if the opportunity arises. A good book on this topic is by Lori Ernsperger, <u>Keys to Success for Teaching Students with Autism</u>. There are many others, and you can look them up right in the bookstore. I like working this way because I get to relax and make it into a nice afternoon or evening.

Take time to explain to the committee that initial work with children with autism can be difficult because there is no clear set of symptoms or behaviors that separate this child from any other. The student may seem to be the same as any other child. Speak directly to how you will need to work with the home in trying to understand more precisely what behaviors to look for and what seems to be the best ways to work through them. In all cases, experts suggest that the home is a lynchpin in developing an overall plan to work with children on the spectrum. Address how you will work with other professionals and family members to understand the best ways to comfort children with autism when they have an outburst or temper display. Most importantly, let the committee know that you know how positive, soothing, and supportive teacher moves will produce far better results than corrective or confrontational postures. Such behaviors have their roots in the disease *and not* the lack of personal discipline.

239

The last segment of your answer should speak to how you will manage the learning environment. Children with autism need fewer distractions and a far more structured classroom situation than do others. Describe an area of your class that might be specifically designed to meet the needs of such students.

Unless you are already very knowledgeable, you should take the time to research this topic. Use an index card and highlight how you will attack a question like this. As with all the sample questions, it might not be specifically asked. Even so, you will almost assuredly find a place to insert some or all of the information.

 <u>KEYS TO YOUR RESPONSE:</u>

- Begin your response with a background of what you know about the autistic learner.
- Outline specific steps you will take to work directly with the home. Explain why they are the critical link in making the school a success for this child.
- Speak to how you will work with behavioral outbursts and difficult or obstruction behaviors that are likely to occur.
- Describe how you will control the environment.

QUESTIONS FOR THE LEARNING CONSULTANT (LC):

The LC role is essential to every school. Your state may have a different title for this role, but in general, the functions are relatively uniform. In cases where the school is small, one LC may be shared amongst two or more buildings; however, every school should have at least shared services. Principals rely heavily on their LC to organize, monitor, and manage much of the special education activity in their building. In particular, you will be expected to design educational programs, establish consistent communications with parents, be a liaison between families and teachers, serve as a resource for the staff, and assist the administration in working with the special education program. At the interview, you may find there are questions to explore your administrative abilities as well as your knowledge of special education. As a school principal, I cannot tell you how many times I called my LC and had her work with me on planning and special issues in my school.

As an overall goal, you will need to demonstrate an ability to get along with diverse groups of people who often have different needs and competing agendas. These groups include administrators, teachers, parents, and students. Human relations skills, management, instruction, law, testing, and report writing will be important elements of your background the interview team will want to explore.

In the next section, we will examine specific questions you may encounter. Each example is designed to provide specific insight to a critical issue you might encounter and offer a possible approach to your response. The discussion for each question should provide a framework around which you can later customize a personal response.

KEY INTERVIEW STRATEGY: *The final answer to all questions must include the personal insight you have gained through experience along with those distinctive viewpoints and thinking that make you a unique candidate.*

SPECIFIC QUESTIONS:

If you could write your own job description, what elements would you include in your role and why would they be important?

Since most schools will not let you design your own position, this may seem an odd question. It is not. The intent is to determine what parts of the LC role you prioritize and how you would work with other people in the school organization. More specifically, the principal wants to hear you discuss the working relationship you want to forge with the school child study team (CST). He or she needs to know how you will merge your efforts with the CST to diagnose student needs and design effective programs. In some states there are school committees that review all students prior to any referral. They go by a variety of names, and one is a Pupil Assistance Committee (PAC). You should address how you envision your role in assisting with the pre-referral intervention process. A good beginning might sound like this:

> *"Let me begin this answer by addressing one of the central LC responsibilities: identification of student learning disabilities and the design of programs to meet those needs. I will need to complete a review of the record, organize testing procedures, conduct interviews, and arrange appropriate professional involvement. To my mind this work would have the highest priority."*

You may have a different first priority, but whatever that is, your highest priority item is where you should begin your response. Move down your list of priority functions to address the other areas that you see as important to your role. For example, you may wish to outline ways you can assist the planning of co-teaching or inclusion arrangements, organize parent newsletters, conduct student counseling, or engage in other characteristics of good special education programs. You need only include three or four items. When discussing these, the order is not as important as the rationale for your choices.

Before attending your interview, organize your thinking on the all-important role of communications. The principal will rely on you to maintain a sound line of internal communications with school professionals and external communications with parents and other professional agencies. This is an important area of concern for principals, and a well-designed answer that includes this aspect of communication can greatly advance your candidacy.

Discuss ideas on how to maintain the flow of information between staff members. Be prepared to discuss the kinds of teacher meetings you feel are necessary and the frequency with which such meetings should be held. Help the committee understand any methods you will use to communicate with parents about their student. Talk about how you will establish a working relationship with local and state agencies that may be needed to help the school carry out its mission. These responses will help establish your role as a key member of the special education team.

Now add something to make your answer stand out! Get the attention of the principal by adding ideas about roles you might undertake that will assist him or her with the administration of the special education program. For example, you might suggest how you could collegially develop ways to streamline administrative involvement in the annual IEP development process. Identify ways you can help with the spring scheduling process. Offer to sit on an administrative council whenever your participation would be helpful. In short, describe the part you can play in facilitating the decision-making process for special education programs. The attitude and cooperative spirit is something that will be noticed and markedly improve your stock!

 ## KEYS TO YOUR RESPONSE:

- Begin your answer with a description of the priority areas you see for a learning consultant.
- Describe how you will promote sound working relations with the child study team and other key groups.
- Describe the importance of your role in communications with teachers and parents.
- Conclude with a discussion of your willingness to assist the principal or other school personnel with special education decisions.

> *What steps would you take to establish an inclusion class in science that will utilize a co-teacher for the first time?*

Generally, this is a responsibility of the administration and principal. The LC, however, can also have a role in facilitating the successful implementation of this teaching design. For that reason a question on co-teaching might be on your interview. Your role in this task will focus on steps necessary to insure teachers are well supported, trained, and informed. In cases where co-teaching was unsuccessful, an underlying reason was often poor teacher selection and preparation. An LC can have a profoundly positive influence on this process.

Begin your response with how you will assist the principal in making the selection of teachers who might best work together. Describe the kinds of teacher planning meetings you would facilitate. Tell how such meetings will help provide the necessary groundwork for constructing a successful teaching relationship. If the teachers are new to inclusion teaching, you can offer to research worthwhile workshops the teachers might attend. Offer to assemble pertinent articles or other print information that can help the teachers prepare for their role. One LC I interviewed described a handbook she had prepared for all teachers who were participating in the inclusion model. That was a very persuasive addition to her answer.

The program planning for included students will also need your help. Specify ways you will work with the teachers to assemble program recommendations and design required modifications to be used in class. Explain how you can assist in designing assessment strategies that will promote student success. You are the primary resource for teachers, and the committee will be interested to hear how you will organize your support.

Before ending your response, be sure the committee is aware of your willingness to support the administration and teachers in the planning process. The planning and teacher support process are key ingredients for a successful in-class experience. Your role in facilitating that process is the central element of this answer.

KEYS TO YOUR RESPONSE:

- Outline how you would assist in the organization of a planning process for teachers who will be working together.
- Emphasize how you might facilitate the communication between teachers and the flow of information to all parties.

243

- Explain ideas you may have about workshops or staff development to assist the teachers in defining their roles.

> *A parent calls <u>you</u> to complain that her son has made no progress over the year. She is frustrated by the treatment he receives in his mainstream classes. The student feels left out, always unsure of what is expected, and completely unhappy. She wants an urgent IEP conference, and if immediate and productive changes do not occur, she will involve her lawyer. How will you proceed on this matter?*

Oh boy, this is one of those hot cases that always seem to come up at just the wrong time (is there a right time?). It is a situational question designed to see how you handle difficult, volatile conferences. Here is the bad news. This situation is becoming more frequent, and if you have not dealt with this already, you can expect to encounter it at some point in your career.

PARENT CONFERENCE TIP: *When faced with any questions that involve a hostile parent, begin by analyzing the real concerns that underlie their comments.* Following this advice, there appear to be three concerns: (1) student unhappiness and alienation, (2) insufficient communication, and (3) the possibility of instructional inequity. The results of your analysis will help clarify what your meeting goals should be. In this case, your goals must include an effort to reduce parent frustration and anger, conduct an open and objective review of the student's program results, and an identification of what each party can do differently to achieve better results in the future. Before winding up the conference it will be important to explore ways you might improve communication with the home and institute an improved support system for the student. These steps will help reduce the probability that this kind of frustration will reappear. In phrasing your response, it is important that you have provided a specific action to achieve each meeting goal.

Before you begin to draw any conclusion regarding what is taking place, make certain that you explain how you will speak directly with the teachers involved and hear what they have to offer. There are at least two sides to these issues, and you will need a complete picture before you design a conference strategy. Parents are reacting to what they hear and see at home, which makes it unlikely that they have all of the facts and information. This step is considered essential, and its omission can significantly undermine the quality of your answer.

Let the committee know that you will have a plan in place before you approach potentially confrontational meetings. The first part of any such plan is to listen, listen, and listen. Explain how you will use your listening skills to allow the parent to fully describe his or her problem BEFORE you begin to respond or seek solutions. The goal of the parent in this meeting is to make the class situation more rewarding and pleasant for their son. Identify this as a mutual goal. The situation described in the question is volatile, but let the committee know that with your good human relations strategies, you feel more than equal to the task.

As the parent mentioned her lawyer and possible litigation, be sure to let the committee know of your intention to keep the principal informed. If there is a director of Special Services, you will make that call as well. Explain that your conference approach will be to remain moot on the subject of lawyers or litigation unless the parent reintroduces the subject.

The last point you want to speak to in this answer is your intent to insure first-rate documentation. In addition to the conference notes, explain how you will ask the teachers to maintain their own documentation within the class. This record will be important to reduce school liability.

KEYS TO YOUR RESPONSE:

- With situation questions, begin by identifying the real issues for the committee.
- Discuss how you will interview the teachers and other school personnel to get the entire picture before you draw conclusions.
- Link the central issues of contention that your meeting goals must address.
- Underscore the need to listen and then find a mutual goal on which all parties can agree.
- Cite your intention to inform the appropriate parties regarding the parent comment on litigation.
- End with a clear statement regarding your intent to document and maintain court-suitable records.

As a case manager, what steps do you take to monitor the progress of assigned students and the success of their programs? What alternatives do you consider when programs are ineffective?

This question was on several of the gathered interviews, and although rather straightforward, it requires the candidate to provide a sound answer. A poor answer on this item can critically damage your candidacy. Recognize the two parts to this question. The first part is how you monitor progress, and the second part is what you might alternatively do when programs are unsuccessful. The response you offer will be based on your past experience, and only you can determine what should be included in the answer. Below is a list of ideas around which you might shape an answer.

STEPS TO CONSIDER FOR MONITORING SE PROGRAMS:

MONITORING STUDENT PROGRESS:

- If there are scheduled planning meetings, decide how often you should attend and for what purpose.
- Recommend a portfolio of student work and ways to link it to the student's IEP goals.
- Include a record sheet at the front of the portfolio to provide a snapshot identifying student progress towards essential skills.
- Identify the informal ways you will meet with teachers to review progress.

DEALING WITH THE INEFFECTIVE PROGRAM:

- Describe how you decide that a student's program is ineffective.
- If you find that programs are ineffective, identify a process to use to determine possible reasons.
- Catalog specific interventions you might recommend when the instructional program is not meeting the student's needs.

1. **INITIAL POSSIBLE ACTIONS:** Consider how you might alter: amount of support, utilize PAC intervention, adjust program goals, utilize more technology, or adjust class or school time.
2. **LAST RESORT ACTIONS:** Change teachers, adjust the IEP with the parent, or re-evaluate the appropriateness of your placement.

You can organize your own thinking on this question because it will differ for each LC. The important concern is that you convey a sense of thoughtful organization to the committee. Your ability to answer this question with precision and authority may well advance you to the top of the class. It is for that very reason that you should pre-think this answer. Even if you leave out an item the committee had in mind, and such an omission is fairly common, the answer will still have its desired impact if it is well organized and concise.

KEYS TO YOUR RESPONSE:

- Begin with a brief reinforcement of how you see this as a central responsibility of your position.
- Address the steps you would take to monitor each student's progress.
- Highlight a variety of alternatives you might consider when a program is not working.
- KEEP YOUR ANSWER CONCISE AND ON TARGET.

CONCLUDING THOUGHTS:

Special education has become an important part of every public school. The principal and school committee will want to know you are a person who uses good judgment and understands the various added constraints that bear on professionals in this field.

An important impression to leave in everyone's mind is that you are an empathetic and child-centered person. Convince the principal that you have the adaptability and flexibility to deal with difficult student issues as well as the day-to-day problems that arise. Let the committee see that you possess the human relations skills necessary to successfully work with a wide variety of people. It is very important the principal see you as a genuine team player on which he or she can rely.

You have chosen a demanding field, but by the end of this interview, the committee will see that you have all the skills necessary to meet this challenge. Be upbeat and optimistic. Stay positive and believe in yourself. Showcase your dedication and persistent pursuit of student success. Accomplish this and you will emerge as a top candidate. Now go for it and let people know what you can do!

"The primary job of the teacher is to create conditions in which students become emotionally and intellectually engaged in the pursuit of solutions to problems and in the exploration of possibilities."

— Phil Schlechty, **2010**

HANDLING YOUR OFFER

17

GENERAL INFORMATION

The highlight that concludes any job search is notification you have been chosen for the position. You prepared an excellent cover letter and resume, presented a professional image, answered the interview questions with insight and enthusiasm, closed the deal with a knockout portfolio, and now you have been offered the post. What do you need to know about the next steps?

At first glance, there seems to be an easy answer – one gratefully accepts the offer, asks when to report, and immediately books reservations for the celebration dinner! In some cases, that may be just what you will do. But once the interviewing process has concluded, you will confront three different phases, and each one has its own set of questions. It is worth your time to look at these questions and pre-think how you will approach each one.

ANSWERS TO YOUR QUESTIONS ON
WAITING FOR THE OFFER:

After the interview, should I use a follow-up call or email to determine my status in districts where I am most interested?

This seems a reasonable and innocuous thing to do. After all, you are simply showing interest. Should you not have the right to know where things stand, particularly if you are an applicant in other districts? I have spoken to many principals and superintendents on this matter, and there seems to be unilateral agreement – follow-up calls are not always well received if they are too close to the interview date. Let me say that again, "not always well received." A number of reasons were offered as to why these calls were less than welcome, but the most frequent reason was that: the process has to have sufficient time to run its course before feedback is available to candidates. Principals generally advise that you be patient and wait to be contacted after a decision has been made. Unless special circumstances exist, it is preferred that candidates refrain from appearing to force the issue.

Most principals have had experience with candidates who call two or three times in a week to ask when the results will be available. In those cases, you can be sure each call has weakened the candidate's viability. Secretaries develop a severe patience deficit for those who call too often, and one should not underestimate the influence of the principal's or superintendent's secretary. Understand that interviews may include ten or more candidates and you should consider the impact if each person called two or three times. The line between "interest" and "pest" is very fine and best left untested.

There are exceptions to this advice. During the interview, your candidacy in other districts may be discussed. At that point, the principal may ask that you contact him or her before you make any decision to accept another position. If this occurs, then the candidate can be sure he or she is under serious consideration and should call the principal's office in accordance with whatever arrangements have been made.

There are, however, two ways you might approach this concern that will yield worthwhile information. A question you should ask at the conclusion of the interview is where the process is and if there are any timelines they can share regarding when you might hear from them. Principals will often provide that information. You might also send off an email if an uncomfortable amount of time has passed. The email should simply say that you continue to be very interested in the opportunity and are available if there are any further questions.

There will be times when you do not hear the outcome of an interview for what seems to be a long time. At the interview, the school may have indicated they wanted to conclude the process by a specific date. That day passes and you have heard nothing. Should you call? Here is the bad news: if you have not heard, there is probably a reason. The best advice is to continue your job search, and let this district continue with what it needs to do. You might still be under consideration, nonetheless, stay active in the interview process and keep your options open. If you receive another job offer, feel free to call the first district and advise them of your situation. We will discuss what to do with multiple job offers later in the chapter.

What should I do if I am a finalist in more than one district?

First, congratulations on placing yourself in this enviable position but be careful. Until you have a firm offer of a contract in hand you are still only a candidate. Districts may advise you that you are one of only two they are considering. The principal might convey that he or she is strongly interested in having you on the staff and is about to call your references. Things may look great and you may feel very positive about a school's interest. I offer a word to the wise. Without a *definite contract offer*, there continues to be at least some potential for this decision to go another way. Unless you have an agreement to contact a prospective district before accepting another position, it is best to wait for a firm contract offer before you begin to notify other districts where you may still be a candidate. Consider why this might be the best course of action. When you call a principal or school office to advise them you are a finalist in another district, it is possible they may assume you are more interested in taking the other position. If their process is not yet complete, such assumptions can compromise your viability because of questionable availability. It has sometimes happened that a candidate announced to a district that he or she was a finalist at another school and later had to call back when the position was not offered to renew his or her candidacy. You can easily see how this would undermine a person's chances.

A second concern is how such declarations might be construed as a subtle way to exert pressure for a decision. Even though this may not be your intention, if something in your voice or words you choose is interpreted as pressure, it can damage your candidacy. Unless there is a compelling reason to take that risk, it is best to avoid.

In sum, unless you have agreed to let the principal know if you become a finalist elsewhere, then you should wait until an offer is tendered before contacting other districts where you are still a candidate.

ANSWERS TO YOUR QUESTIONS ON HOW TO HANDLE THE OFFER WHEN IT ARRIVES:

What if I receive an offer that is not my first choice and am still waiting on a decision regarding a more attractive position?

It is likely that good candidates will find themselves in this position at some time in their career. It is one of the most sensitive and difficult decisions a professional may face, and you need to pre-think what you will do should that circumstance present itself. You may have heard the maxim, "A bird in the hand is worth two in the bush." That goes double in a professional job search. Be aware that the window of opportunity is open ever so briefly. In interviewing numerous principals and superintendents, they are generally unimpressed by candidates who receive their offer of a position with reservations. When a candidate responds to a job offer by announcing, "I am continuing to consider another offer; can I have the weekend to think this over?" principals or superintendents are led to question their decision. If they sense a candidate is stalling, they may assume he or she is waiting for a "better position." No matter what you may think or how you rationalize the delay, realize it is not helping your situation. In fact, there have been occasions when principals have withdrawn an offer after a candidate hesitated too long. It has happened that good candidates with multiple possibilities have ended up with no job because they mishandled the offer. I must add that many principals and superintendents feel a few days to consider an offer is perfectly reasonable, but unless you know this is the case, you may be taking a chance.

With these thoughts in mind, only you can decide whether you want to risk losing one position to possibly win the prize position. No one can answer this question for you. If you have thought the issue through in advance and developed a clear course of action, it will help you deal with the call when it arrives. The advice is – have a game plan already in mind.

If you decide you will accept the first position where an offer is made, then be happy and accept that offer enthusiastically! Remember, it was *you* who applied for the position and told the committee all the great things you would bring to their school. When the principal calls to offer the position, he or she expects to hear that same great candidate on the other end of the phone – BE THERE!

Here are a few final insights on accepting jobs that may not have been your first choice. A teaching position will be exactly what you make of it. Often that "must have" job in the great district will not turn out to be what you envisioned; while, those "second-tier jobs" become much more than you had ever hoped. So, if you decide to take the first position on the table, you did not make a mistake. Congratulations and go make a difference to every child you teach!

What if I decide this is not the job for me, how do I gracefully refuse?

This can happen, and it is not totally unexpected. The important issue in this decision is its timing. If you complete the interview process and come away with the feeling this may not be the right school, you should take immediate steps to clarify those thoughts. If you choose to withdraw, the best time to act is *prior* to the district's selection of final candidates.

The withdrawal process is reasonably simple. First, call the district and attempt to speak with the principal or head of the interview committee. This is a professional courtesy that most school leaders appreciate. The principal may ask you for a reason so be prepared to offer an honest but diplomatic response to the question. There is no need to burn any bridges. If the principal is not available, it is perfectly acceptable to leave a message with the secretary. You may or may not receive a follow-up call from the principal, but you should be prepared for either event.

Although you have advised the school by phone, you are not quite finished. You should write a short letter of withdrawal and extend your appreciation to the principal and committee for their consideration. Address your letter to the principal of the school. In this letter, it is not necessary to cite reasons for withdrawing although some candidates do. The importance of the letter is its ability to demonstrate your professionalism and courtesy.

Take a look at what might be contained in this letter. **NOTE:** *Use the sample letter as a starting point for what you will write, but you should use your own words.* The model is intended to give you some ideas as to how you might structure your own document.

Mr. John Hopeful
23 Brandon Lane
Brighton, PA 55520

Dr. Robert Andrews
Brighton Elementary School
101 Elm Street
Brighton, PA 55520

May 2, 2011

Dear Dr. Andrews,

I would like to thank you and the interview committee for providing me the opportunity to see your school and interview for the position of Science Teacher. I found the time we spent together to have been both informative and enjoyable. The steps taken by your staff to make me feel comfortable and welcome were most appreciated.

In light of a number of issues now before me, I must regrettably ask that you withdraw my application from further consideration. I would like you to know that this decision is not predicated on any dissatisfaction with your school or our time together. There are other matters that make my continued candidacy impractical at this time.

In closing I wish you the best in finding the right candidate for your 5th grade science position. I am honored to have been a candidate.

Sincerely,

J. Hopeful

As you can see from the model, there are three separate paragraphs. The goals of the first paragraph are to identify the position for which you applied, demonstrate your appreciation for their time, and set a pleasant tone to the letter. It need not be long or gush about how wonderful you found the school. Remember, you are withdrawing from consideration.

The second paragraph withdraws you from further consideration. As mentioned before, a specific reason is not necessary; however, you want to make clear that you have thought this through and made your decision based on a particular reason. If, unlike the model, your reason for withdrawing is specific to the interview or some perceived shortcoming of the school, you are not obliged to provide those details in your letter. Most often, it is best to remain moot on the subject and move on to other opportunities. There is nothing to be gained by risking antagonizing the school principal or committee. If, on the other hand, you feel obligated to include your reason, *be diplomatic.*

The last paragraph is a simple closing you will find in most letters of this nature. It wishes the district well and restates your appreciation. As in the first paragraph, it should not be overdone.

A final word on the subject is to keep your letter short and to the point. The entire text should fill no more than one side of a single sheet of paper. If it exceeds one side, it is probably too long.

What if the offered position is different than the one for which I applied?

This happens from time to time and can be disconcerting if you have not given the idea advance thought. There are a number of changes that can occur to prospective teaching assignments between the time of your interview and the time of your offer, but a few seem to predominate. The most common changes include an amendment from a tenure-track contract to leave replacement, an alteration of the grade level to be taught, or a revision of the subject areas to be taught. We will treat each individually.

There are times when you believe you are applying for a tenure-track post and later find the position is for a teacher who is on leave. Ads in the newspaper usually indicate a position is for "leave replacement" when that is the case. On other occasions, a change may have occurred after the posting and you will not find this out until the interview or later. You need to realize that teachers on leave sometimes unexpectedly announce their intention to return and reclaim their position. While it is also true that some teachers do not return, you cannot count on such good fortune. Therefore, if you have a tenure-track offer from another district, you may be best advised to accept it and leave the replacement position for someone else. If you have no other offers, then by all means consider the replacement position. Should you perform well, the school may take steps to try to keep you even if the original teacher returns. At worst, you have one year of experience and a good recommendation for your next search.

Elementary teachers are sometimes faced with a change in their grade placement. They applied for what they believed was a 1st grade position and were later asked if they would be interested in teaching 4th grade. The best advice is to accept the position if it is offered and disregard the grade level change. Once you are on the staff, the principal has the prerogative to change you to any grade within your certification. Again, if you provide good service, a transfer to your preferred grade level may be made later. In the meantime, you have a fine position in a good school.

With secondary teachers, changes to the teaching schedule can easily occur. You originally thought you would teach three classes of sophomore English and two Honors English classes. When the job is offered, you are told your schedule will include two freshman composition classes instead of the Honors English. As with grade level changes, principals can assign you to any subject for which you are certified. Once you join the staff and show everyone what you can do, schedule changes can be requested. Unless there is a very good reason to object, subject changes in the offered position need not be deal killers. You can often improve your standing with the principal by demonstrating flexibility and making this change work. In sum, do not let class assignments stand between you and a good school.

ANSWERS TO YOUR QUESTIONS ON WHAT TO DO AFTER YOU HAVE ACCEPTED THE OFFER:

What if I accept one of my second choice positions and my first choice school then offers a contract?

This is another problem that can present itself and is closely related to the last question. In this case, however, you committed yourself to one district and the more desirable school offered at a later date. There are two possibilities regarding your current circumstance. One possibility is that you have made a formal commitment to the first district and have a signed contract for the coming year. The second possibility is that you have only made a verbal acceptance with the principal or superintendent.

If you have signed a contract, you are legally committed to the first district. If you call them and ask to be released from your contract, it is unlikely you will be successful. Understand; other candidates whom they might have employed have been notified of the decision and may no longer be available. The school will not want to reopen the entire search process because you now have a "better offer." Be certain, your request will be negatively received and place an unnecessary shadow over your employment at the school. Avoid starting in a new school with negative baggage whenever possible. Once you sign a contract, you should consider yourself committed and proceed with enthusiasm and energy.

In the second case, you do not have a signed contract, and a clear legal bind has not yet occurred. Again, however, you have given your word and the district has probably acted on that by notifying the other finalists of the school's decision. Should you withdraw to take a better offer, be aware it will be considered somewhat a violation of your professional ethics. Whereas there may be no *legal* recourse for the district, your professional reputation is now in question. You need to decide how important that is as compared to the prospects of the new position.

These are not easy or inconsequential matters. You should keep your overall goals in mind, weigh the relative strengths and weaknesses of each choice, and make your decision. Most importantly, do this *before* any calls arrive. If you try to make these decisions over the phone as an offer is made, you place yourself at risk of making a costly mistake.

What if I accept the position but I have a 30-day or 60-day notice requirement?

This is often the case when teachers change positions at times other than the end of a school year. It can also occur with **alternate route candidates** who are leaving the business field to enter teaching. In such cases, it is customary to provide notice to employers at the time or your resignation.

Teachers have an almost universal 60-day notice clause in their contracts. As such, there are some precautions you will want to take. **RULE #1:** *Never submit a resignation until you have a signed contract in hand.* Many districts will suggest that their "verbal offer" is good and that you can provide notice. If you follow such advice, do so at your own risk. Boards of Education have been known to reject the hiring recommendation of the superintendent, and a candidate who thought he or she had a firm job offer was left in a very awkward position. You need to have a written confirmation that you were appointed by the Board prior to any formal action to resign your current position.

If it is mid-year or toward the end of the summer, your new district will likely want you to start as soon as possible. In this case, you will need to make a request for an early release. As a general rule, principals and districts are unlikely to grant an employment release until a suitable replacement is found. If your resignation occurs in June or July, the possibility of early release rises dramatically because schools rarely like to start the year with a temporary teacher. Prospective employers understand the 60-day clause, and if they are prepared to hire you, this impediment should not present a problem.

If you are a long-term substitute or occupy a position other than regular contract, examine the agreement for any "due notice" arrangements. Even if there is no formal clause to govern your release, you should notify the current school as soon as possible and give them time to provide a suitable replacement. If you are a daily substitute, no notice is required other than to inform the substitute caller of your last day of availability. That is simple courtesy and good professional conduct.

What should I put in my letter of resignation?

Once you inform the principal that you intend to resign, you will be asked to submit a letter of resignation for Board action. In all matters concerning a job change, the best policy is to leave your district or position on the most positive terms possible. Even if you are leaving because of dissatisfaction, be professional and gracious on your exit. The good impression you leave can only assist you in the future.

Your letter should be positive and brief, less than one page. There is no need to detail your reasons for leaving the district. The Board only needs to know that you plan to leave and the termination date you request. Look at this sample letter and you will see that there are only a few important items included.

Mr. Robert Hopeful
23 Brandon Lane
Anytown, MA 55555

Dr. John Coppola, Board President
York Valley Schools, Board of Education
100 Main Street
York Valley, MA 55520

March 2, 2011

Dear Dr. Coppola,

This letter is to advise the Board of Education that I will be resigning my position as 7th grade Science Teacher at the Valley Middle School effective Friday, March 11, 2011. I fully understand that my continued service for 60-days is required to insure a smooth transition for my students.

I would like to thank the Board of Education and the community of York Valley for the opportunity to have worked in such a fine school with so many wonderful children. I have many happy memories to cherish.

Please accept my best wishes for the future. It has been a privilege to teach in this district.

Sincerely,

R. Hopeful

As you can see, the only required information is the resignation date and your understanding of the 60-day clause. The remainder of the letter consists of pleasantries and appreciation. Feel free to make adjustments that suit your situation.

Once I accept the position, what steps do I need to take prior to beginning work?

The first step will be to make an appointment through the superintendent's secretary to go to the board office and sign the necessary paperwork required for your employment. Usually the superintendent's secretary will notify you of a time and date for this, along with a list of items you will need. You generally need an original copy of your teaching certificate, two forms of ID for the I-9, and possibly a set of official college transcripts if you are a new teacher. If you have not already been fingerprinted and had a background check, that is likely to be required and can be arranged by the district. Some districts also require a physical examination, and you should be prepared to make arrangements with either the school doctor or your own physician. The HR Department or superintendent's secretary will advise you of any additional requirements, and you should rely on them for guidance.

Try to arrange a visit to your new school through the principal's office. Do this as soon as possible so you can obtain copies of any materials you need to begin planning for your classes. If possible, meet with the person who will be supervising you or helping to direct your efforts. This could be a grade level leader, team leader, department head, or supervisor. Even if you met this person at the interview, now that you are hired, a more detailed conversation regarding your role should be held as soon as it is convenient.

If you have not arrived and are fulfilling a 60-day clause, touch base with your new school on a regular basis. If there are monthly bulletins or other announcements the school regularly provides, you may want to read those and keep abreast of school news. If there is an evening performance, it is a good idea to attend if at all possible. These small steps will help you garner necessary knowledge of your school and ease the transition. When you arrive for your first day, you will want to be as fully prepared as possible.

Congratulations on your selection and good luck!

PUTTING IT ALL TOGETHER

Congratulations on completing this book and taking the initiative to maximize your chances of securing a great new position in teaching! With the information you now own, you will be a formidable candidate in any selection process. You have no doubt realized these pages contain too much information to memorize, but that was not the goal when we began. What you now have are critical understandings on how to get noticed, prepare for the tough questions, and avoid costly mistakes. These larger issues and insights will stay with you while you formulate an interview style that is uniquely yours.

At this point we must turn our attention to assembling all of our information into a winning strategy to get hired. When I was a young naval officer, my captain used to say something that has rung true over the years. "It is one thing to have the knowledge but still another to put it to good use. Many people may *know* but only a few *do*." Now that we have the knowledge, we need a deliberate, well-formulated plan to place you in the right school. The best way to accomplish that goal is to break our task into manageable parts. These parts include the search, preparation, interview, and follow-up.

You will want to go back and reread certain chapters or passages during your preparation. In so doing, you will discover new ideas and gain additional insights you may have missed the first time. Allow this creativity free reign and jot these ideas down as they appear. New thoughts are very perishable and when trying to remember them later, they can be difficult or impossible to recall. If you wrote a few notes, your ideas will spring back instantly.

HOW TO CONDUCT AN EFFECTIVE SEARCH PROCESS:

This task is often done in a way that lacks thinking and planning. Many teachers simply scan the newspaper for jobs that fit their title and send off their resume. Occasionally, you can get lucky, happen on just the right position, have a successful interview, and receive a job offer. More often than not, however, a haphazard search has a most unsuccessful ending.

Since this decision carries such importance, take your time and do it right. Remember, school districts are looking for you; it was they who placed the advertisement. Avoid the temptation to "blanket" the marketplace with resumes. Be deliberate and selective.

ALTERNATE ROUTE CANDIDATE: For you, the search for employment might seem a bit of an uphill battle. Unless the advertisement clearly states "standard certification required," you should consider yourself just as qualified as any other applicant. Remember, your cover letter and resume are designed to maximize your match to the district. This alone will place you ahead of many less informed candidates.

CREATE A HARD-HITTING PLAN OF ACTION:

In what community or location do I want to live?

This is a *very* important question, and you need to be honest with yourself. If you have family commitments and strong ties, you may wish to draw a radius circle on a map that identifies the geographic region you want to target. You must decide if you like rural, suburban, or city lifestyles. If you like the arts and shopping available in the larger cities, you need to think about schools within a reasonable distance of those amenities. If you are married, you need to discuss the matter of location thoroughly with your spouse. You will want to make certain your prospective schools are located where you will both be well-served and happy.

If a specific state or general location is not of prime importance, then you have a much wider field to explore. I know of many candidates who found outstanding positions by simply expanding into less populated areas of the country. If you are considering other states, be sure you know their certification process and requirements. Most often you will find that having a certificate in one state will make it easier to obtain one in a different state. You definitely want your certification status to be clear *before* you begin applying out-of-state.

What would be the ideal school for me?

I remember one of my college classmates at the University of Tennessee who answered this question by saying, "Any district that has a job and will hire me." Even then I thought that to be a shortsighted approach to establishing a professional career. Unfortunately, that philosophy continues to predominate in young teachers looking for positions. It is especially true with **alternate route candidates**. This is due in part to the fact that new and alternate route teachers may still be somewhat insecure and uncertain about their market demand. Let me assure you, the profession has a high demand for skilled teachers and good candidates like you. You do not need to take just any opening that comes along the way.

Pay scale is another reason candidates might choose a district, but this too lacks clear thinking. Let me share this advice I received from William Librera, former Commissioner of Education for the State of New Jersey; "Never leave or take a position on the basis of money alone. You almost always regret it." I found his words extremely valuable, and I hope you will as well. Within a geographic area or state, there are always differences; however, most districts are reasonably competitive and the salary differential is unlikely to make much difference in your lifestyle. Let us hypothetically take District A that pays a starting salary of $43,500 and District B that only pays $36,100. Adjusted for taxes and other deductions, the difference will be in the $200/check range at most. If you adjust for regional cost of living expenses, you are lucky to be ahead at all. Of course finances are important, and with all other things equal, you would be foolish to totally ignore salary in your decision-making. The point is, money should not be the *primary* reason for choosing your school. It makes more sense to focus on districts that offer you the kind of position and working conditions you seek.

To identify schools that meet your criteria, you should do some investigation. Once you have identified a geographic area, find out what school districts are in that region. There may be a county education office that can supply all the information you need in one stop. Get copies of annual school reports, brochures, state report cards, websites, and other items that will provide sound insight. As you review these materials, certain schools will begin to emerge as good matches for you. Keep this information in a set of files. It will be important if a later opening exists and you decide to apply.

How do I go about finding the right vacancy?

Now that you have identified the area and types of schools to which you will apply, it is time to look for a vacancy. The first obvious place to look is the newspaper. There are generally at least two papers that service a particular geographic area, and you should get both papers on a weekly basis. The Sunday paper generally carries the ads you need, but there may also be ads in the daily paper. This varies from location to location.

Check with the county education office. They may receive listings that are posted. Professional magazines, Education Week, and other periodicals also run ads, but in my experience, they are not always current. Therefore, you may find yourself entering the process too late.

Job boards and Internet employment sites have not always yielded much in the way of legitimate openings. As we mentioned way back in the beginning of the book, the limited results tend to be outweighed by the other concerns and risks. Your better use of the Internet would be to scan each district's website. Often they will have position postings right on their own "employment" page.

Many states such as Maryland and Tennessee are organized by counties. County websites will generally list all of the vacancies, and you might be required to apply through the county website. In that case, you will need to follow the established protocol.

A final word on this matter is to extend your search over a four or five week timeframe. As stated above, the spring season is the best time, but there are numerous job openings through the summer and school year as well. Whereas, you should not send out 75 applications all over the region; I recommend you apply to at least five districts if possible.

What if there are no posted vacancies in the geographic areas and schools I have selected?

This can happen, especially if you are applying during the academic year when most good schools are fully staffed. In this case, there are two avenues to consider. Perhaps you can consider a job outside your desired travel range or a school that is not exactly the type you want. In this instance, you need to decide how important the experience might be. Keep in mind that any teaching skills you acquire in this school will make you a more attractive candidate in the future.

Another alternative you should consider is substitute teaching. I finished my MA degree at Indiana University in January. When I arrived home there were no jobs in my subject so I accepted a substitute teaching position. Within five weeks, I learned of a science teacher who was going on maternity leave in a neighboring district. *Voila!* I was in the door. Many teachers take this route, and it is an excellent way to gain valuable experience. There is another benefit. If you are substituting in a school where you would someday like to work, you gain exposure and an inside track to the next position. You will know about the vacancy well ahead of everyone else and the administration will be acquainted with your work. It has happened where a substitute teacher was offered a position before it ever reached the paper. We all recognize the life of a substitute has its shortcomings. Do not overlook its positive features as well. *I particularly recommend this path to any* **alternate route teacher** *who does not find a full time position for the fall.* Just so you know, I personally hired two **alternate route candidates** who had been substitutes in my school. I knew them. I knew what they could do. Most of all, they were excellent teachers. And who knew? If all else fails, try it.

THE PREPARATION:

1. *RESEARCH:* Once you have selected a few districts to which you will apply, you need to prepare a plan of action. First, go back to your files and retrieve the information you gathered on each district. If this has not yet been done, do it now. Study each school and prepare a short list of facts regarding its demographics, programs, district initiatives, and other items that may be used in an interview.

2. *COVER LETTERS:* Write a separate cover letter for each district and include the executive summary to match your background with their stated requirements. Those requirements may be listed directly in the advertisement. Take care to address each one. If the ad is not specific as to its needs, then use one or two items from your research and add those to create impact.

3. *SHARPEN THE RESUME:* Tailor your bullets to meet district needs or initiatives. Look in the newspaper to see if the same district has placed ads for co-curriculum positions. If they have and you can fulfill one, be sure to highlight that in your cover letter and resume.

4. *PREPARE THE INTERVIEW PORTFOLIO:* I suggest you use a large three-ring binder that will lay flat. Put documents and pictures in page protectors. Place marked dividers between each section so that you know where everything is located. There is nothing more frustrating than looking through 20 or 30 pages for a document or picture while saying, "Gee, I know it is here somewhere." By the time you reach it, the impact is greatly reduced. *Tailor your portfolio to what you know the district is seeking!*

5. ***PUT YOUR INTERVIEW ATTIRE TOGETHER:*** This means having clothes cleaned and shoes shined. Take care to have your hair and nails neatly cut and cleaned. If you are not sure, reread the chapter on this subject. Have someone who can be objective check your selections.

6. ***ASSEMBLE YOUR BRIEFCASE:*** The day before the interview, assemble your briefcase. It should contain a file folder with additional resumes, pad, pen, and the interview portfolio. Leave out anything that is not pertinent to this interview.

7. ***PREPARE FOR THE INTERVIEW QUESTIONS:*** Prepare a few index cards with points you would like to make during the interview. There are numerous places in the book where I suggest you pre-think an answer. In addition, there are **KEYS TO YOUR RESPONSE** sections for every question. These are handy in the review process. Place your prepared questions on one side of the card and a few bullet-type comments on the opposite side. **WARNING:** *Do not show these at the interview.* Candidates often leave this step out because it is more work than they want to expend. Believe me; the little extra effort this takes will pay big dividends at the interview.

8. ***ALTERNATE ROUTE CANDIDATES:*** In an earlier chapter, I noted the books, The Passionate Teacher and Teach Like a Champion as "strongly recommended." I have repeatedly said that they key to your success is to prove your *capacity to teach and fill the position.* These two books hold a wealth of teaching ideas and practical classroom strategies that, if you can articulately present them, will more than give evidence of that capacity. Teach Like a Champion has dozens of classroom practices and strategies that will set you apart from the average applicant. Better yet, there is a DVD that shows the ideas at work in real classrooms. As part of *your* preparation, I cannot stress strongly enough, the need for you to get as many good ideas as you can from the classroom giants of today. Take this one extra step as it may prove to be the real difference maker in obtaining that important job offer.

MASTER THE INTERVIEW DAY:

The day of the interview is always one that has a little added stress. For that reason, do all of the preparation beforehand. If it is a morning interview, have the rooster get you up in plenty of time and leave the house a little early. Traffic, road construction, and other unforeseen problems can occur and turn your trip into a nightmare. Oh, once you are in your interview attire, do not eat or drink. That cup of coffee or jelly doughnut is just waiting to get on your jacket or blouse. Inanimate objects LOVE to destroy your day! Besides, you will enjoy those more *after* the interview is over. I always treated myself to a nice lunch or dinner after I had completed an interview session.

Before you leave the house, flip through your cards one last time, check your briefcase, and insure yourself that you have everything. You probably do, but the ride is more relaxing if you *know* everything is ready.

Try not to arrive at the school more than ten minutes early. If the interviews are not on schedule, they are almost surely running late. Ten minutes gives you time to go the men's or ladies' room and check your appearance one last time. When you go into the office, announce yourself to the secretary and tell her you are there for the interview with Mr. or Ms. Jones. Then take a seat and patiently wait for your turn. DO NOT PACE IN THE OFFICE LIKE A CAGED TIGER!

Also, secretaries are generally very busy so resist the temptation to engage them in casual conversation unless initiated by them. Smile and use courtesy remarks such as thank you and please. You may be offered coffee or a drink. In most cases, it is best to gracefully decline. The cup can be a nuisance if you are invited into the office and you are not finished. There is also the chance for spillage.

Once in the office, offer everyone a smile, handshake, and greeting. A simple "pleasure to meet you," is sufficient. Keep it professional and upbeat. The principal or designee will generally tell you where to sit, but if they do not, it is customary to ask, "Will this chair be all right?" Once in your seat, you can retrieve a pad and pen from your briefcase. Leave everything else alone unless it is needed. You might ask if anyone would like a copy of your resume. Most often copies have already been made, but occasionally someone will say "yes." In either case, it makes a good impression that you were planned enough to bring extra copies.

 Now sit back, take a nice deep breath, plaster on that smile, and just do your best with the questions. If you read the chapter on general questions, you already know the first one they are likely to ask. This should get you off to a great start, and you can build from there. Do your best to keep that upbeat demeanor, relax, and be yourself. Remember, as we have said, your enthusiasm and energy can offset any small omissions or technical errors.

After you have answered the last question, remember to ask the committee if they would have just a few minutes to look at the portfolio you have put together for them. Phrase it that way because you want them to know you made special preparations just for them. This knowledge increases the probability that they will give it some attention and adds to your stature as a serious candidate. Now close the sale and slam the door on any would-be applicants still cooling their heels in the outer office!

Once the portfolio review is finished there will be a signal that the interview is over. Sometimes the principal or committee will stand and at other times, someone will simply say, "If there are no more questions…." Stand, shake hands again, and thank them for the time you have had together. On your way out, remember to *thank the secretary* and say goodbye.

THE RIGHT WAY TO FOLLOW-UP:

After a day or so, be sure to write a short note or email to the principal thanking him or her for the opportunity to meet. This is not just a nice gesture, it is a professional courtesy, and its omission will not help. Keep your note or email simple and to the point. Resist the temptation to go back and oversell yourself by reprising the details about how you are such a perfect match for the school. The letter is a "thank you" and should be left at that. I know there are other books on the subject that advise you to do just the opposite. But, I never liked it, and most of the principals to whom I have spoken did not think highly of that strategy either.

While you are waiting for the results, keep your search activities alive and active. Do not be impatient. Know that you did well and are receiving full consideration.

When the offer arrives – and at some point it will – be ready with your answer.

CONCLUSION:

Here is my last word. Be positive and believe you will succeed. You have all the information, all the skills, and all of the education necessary to acquire the position you want. By the very fact that you took the time to read this book and follow its advice, you have made yourself into a candidate that will impress *any* interview committee. Even if you remember only a small portion of what you have read, you will be ahead of the other candidates who just showed up hoping to do well.

I wish you all the luck in the world and look forward to hearing about the success you are sure to find. More than that, I welcome you to one of the noblest professions in the human endeavor. I welcome you as a colleague and a *teacher!*

APPENDIX A

RUBRIC DESIGN

The scoring rubric is an assessment device that provides very specific information about what criteria will be judged and the specific performance factors required. Generally, a rubric has from three to five levels of performance that move from a near absence of quality to exemplary performance. The strength is that specific indicators are listed for each level of performance and both the student and the teacher are clear on the expectations.

Rubrics are used as both formative and summative evaluative tools. As the work is progressing, students can be informed of precisely what level of work is present. By examining the rubric, the student can also see what improvements must be made to reach the exemplary performance level. Peer evaluation is made possible through this tool, and small group discussions can often lead to improved performance.

Another strength of rubrics is their ability to focus student attention on just the elements that the teacher sees as important. A simple rubric for a 5th grade short story assignment might list such criteria as: Use of Opening, Story Development, Conclusion, Mechanics, and Overall Story Interest. The items included would be those the teacher has taught and has a reasonable expectation for student understanding. The teacher can also simplify or sophisticate the rubric by adjusting the number of performance levels.

Look at the example below which tries to simplify the short story assignment.

Criteria	1	2	3	Your Score
Use of Opening	Story has little or no opening.	The opening somewhat sets the stage for the coming events. Uses one or two of our devices to wet the reader's appetite.	The opening lays all essential ground-work for the coming events. Uses all three of the devices to stimulate reader interest.	1 2 3

As you can see, the teacher has taught students to provide the story setting and use three specific devices to raise reader interest. Those are the performance issues he or she assesses with the rubric.

Three additional sample rubrics from TaskStream.com are included for your review.

BOOK REPORT

Criteria	1	2	3	4	Your Score
Brief Plot Summary	Inaccurate plot summary	Incomplete plot summary or re-telling of entire story	Adequate plot summary without drawing attention toward significant events	Complete plot summary with attention focused on significant events	1 2 3 4
Main Characters	Incomplete description of main characters	Adequate description of main characters, but no sense of character comparison	Descriptions of main characters including some character comparison	Complete descriptions of main characters and full comparative analysis	1 2 3 4
Mechanics	Frequent errors in spelling, grammar, and punctuation	Errors in grammar and punctuation, but spelling has been proofread	Occasional grammatical errors and questionable word choice	Nearly error-free which reflects clear understanding and thorough proofreading	1 2 3 4
Originality	Report displays no evidence of original thought	Basic information and plot summary with little or no evidence of new insight	Report demonstrates a clear understanding of the book's content and offers some original insight	Evidence of high level reading comprehension is demonstrated through telling description, originality and fresh insight	1 2 3 4
Setting	Incomplete or inaccurate description of setting	Adequate description of setting, but no apparent sense of its relation to events and/or characters	Description of setting with basic sense of its relation to events and/or character motivations	Thorough description of setting and its relation to the plot, theme, and/or character actions	1 2 3 4

MULTIMEDIA RUBRIC

Criteria	1	2	3	4	Your Score
Content	Information is cursory or incorrect. Little understanding of content is evident from presentation.	Some solid information presented; however, some information is incorrect or cursory.	Information is clear and correct throughout most of presentation.	Information is well presented, clear, and correct throughout.	1 2 3 4

Effects	Effects are limited or not present.	One or more than one type of effect is used; however, some or all effects detract from presentation.	More than one type of effect is used. Effects enhance presentation.	Effects are varied, yet cohesive, and they significantly enrich the presentation.	1 2 3 4
Graphics	Images do not connect to text and/or are not relevant.	Images are not always relevant. Text citations are not always present and do not connect to images.	Images are mostly relevant. Text citations are usually present and identify the images.	Images are relevant, and complement the text. Each image is cited in the text and identified. The number of images is appropriate.	1 2 3 4
Mechanics	Text contains many spelling/grammar errors. Sentences seem disconnected, and there is carelessness throughout.	Text contains some spelling/grammar errors. Little logical structure or flow to sentences. Evidence of carelessness in writing.	Grammar and spelling are nearly flawless. Logical sequence apparent. Some wording is careless. Inconsistency in style.	Grammar and spelling are flawless, and the flow provides a logical pathway of ideas. Consistent and engaging style throughout.	1 2 3 4
Navigation	Many necessary buttons or tools are missing or difficult to use. Navigation from page to page is difficult or even impossible.	Not all necessary buttons are present. Navigation from page to page is confusing.	Navigation from page to page is typically easy.	Navigation from page to page is consistently easy and logical.	1 2 3 4
Page Design	Many pages are either cluttered or empty. There is no text/image balance. No attention paid to variation in design.	Some pages are either cluttered or empty. Inconsistent attention paid to sizing of graphics, placement of graphics and text, and text wrapping.	Most pages contain well-placed objects, with thoughtful text/image balance. Inconsistent text wrapping.	Objects on all pages are well placed and sized. Pages are not cluttered or empty. Imaginative and logical text wrapping.	1 2 3 4
Planning	Storyboard is incomplete. Little or no details about graphics, content, formatting, or effects are provided.	Storyboard lacks some important details about graphics, content, formatting, and effects.	Storyboard is mostly complete. Includes many important details about graphics, content, formatting, and effects.	Storyboard is complete. All necessary information about graphics, content, formatting, and effects is included.	1 2 3 4

ORAL PRESENTATION

Criteria	1	2	3	4	Your Score
Attention to Audience	Did not attempt to engage audience	Little attempt to engage audience	Engaged audience and held their attention most of the time by remaining on topic and presenting facts with enthusiasm	Engaged audience and held their attention throughout with creative articulation, enthusiasm, and clearly focused presentation	1 2 3 4
Clarity	No apparent logical order of presentation, unclear focus	Content is loosely connected, transitions lack clarity	Sequence of information is well-organized for the most part, but more clarity with transitions is needed	Development of thesis is clear through use of specific and appropriate examples; transitions are clear and create a succinct and even flow	1 2 3 4
Content	Thesis is unclear and information appears randomly chosen	Thesis is clear, but supporting information is disconnected	Information relates to a clear thesis; many relevant points, but they are somewhat unstructured	Exceptional use of material that clearly relates to a focused thesis; abundance of various supported materials	1 2 3 4
Creativity	Delivery is repetitive with little or no variety in presentation techniques	Material presented with little interpretation or originality	Some apparent originality displayed through use of original interpretation of presented materials	Exceptional originality of presented material and interpretation	1 2 3 4
Presentation Length	Greatly exceeding or falling short of allotted time	Exceeding or falling short of allotted time	Remained close to the allotted time	Presented within the allotted time	1 2 3 4
Speaking Skills	Monotone; speaker seemed uninterested in material	Little eye contact; fast speaking rate, little expression, mumbling	Clear articulation of ideas, but apparently lacks confidence with material	Exceptional confidence with material displayed through poise, clear articulation, eye contact, and enthusiasm	1 2 3 4

Courtesy of TaskStream.com

APPENDIX B

THE TASK ANALYSIS

A *task analysis* is the clinical analysis of the sub-tasks that a student would be required to master before he or she would be able to demonstrate competence of more complex objectives. For example, assume that you want students to be able to divide simple fractions and that was your overall objective for the day. There are a few concepts and tasks in which students would first need competence in order to master the skill of dividing fractions. Here is a possible breakdown of those tasks.

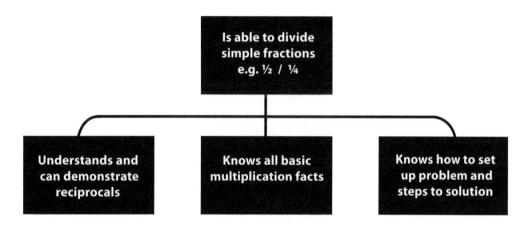

As you can see, if a student were not certain on any of these subtasks, then mastery of the final objective would not be within reach. When dealing with a more complex objective, a task analysis will allow you to diagnose both student readiness and where learning blocks may be preventing mastery.

A second advantage to a task analysis is that it lays out your lesson design in clear terms. You simply take each step of the analysis and that becomes a small teaching segment of its own. In your design, you move from the simplest to the most complex and, voila, you have your lesson. Note that in this example, "knows basic multiplication facts" likely will not need to be taught. But, depending on the age and your previous knowledge of the students, you might build in a quick check for understanding. Look below for how the task analysis leads to a lesson design.

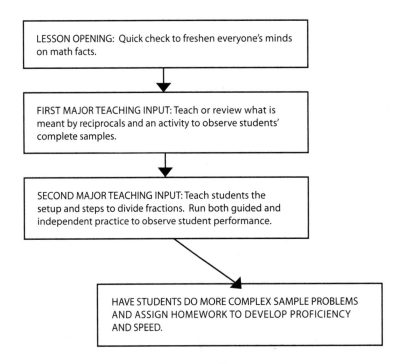

You can see how this simple design allows the teacher to prepare a clinical approach to the lesson and diagnose any learning difficulty with precision. Remediation or other teacher interventions can be built in exactly where they are needed. The *task analysis* is a vitally important skill for every classroom teacher, and you should use it on any complex task.

APPENDIX C

TASKSTREAM.COM

The Learning Achievement Tools by Taskstream, www.taskstream.com, is listed as a separate appendix because it is one of the more valuable online resources. TaskStream provides a number of valuable tools and includes resources you can access with a modest subscription fee.

One of the features available at TaskStream is the e-Portfolio tool. The ability of **e-Portfolios** to upload work in any digital format — including text, images, videos of classroom teaching, and slideshows — allows prospective teachers to showcase their accomplishments.

The **"Standards Wizard"** is a tool that provides a comprehensive list of regional and national standards with information on the specific proficiencies for each state. It permits you to select the level of standards detail you desire. For example, if you select the Illinois State Standards, the discipline areas will appear, and you can select your subject area. If you click on "English/Language Arts," it provides a variety of subjects such as Reading, Literature, Writing, and so forth. Continue this process until you reach specific learning proficiencies.

The site also has the **Standards-Based Lesson Planning** tool to help ensure you address appropriate state and national standards in your classroom. With this feature, you can create custom lesson plans, organize all of your instructional materials, request feedback from mentors, and create a library of units and lessons. TaskStream's **"Cybrary"** gives you access to a large collection of lesson plans that are published by other TaskStream subscribers along with the ability to view and download these lesson ideas. This is an excellent lesson design resource.

TaskStream also provides authentic assessment tools to monitor student performance on higher-order skills. Reporting tools are included to help you analyze student performance against each standard. You would be wise to take the time to investigate this Web-based tool.

REFERENCES CITED

Andersen, H. O. (1970). Readings in science education for the secondary school. New York, NY: Macmillan

Anderson, L. W., Krathwohl, D. R., Airasian, P. W., & Cruikshank, K. A. (2000). A taxonomy for learning, teaching, and assessing: A revision of Bloom's taxonomy of educational objectives. Boston, MA: Allyn and Bacon

Armstrong, T. (1998). Awakening genius in the classroom. Alexandria, VA: Association for Curriculum and Development

Armstrong, T. (2009). Multiple intelligences in the classroom. Alexandria, VA: Association for Curriculum and Development

Armstrong, T. (2006). The best schools. Alexandria, VA: Association for Curriculum and Development

Arter, J. A., & Chappuis, J. (2006). Creating & recognizing quality rubrics assessment training institute. Boston, MA: Allyn and Bacon

Beshara, T. (2008). Acing the Interview: How to ask and answer the questions that will get you the job! New York, NY: Amacom

Brooks, J. & Brooks, M. (2001). In search of understanding: The case for constructivist classrooms. New York, NY: Prentice Hall

Burke, K. (2009) How to assess authentic learning. Thousand Oaks, CA: Corwin Press

Burns, K. The Civil War. Classroom Activities: What teachers are saying. Available: http://www.pbs.org/civilwar/classroom/activities

Canfield, J. (2002) Chicken soup for the teacher's soul: Stories to open the hearts and rekindle the spirit of educators. Deerfield Beach, FL: HCI

Ernsperger, L. (2003). Keys to success for teaching students with autism. Arlington, TX: Future Horizons

Fried, R. L. (2005). The game of school. San Francisco, CA: Jossey-Bass

Fried, R. L. (2001). The passionate teacher. Boston, MA: Beacon Press

Hunter, R. (2004). Madeline Hunter's mastery teaching: Increasing instructional effectiveness in elementary and secondary schools. Thousand Oaks, CA: Corwin Press

Jacobs, H. H. (2010). Curriculum 21: Essential education for a changing world. Alexandria, VA: ASCD

Kentucky state standards for mathematics. Retrieved January 15, 2011, from http://kentuckymathematics.org/resources/standards.asp

Lemov, D. (2010). Teach like a champion: 49 techniques that put students on the path to college. San Francisco, Ca: Jossey-Bass

McGuire, C. & Abitz, D. (2001). The best advice for teachers. Kansas City, MO: Andrews-McMeel

National Commission on Excellence in Education. (1983) A nation at risk. Washington, DC: U.S. Government Printing Office

Novelli, J. & Meagher, J. (1999). Interactive bulletin boards: Language arts. New York, NY: Scholastic

Opitz, M. (1994). Learning Centers: Getting them started, keeping them going. New York, NY: Scholastic.

Palmer, P. J. (1998). The courage to teach. San Francisco, CA: Jossey-Bass

Royal, D., Culpepper, P., Pryor, C., & Wheat, J. (2005). Coach Royal: Conversations with a Texas football legend. Austin, TX: University of Texas Press

Saphier, J., Haley-Speca, M. A., & Gower, R. (2008), The skillful teacher: Building your teaching skills 6th edition. Boston, MA: Research for Better Teaching

Siegel, D. (2001). The developing mind: How relationships and the brain interact to shape who we are. New York: Guilford Press

Sousa, D. A. (2005). How the brain learns. Thousand Oaks, CA: Corwin Press

U.S. Department of Education. (2002, January 7). Executive Summary: The No Child Left Behind Act of 2001. Washington, DC: U.S. Department of Education

Vatterott, C. (Jul 2, 2009). Rethinking homework: Best practices that support diverse needs. Alexandria, VA: ASCD

Watson, J. D. (2001). The double helix: A personal account of the discovery of the structure of DNA. Austin, TX: Touchstone

Wiggins, G. & McTighe, J. (2005). Understanding by design. New York, NY: Prentice Hall

Wolff, M. (1997). Netstudy, your personal net. New York, NY: Dell

Yate, M. (2010). Knock 'em dead 2011: The ultimate job search guide. Cincinnati, OH: Adams Media

INDEX